BORLASE SMART

BORLASE SMART

St Ives Artist - Man of Vision

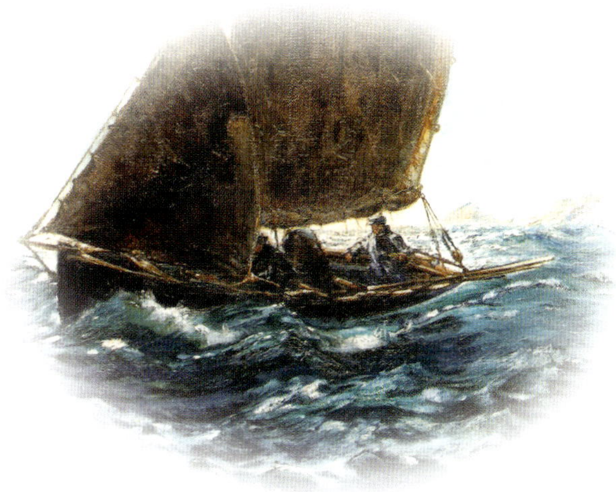

Marion Whybrow

HALSTAR

First published in Great Britain in 2012

British Library Cataloguing-in-Publication Data
A CIP record for this title is available from the British Library

ISBN 978 1 906690 41 0

HALSTAR
Halsgrove House,
Ryelands Business Park,
Bagley Road, Wellington, Somerset TA21 9PZ
Tel: 01823 653777 Fax: 01823 216796
email: sales@halsgrove.com

Part of the Halsgrove group of companies
Information on all Halsgrove titles is available at: www.halsgrove.com

Printed in China by Everbest Printing Co Ltd

Foreword

By David Lay FRICS

IN 1981, AS A YOUNG AUCTIONEER, I was so pleased to be approached by Brian, the son of Borlase Smart to sponsor a commemorative exhibition. Of course I was familiar with the artist's work but in those days, sponsorship by auctioneers was a new idea. However, it proved a most rewarding experience.

Before the exhibition I was given a tour of the show with Brian. Together, we discussed each picture and I learnt about the artist's skill, his unique blend of architectural precision, combined with his ability to capture the Cornish light. Also during this very privileged guided tour, I learnt about his valuable contribution to the population of St Ives, especially to the artists who he particularly served through the St Ives Society of Artists. I learnt how he had played a major role in accepting the young 'Moderns' with their new abstract ideas and concepts on art.

It was this group that began to form before the beginning of the Second World War, which brought international fame to St Ives and now, thirty years later, I feel privileged to be paying tribute to Borlase Smart again.

Over the years I have sold perhaps 100 paintings by Borlase Smart through my auction house, along with the work of all of his friends and contemporaries. Borlase Smart offered help and encouragement to the new, often controversial, band of abstract artists. He helped by giving access to his studio, by organizing exhibitions, providing hanging space in the St Ives Society of Artists gallery and by helping to secure the Porthmeor Studios for future generations. He did all this against a clamour of disapproval and charges of disloyalty from Royal Academicians. Their traditional style had held sway from the 1890s and earlier; a style which was easily understood and publicly acceptable.

Today, appreciation of his commitment to a broad artistic church has been recognised in the founding of the Penwith Society in his name, and the Borlase Smart Trust to safeguard the Porthmeor Studios. This has happened in the most spectacular way through major national and international grants and locally, 'Smart Regeneration'.

This book will help us all to recognise the importance of Borlase Smart in the development of art in St Ives and its importance to the progress of the modern movement.

Borlase Smart was truly 'A Man of Vision'.

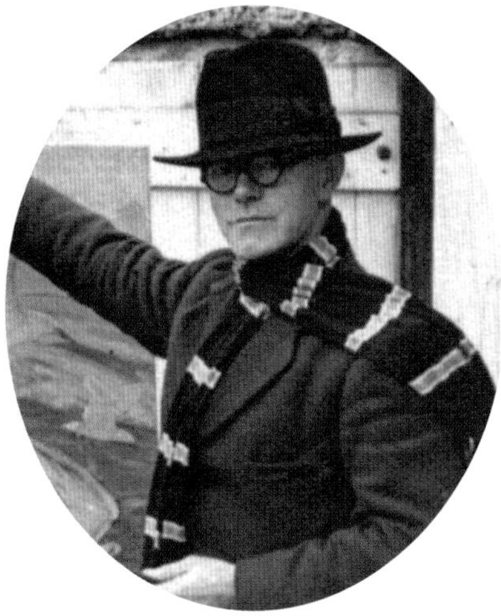

Contents

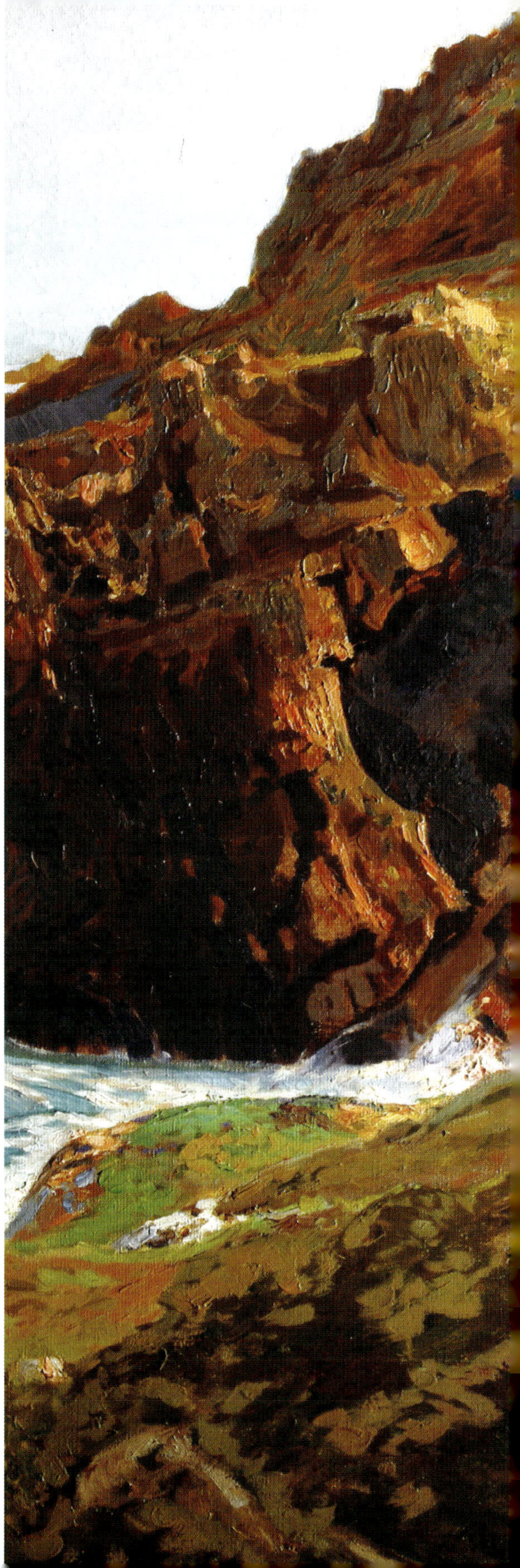

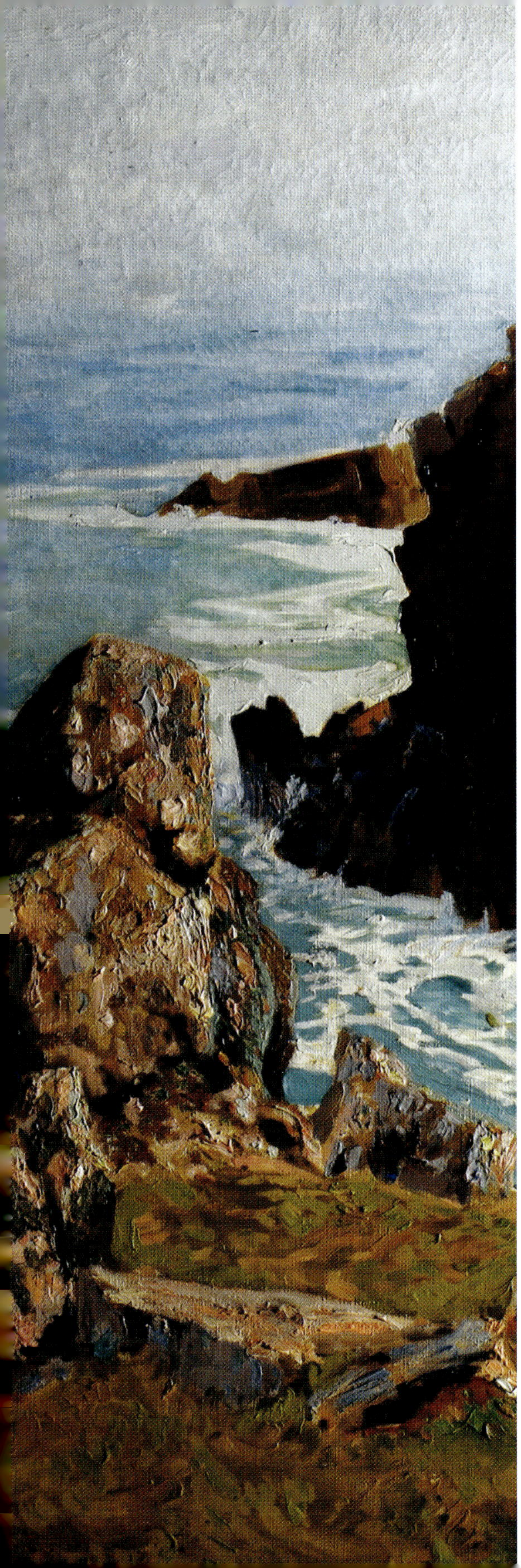

Introduction

BRIAN SMART 6.4.1929–31.12.2010

I WAS ONLY 18 WHEN FATHER DIED. His work took him away from home almost it seemed into another world. I never went with him, just occasionally visiting him in his studio, but never for long.

Mother was dead against either of her sons becoming artists. Perhaps it was her early married life in Ocean Wave Studio, off St Andrews Street. It was just a simple studio where the local fishermen gave father old sails. These were used as compartments for the kitchen and other rooms. In the early days they were very poor, and Mother would tell me the story of asking the local grocer, Mrs Hosking, if she would let mother have groceries in exchange for one of father's pictures; and as soon as they had some money she would come and pay and collect the picture. When that time came, Mrs Hosking said she would rather keep the picture.

My brother Michael and I went away to boarding school. During our holidays, Father would often read to us before bedtime. After that he would go downstairs and play on our piano. He couldn't read music but had that natural talent of playing by ear. He told me his father had been headmaster of a school in Kingsbridge, his mother had been one of the teachers there. Both were disciplinarians, and at weekends and during school holidays, father and his sister were taught to play the piano; when they weren't at the piano they had to draw or paint. Father developed into a painter who could play the piano, and Auntie Hilda a concert pianist who was good with her watercolour paintings of flowers.

From Plymouth College of Art, Father went to study at the Royal College of Art. In his holidays he was drawn to St Ives and studied under Julius Olsson there. His great ambition was to move to, and work in St Ives. Little is known of his life before 1914, but he was quick to join up when the war started. He joined the 21st London Regiment, and became an active member of the Artists Rifles. These were fellow artists who developed a keen knowledge of camouflage. Father told me a story of constructing out of timber, soldiers standing, kneeling and lying down; a large number of them, to be strategically placed near the front line. At a given signal, every one of them would be raised into a firing position. This action took the Germans by complete surprise. They immediately turned their firing on to the figures, which by then were lowered out of sight.

One of Father's newly-made friends was fellow officer Leonard Fuller. Both expressed their interest in moving to St Ives after the war. They were two of several artists who were posted out of France and sent to Grantham to work on drawings of the newly designed Lewis Machine Gun. During leave in England Father took it upon himself to visit all next of kin of those in his company who had been killed. He met up with the parents of his sergeant, Stuart Godson. George Bird Godson was a successful London Builder and had recently moved from Bloomsbury Park to Bletchingley in Surrey to avoid the German aircraft which were bombing London.

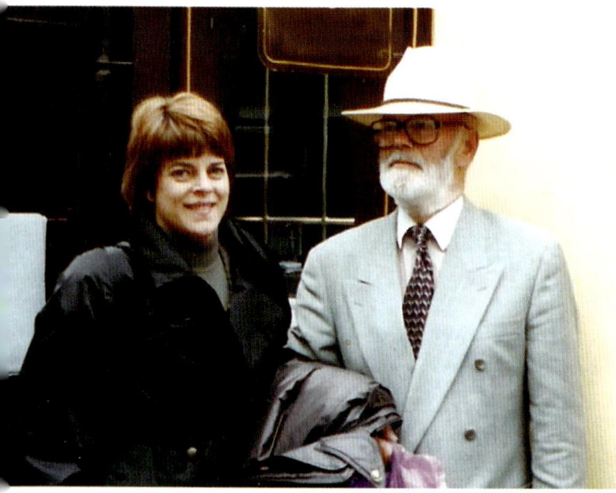

Brian and Genie Smart.

The Godsons had four attractive daughters, and Father fell for the second one, Irene. At this time Father was 36 and Irene was only 18. Her parents would not give their approval and did not go to the wedding. Soon after Borlase and Irene moved to St Ives. Many years later George Godson came down to stay with them and was horrified at this impoverished world.

After he had returned home, Mother and Father received a huge package in the post, on opening it they found, not food, but a silver cutlery service from Mappin & Webb.

On the death of her father in the early 1930s, Mother became the Smart 'Bread Winner' and they bought a nice house 'Pendennis' at the bottom of the Belyars. The Lanyon family lived nearby. Mother was near her tennis club and poor old Father was committed to the daily chore of walking the 112 steps down into St Ives and onward to his studio which by then was one of the Studios overlooking Porthmeor Beach. In those years he spent a great deal of time preserving studios as studios and preventing them being sold off as holiday homes.

Genie Smart

Genie became Brian's second wife. They married in1986 and since that time Genie has lived with the legacy of Borlase Smart. Every room in the house, from basement to attic, hallway and staircase has its complement of paintings, drawings, watercolours and etchings. Every cupboard has its boxes and packages of Borlase memorabilia; photos, certificates, letters, sketches, mementos, to which Genie has generously allowed access. After Brian's death, Genie bravely carried on making all this material available, therefore ensuring the publication of the book.

Man of Vision

'Borlase Smart: a sort of artistic admiral who marshaled the columns of waves on to his canvases.' [1]

Peter Lanyon

Captain Robert Borlase Smart 1881-1947

BORLASE SMART, living in Plymouth and working as art critic for the *Western Morning News*, followed the artists' trail to St Ives and found an art colony to equal any that were establishing themselves in Europe and the western world. For Borlase it was an experience to make him realize that St Ives was the place in which he could live among artists and develop his own artistic talents.

In 1912 Borlase's painting 'Moonlight on the Cornish Riviera' was hung in the Royal Academy Summer Show. This may have been the spur to his decision to become a professional artist, and having made that choice, to pursue his goal. In 1913 at the age of 32, Borlase Smart gave up his post as a journalist and came to St Ives to study seascape painting under the expert eye of Julius Olsson.

Olsson had established a School of Painting in 1895. A notice was published in the St Ives Weekly Summary: *'Two young artists, Mr Louis Grier and Mr Julius Olsson, are announcing the opening in St Ives, Cornwall of a School of Landscape and Marine painting. The main idea is to give students an opportunity of studying out of door effects.'*[2] Olsson was keen to establish the rule of vacating the studio and experiencing the outdoors even in extreme weather conditions. He advised the students committed to studying with him that they must be prepared to face a brave fight with the elements, 'which will be frequently against them'.

This philosophy suited Smart, who believed in capturing the spirit and truth of a topic such as the sea, with its constant movement, wind, tide, light, waves and seasons shaping the subject. He wasn't a student in the true sense of the word; he was already a competent artist but keen to develop his skills with a recognized leader of this particular discipline. He was a man equally willing to learn as he was to teach.

Having satisfied himself that he had mastered the techniques of seascape painting Borlase later informed his own students, *'It has always been my endeavor to paint even large pictures out of doors.*

The toil of carrying such canvases, as well as material and easel, is compensated by the freshness one gets in doing a picture first hand from Nature' [3] By 1919 he was listed among the best British Marine Painters in a survey published by the *Studio* magazine.

Smart was by no means a fledgling in the world of art. He studied at Plymouth Art College 1897-1900, and obtained a First Class Honours Certificate in teaching from the Royal College of Art 1900-1901.

St Ives had been attracting artists since the building of Brunel's railway bridge across the River Tamar into Cornwall in 1859. Turner had arrived in 1811, without the benefit of the bridge. Other Royal Academicians such as Sir Lawrence Alma Tadema and Sir Ernest Waterlow, had sojourned here.

In 1877 the branch line to St Ives brought visitors directly into this marine environment and fishing harbour. Whistler and Sickert spent the winter of 1883-84 sketching and observing the resident artists, who were painting nocturnes in the Whistlerian manner and cultivating plein air techniques.

Throughout its history the town has received other visiting painters of renown, Francis Bacon, Vanessa Bell, Peter Blake, William Holman Hunt, Paul Nash, Victor Pasmore, Mark Rothko, Helene Schjerfbeck, William Scott, Graham Sutherland, Stanley Spencer, Christopher Wood and other luminaries.

By 1900 there were over one hundred artists living and working in the town, as well as travelling artists, and those from nearby Newlyn; the latter were the painters who mainly portrayed the working lives and tragedies of the fisher folk. The majority of artists in St Ives were keen advocates of marine and landscape painting and St Ives became established in this representational style. *'Old sail lofts and cottages were sought out, and turned into studios, and large skylights appeared everywhere among the grey roofs of the old town; by the enterprise of the townspeople large studios were built, some of imposing size, and St Ives took its place as a well-known centre of art work.'* [4]

The War Years 1914-1918

The First World War interrupted Smart's permanent move to St Ives. He joined the Artists Rifles, a volunteer regiment of the British army, where he met fellow artist, Leonard Fuller. Their intention was to open a school of painting in St Ives after the war, but it was only Smart who followed his ambition, immediately, to become a professional painter and live in St Ives; Fuller was to arrive eighteen years later.

Captain Smart, now engulfed in this tragic war and experiencing death and destruction among the troops, knew the vital use of his newspaper background and realized that here was a situation that needed to be recorded. He appointed himself an unofficial war artist, before artists and photographers were officially commissioned to undertake this work. He drew and sketched as his company moved through the war zone. His drawings were unique and some of the first to document the disasters and horrors faced by the allied forces.

Smart's very personal drawings in charcoal and wash, reveal the war conditions for the soldiers in the front line and the destruction of towns and villages on the Somme, Arras and at Ypres. The first showing of these drawings, 'Sketches of the Western Front, Vimy Ridge to the Somme' were exhibited in The Fine Art Society, New Bond Street, London, in 1917; at The Harris Galleries, Plymouth; in Lanham's Gallery St Ives in 1919, and other venues. Some of them were gifted to the Imperial War Museum and the National Maritime Museum. A letter to Borlase Smart conveys 'an expression of warm appreciation', and informs him that he has been elected a 'Friend of the National Maritime Museum'. He was given a badge which allowed him free admission. Drawings were purchased by other museums, and Plymouth City Museum and Art Gallery also has a number of drawings of scenes from the Great War.

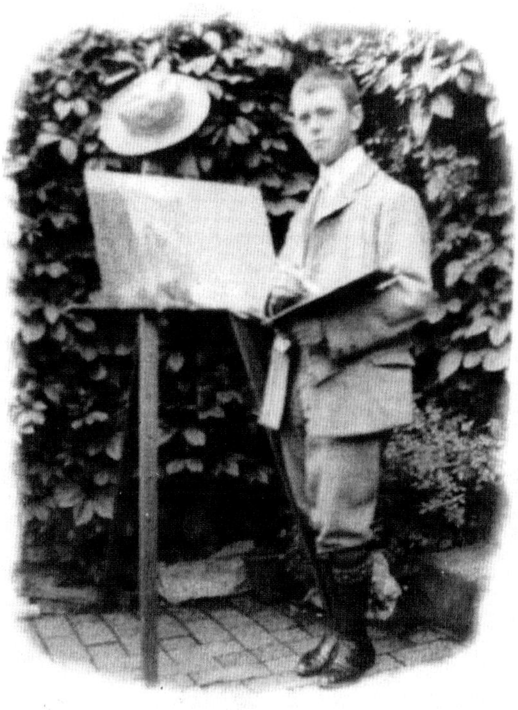

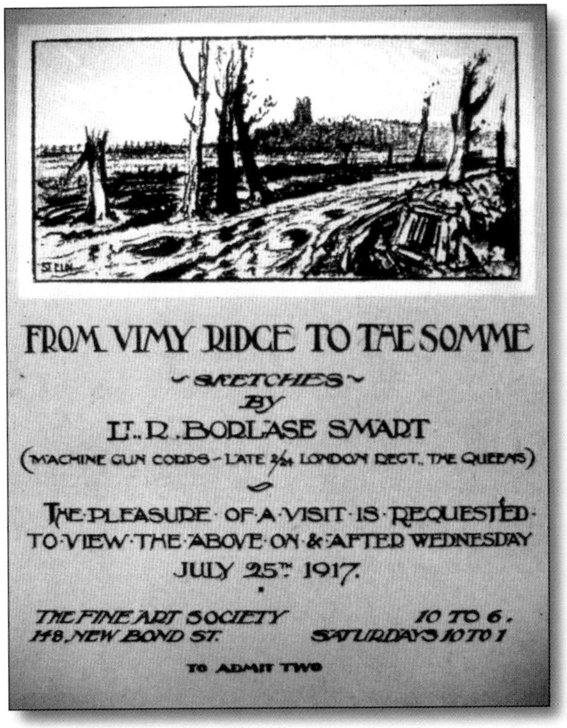

Left: *Borlase as a young man.*

Right: *Poster for the 'Sketches of the Western Front' exhibition.*

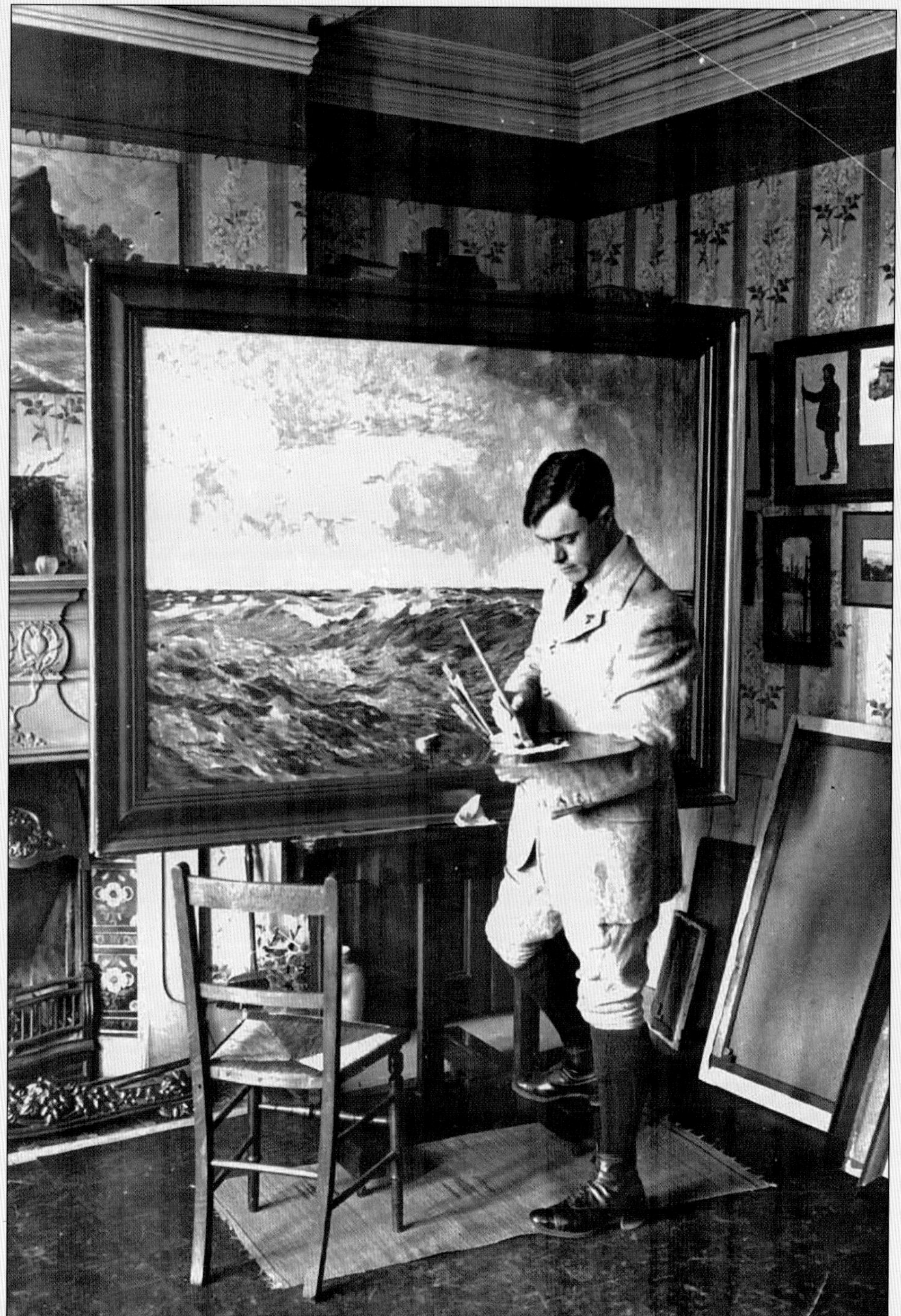

Borlase before 1914.

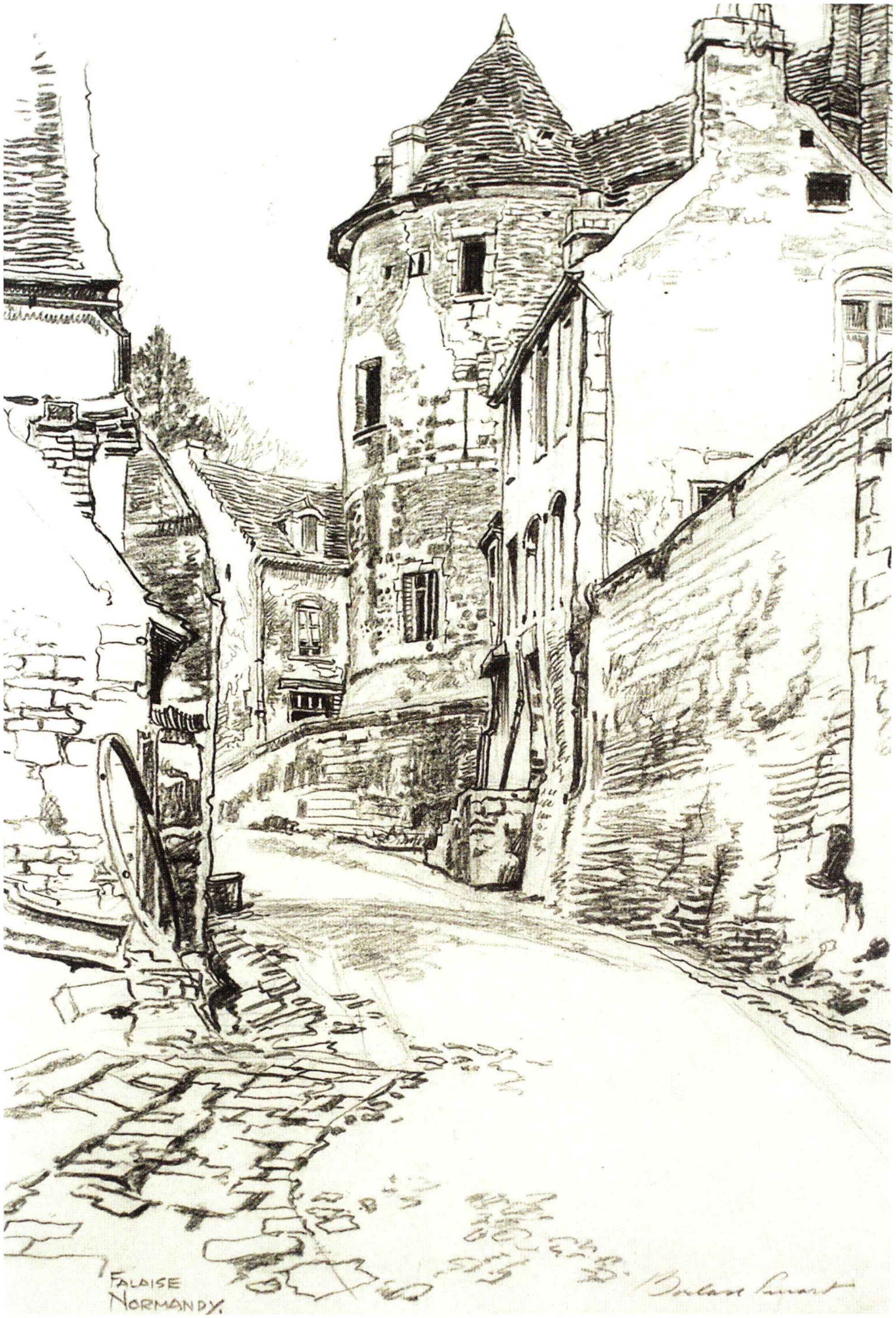

Falais, France.

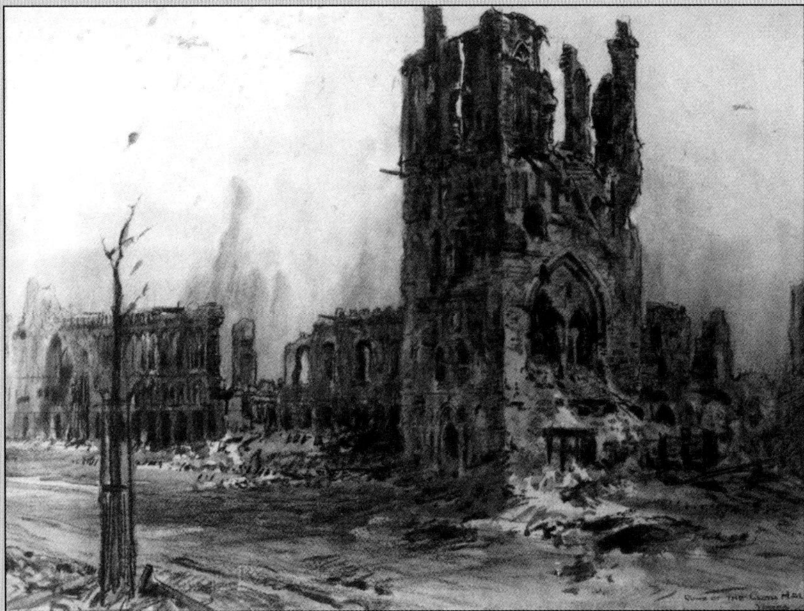

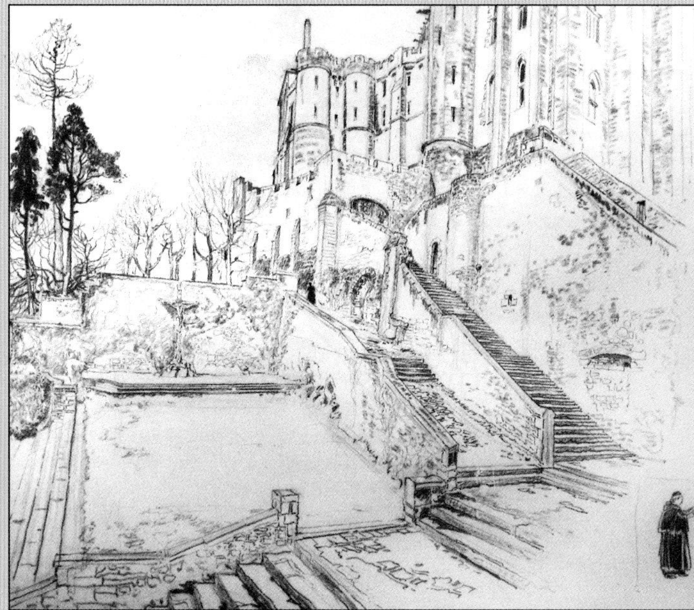

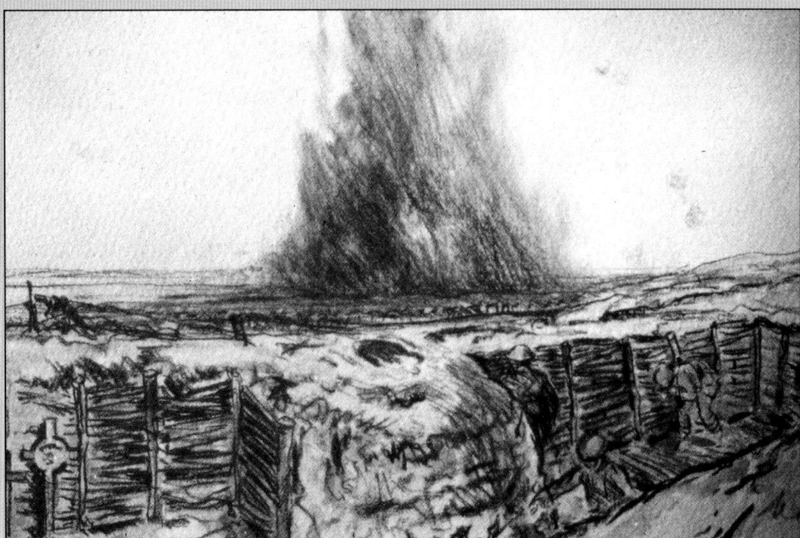

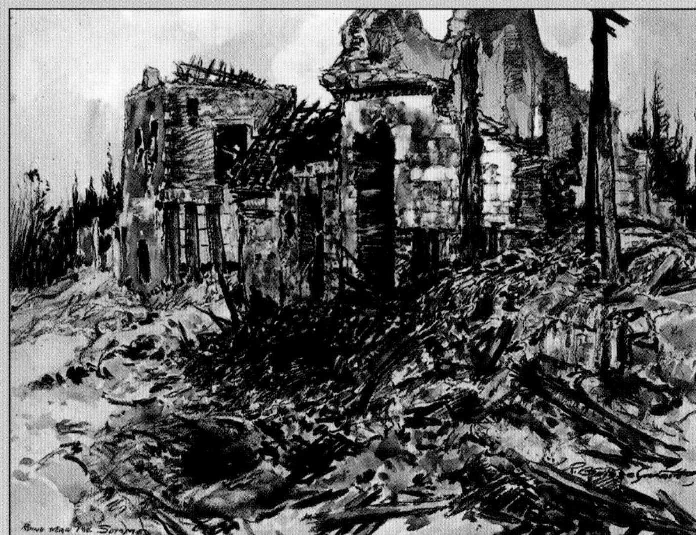

'Sketches of the Western Front' clockwise from top left: *Cloth Hall, Ypres; Mont San Michel; The Somme; exploding shells on the front line.*

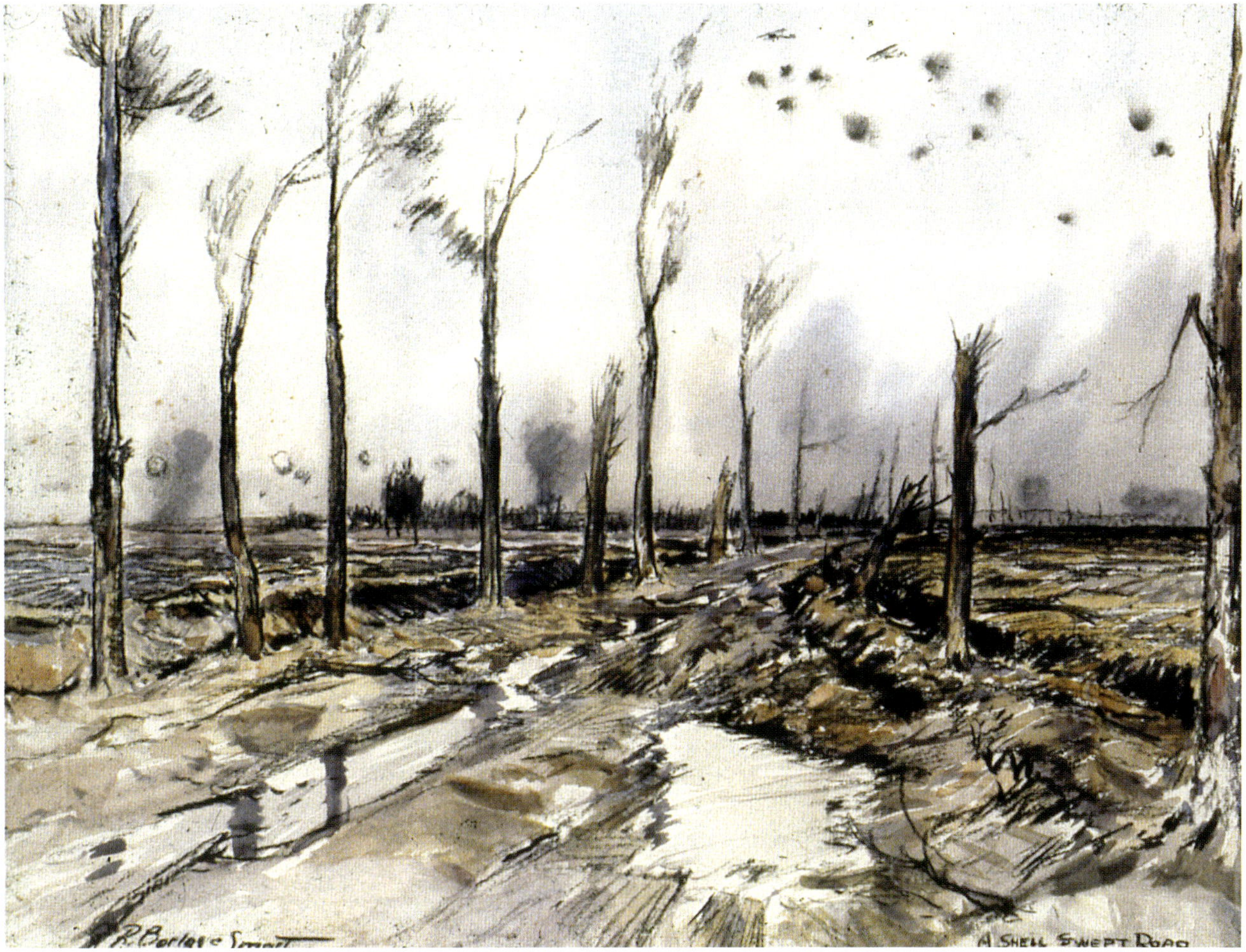

Road near Arras.

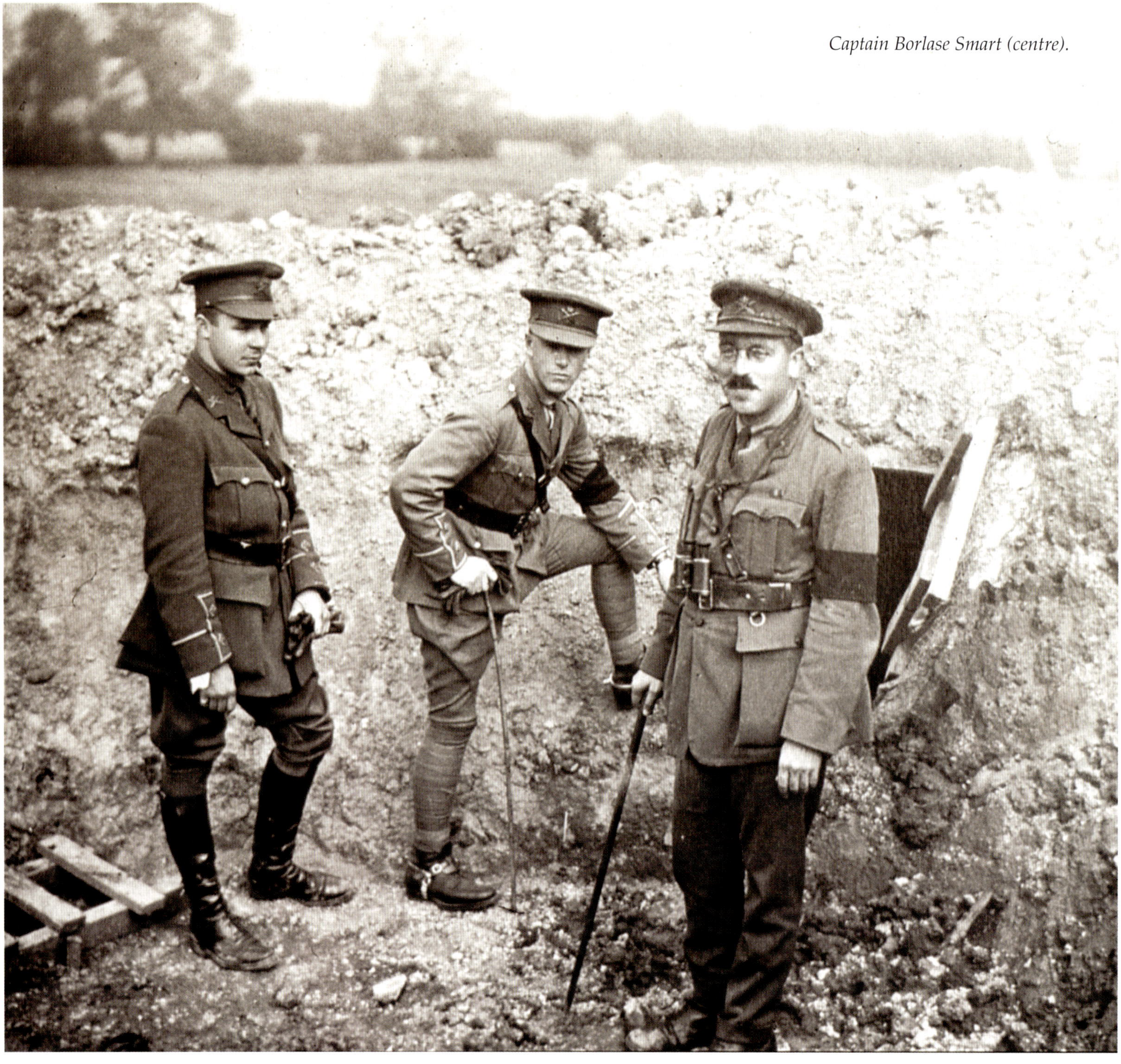

Captain Borlase Smart (centre).

Arriving in St Ives

In 1919, having survived his army experience in the First World War, he arrived with his wife, Irene, whom he married in 1917, to take up residence at Ocean Wave Studio, Pedn-Olva Walk, facing the harbour, where they lived very frugally in one long room. Borlase was given a huge canvas sail by a fisherman friend to divide the room into studio and living space.

Irene was the sister of his friend and platoon sergeant, George Stuart Godson, who had been killed in action at Arras on the eve of his twenty-first birthday. Borlase witnessed this unfortunate death at first hand standing next to Sergeant Godson, who was hit by an exploding shell. He died from loss of blood. When Captain Smart was posted back to England he visited the parents of his young friend to offer his sympathy and relate the circumstances of their son's death. In their house he met and fell in love with one of their four daughters, Kathleen Irene Godson. In spite of objections from her parents, Borlase being nearly twice her age, the couple married. Her parents did not attend the wedding.

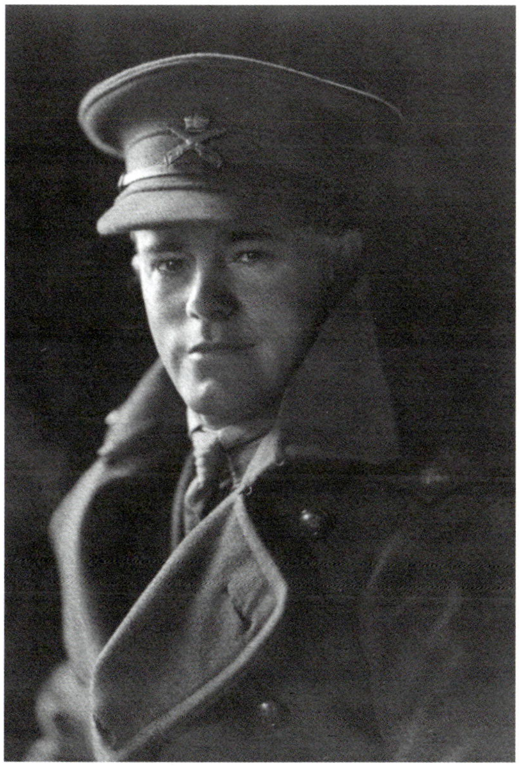

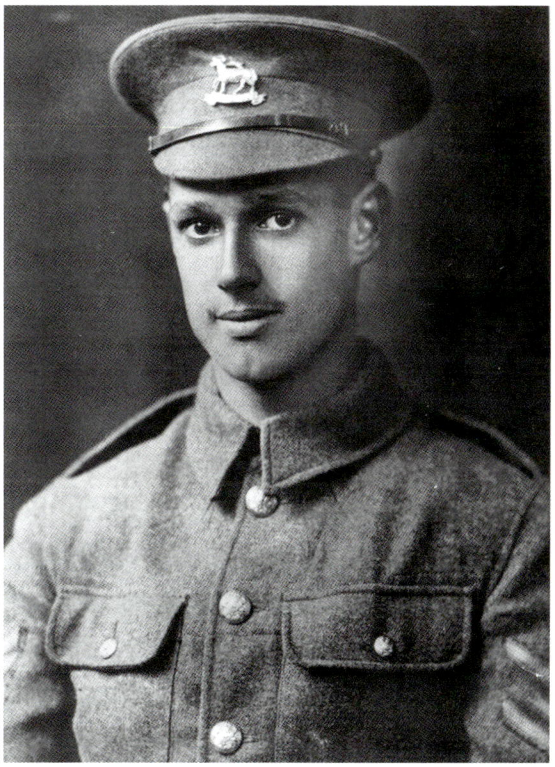

Left: *Borlase Smart.*

Right: *George Stuart Godson.*

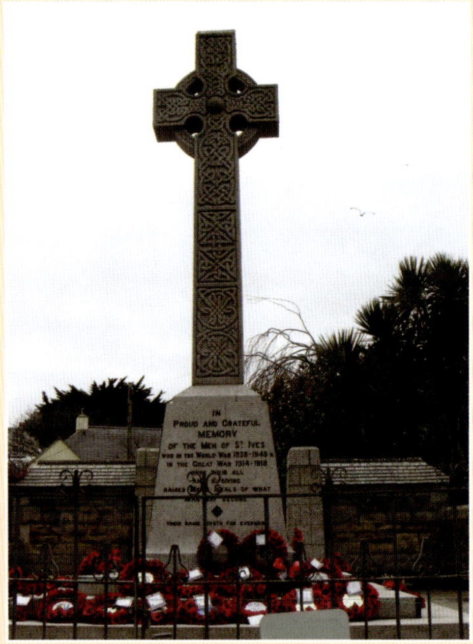

The War Memorial, St Ives.

I REMEMBER

All those long years grandma
Kept your photograph, and wept,
Every Remembrance Day
When poppies fell in the Albert Hall.
There is no keeper now
Of your eternal nineteen years.
Who will cherish your medals,
Letter of regret from the Palace?
Does it seem unkind to say
That now we should let you go?
Bury the noble photograph
As though you had died of old age.
On your stone we would write -
'He lived in the memory of his family
And in the minds of all generations'.

Marion Whybrow

Undeterred by such rejection, and having served on the front line and seen the devastation of the countryside and towns of Europe and recorded such events; having endured and witnessed the terror of fighting and the deaths of many comrades and escaped with his life, he determined to benefit from his good fortune. Borlase could conquer anything civilian life could throw at him.

On arriving in St Ives Captain Borlase Smart brought with him energy and enthusiasm in abundance. He began to capitalize on his training at Art College and his teaching certificate and in 1920, when he was elected secretary of the St Ives Arts Club, he felt well equipped to join and organize the affairs of the artists and form his fellow painters into a formidable group.

His painting 'Munitions 1918' was accepted for the RA in that year. A year later he was elected a member of the Royal Society of British Artists. In 1920 his painting 'Clear After Rain, St Ives Bay' was exhibited at the RBA and at the Paris Salon a year later. It is typical of plein air painting. The picture is now in the possession of the St Ives Town Council.

Other artists who settled in St Ives after serving their country in the First World War were Commander George Fagan Bradshaw, Arthur Hayward and Hugh Gresty; the latter suffered the effects of gassing for the rest of his life. Leonard Richmond, Algernon Talmage and Julius Olsson were officially commissioned as war artists by the Canadian Government, who recruited them to map the effect of the war on towns, villages and the countryside. Also employed by the Canadians in their Cavalry Brigade, was painter of horses, Alfred J. Munnings, who had lived in Lamorna. He was later President of the Royal Academy and of the St Ives Society of Artists. Another painter, who had served in France at the same time as Smart was John Park. He had known Park in Plymouth and had reviewed his paintings for the local paper.

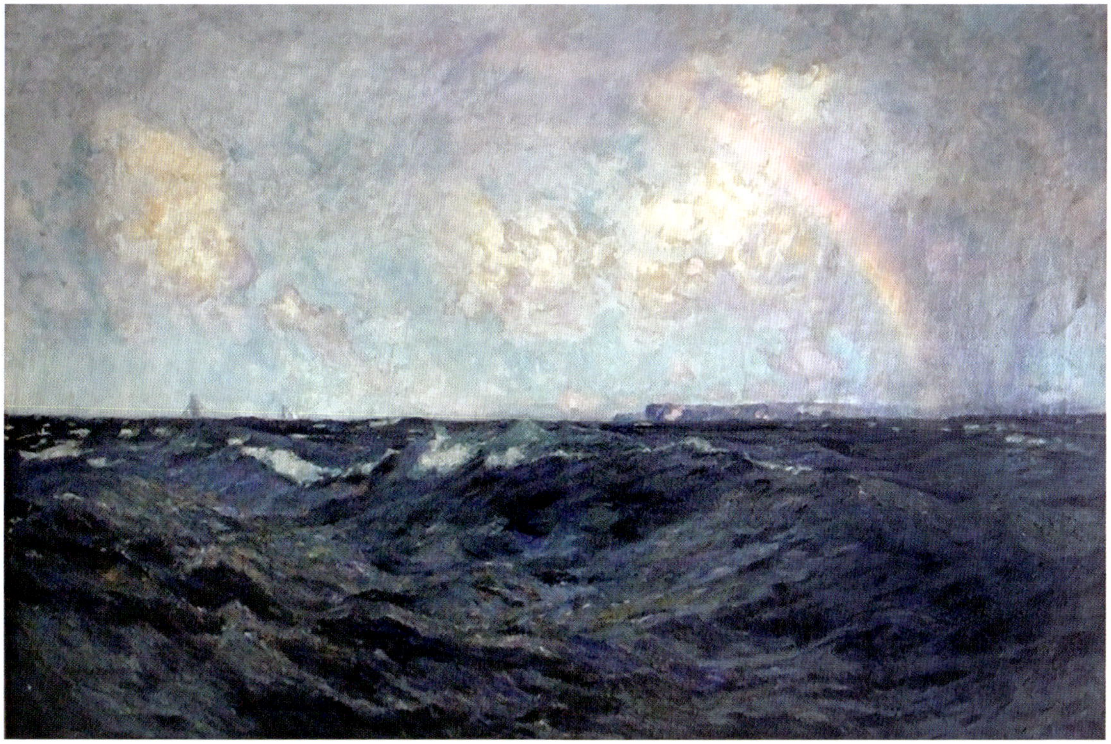

Clear After Rain, St Ives Bay.

Art Gallery and Museum for St Ives

At the Mayor Choosing in St Ives in 1919, Captain John Hain, retiring from office, felt that a gallery hung with pictures from local artists would be a worthy record of the St Ives Art Colony and would represent the town. Borlase Smart tried in vain to support the idea that the town should build a gallery as a fitting memorial to those who gave their lives during the First World War. He felt it would find favour with the inhabitants because St Ives had provided subjects for some of the '*greatest pictures in modern art*'.

However, Borlase Smart and the artists were disappointed; the War Memorial took on the more conventional form in the shape of a cross and was sited opposite St Ia Church. It was designed by architect George Turland Goosey, who was a member of the Arts Club. The surrounding gardens were designed by Will Arnold Forster, then living at Eagle's Nest, Zennor, and later the home of Patrick Heron.

Continuing his success in the art world, in 1922 and 1923 the Royal Academy accepted two of Borlase's marine paintings, 'Morning Light, St Ives' and 'Cornish Cliffs, Zennor', both of which are now in the collection of the Royal Cornwall Museum in Truro. In this same year he was elected to the Royal Institute of Oil Painters and in 1925 was invited to membership of the Royal Institute of Cornwall.

Heartened by his success and his easy acceptance into the established art colony he took his first studio in the Porthmeor complex, occupying number one. The windows overlooked the huge sandy beach and the fierce Atlantic Ocean; a great inspiration for a man who studied the sea in all its moods. His companions were other artists, and also fishermen, who worked below the studios, mending nets and storing their fishing gear.

Morning Light, St Ives.

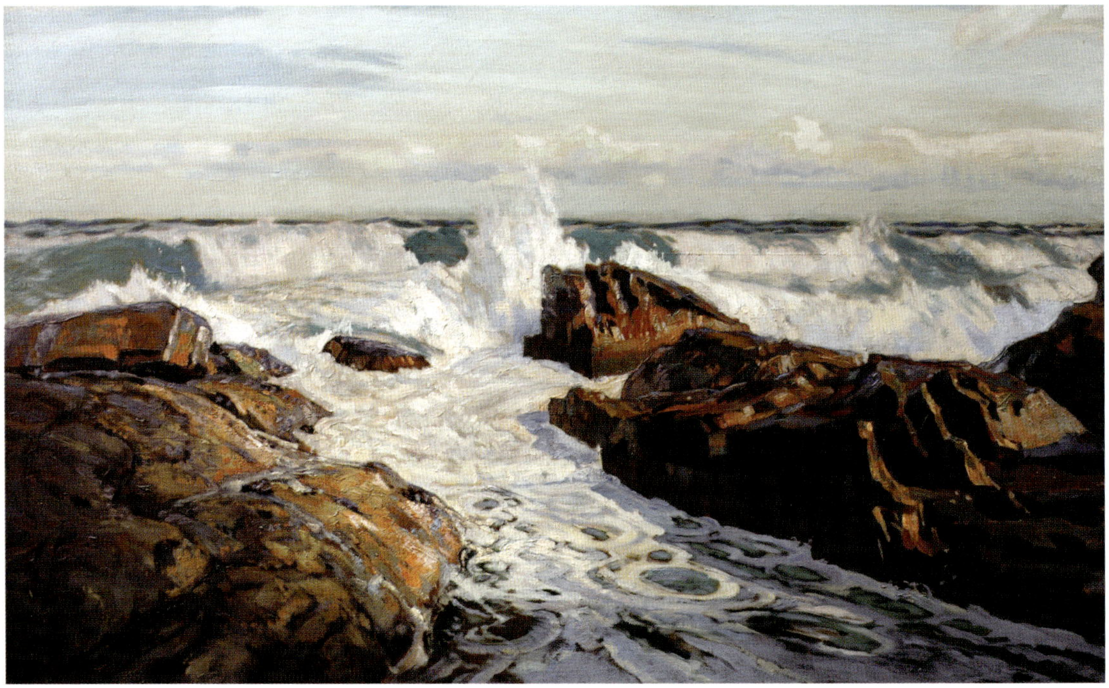

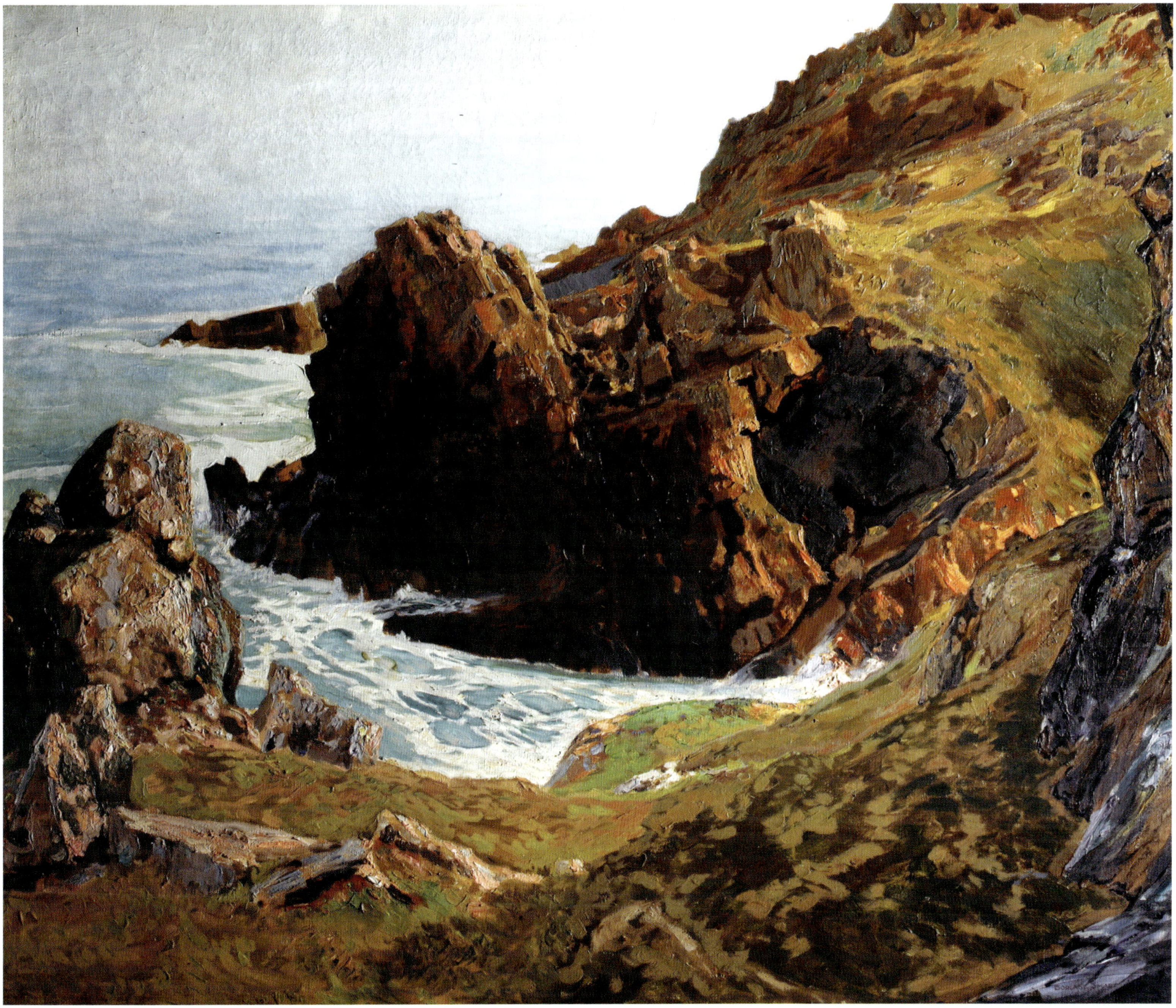

Cornish Cliffs, Zennor.

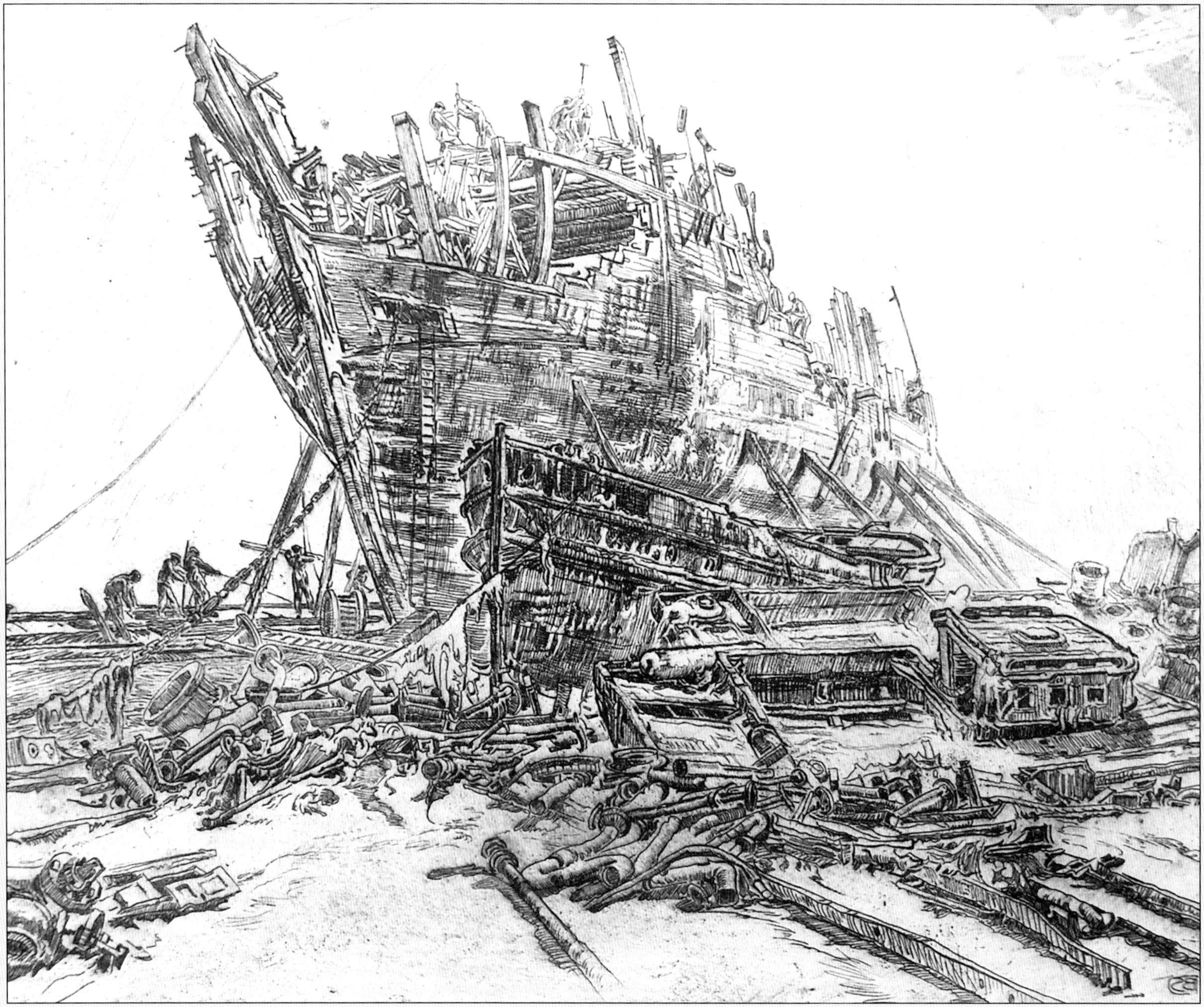

Breaking up HMS Foudroyant, *an etching made from an original chalk and wash study included in 'England's Wooden Walls'.*

He was fortunate in his knowledge of the working of a newspaper and made maximum use of that medium to further his ideas and advertising for the many schemes and events he planned for the artists, bringing their activities to a wider field. His fellow painters benefited from his reports to the *Cornishman*, the local *St Ives Times* and other art magazines and exhibition catalogues. Having worked on the *Western Morning News* from 1903-1913 his association with them lasted throughout his life.

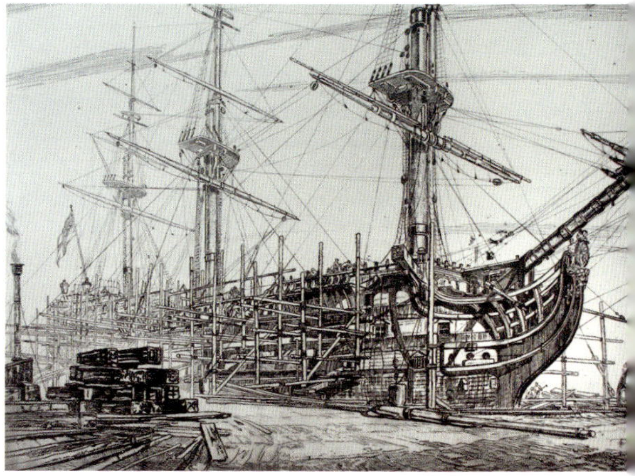

HMS Victory, *included in 'England's Wooden Walls'.*

A decade after the Harris Galleries showed Smart's war drawings, they featured 'England's Wooden Walls', an exhibition of sixteen pictures by Borlase Smart in chalk and wash of the Navy's old wooden vessels, due for destruction. Among those featured were Nelson's Flag Ship, HMS *Victory* (later saved for the nation), HMS *Britannia* and HMS *Implacable*. Many of these heroic ships had been later used as naval training ships for boys and, in typical fashion, Borlase recorded the passing of these vessels as being of great historical importance.

The shattered buildings of war time and the dismantling of the old wooden ships had a profound and long lasting psychological effect on Borlase, and for some years afterwards he found it necessary to record the blitzed buildings of Plymouth and other areas, and many years later the demolition of the old cottages in St Ives, as though his drawings were their epitaphs.

Venice

In 1925 Irene and Borlase travelled to Venice, where they took a delayed honeymoon and prolonged their original stay of two weeks by several months. In Venice he was able to access the paintings by Titian and the Venetian artists; to visit Florence to see Botticelli's 'The Birth of Venus', the Leonardos and the artists in the Uffizi gallery, as well as visiting Rome to admire Donatella's statue of David and Michaelangelo's gigantic David in Florence and his frescos in the Sistene Chapel.

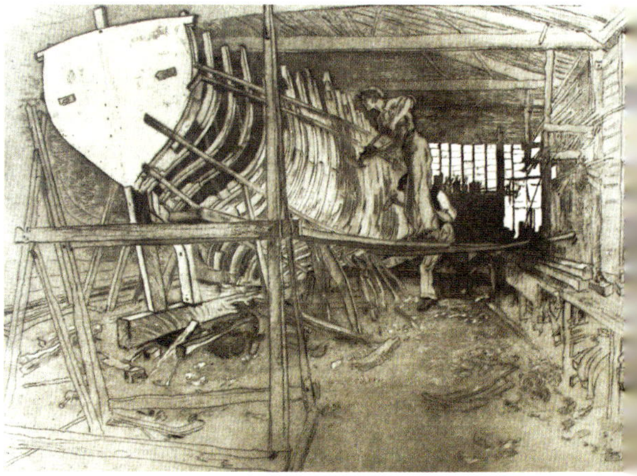

Inside a Venetian boatyard, etching.

Borlase's artistic talent flourished in the inspiring city of Venice. He produced a great number of paintings and drawings celebrating its grandeur, canals, architecture, traditions and art. This was Borlase at his most prolific. He produced sketch books, oils, watercolours, pastels and etchings.

The painting of the hotel Traghetto Della Casson, with Irene standing far right, captures the idea of the romance of the subject matter. They are momentarily in touch with the poet, art critic, writer on architecture, watercolour artist and supporter of the Pre-Raphaelites, John Ruskin, who they understood had stayed in this hotel. Borlase's opinions reflected the philosophy of this man, that all great art should show an appreciation of nature and must be an expression of the artist's moral outlook. Borlase lived by his principles, that art should involve the whole man, his ethics, values and beliefs.

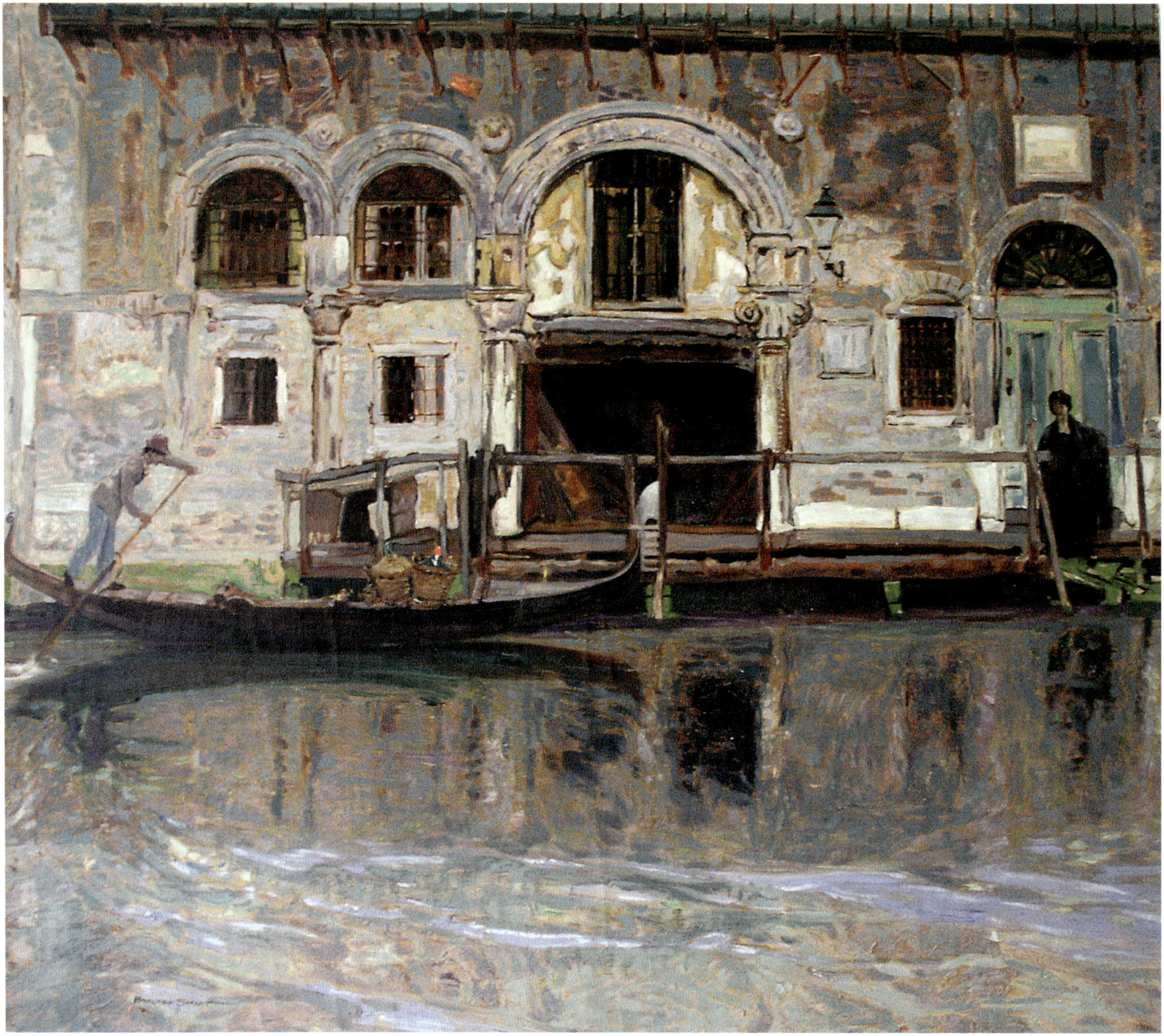

Traghetto Della Casson, Venice 1925.

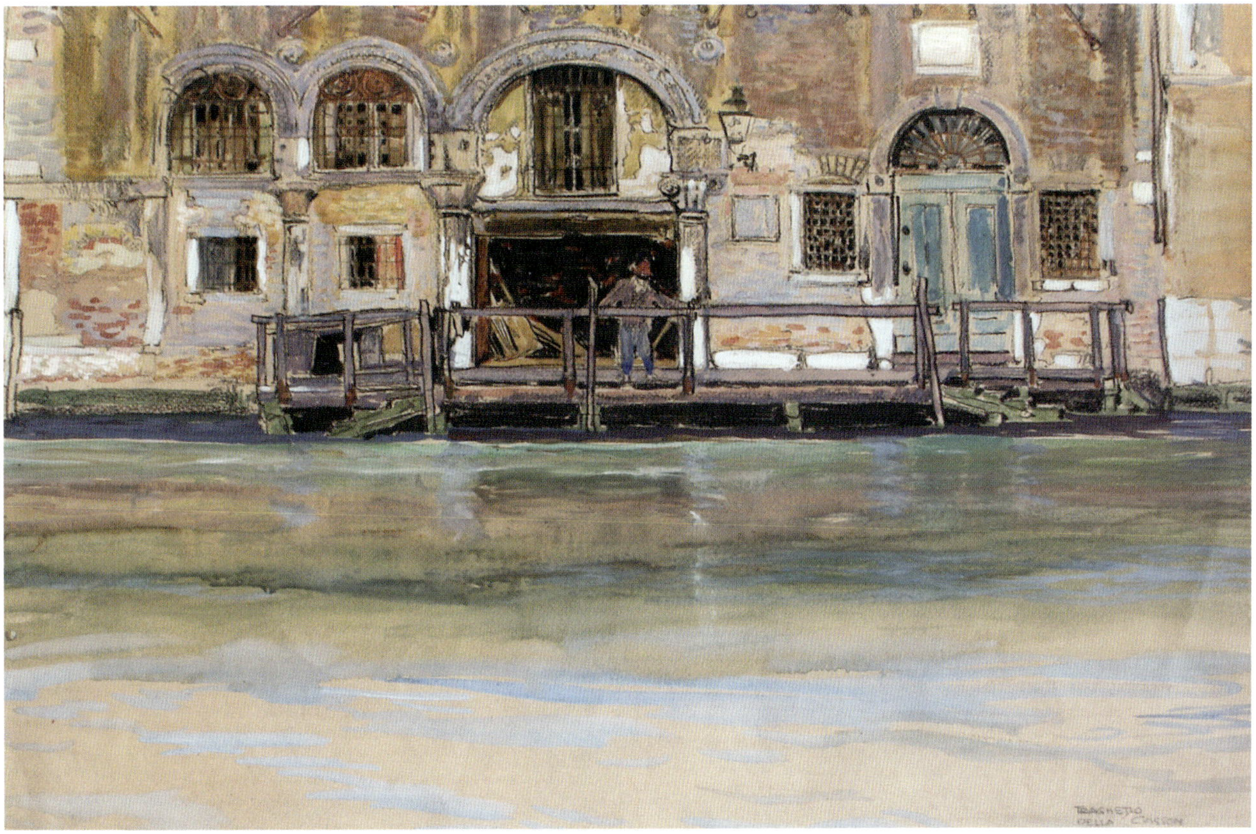

Traghetto Della Casson, Venice 1925.

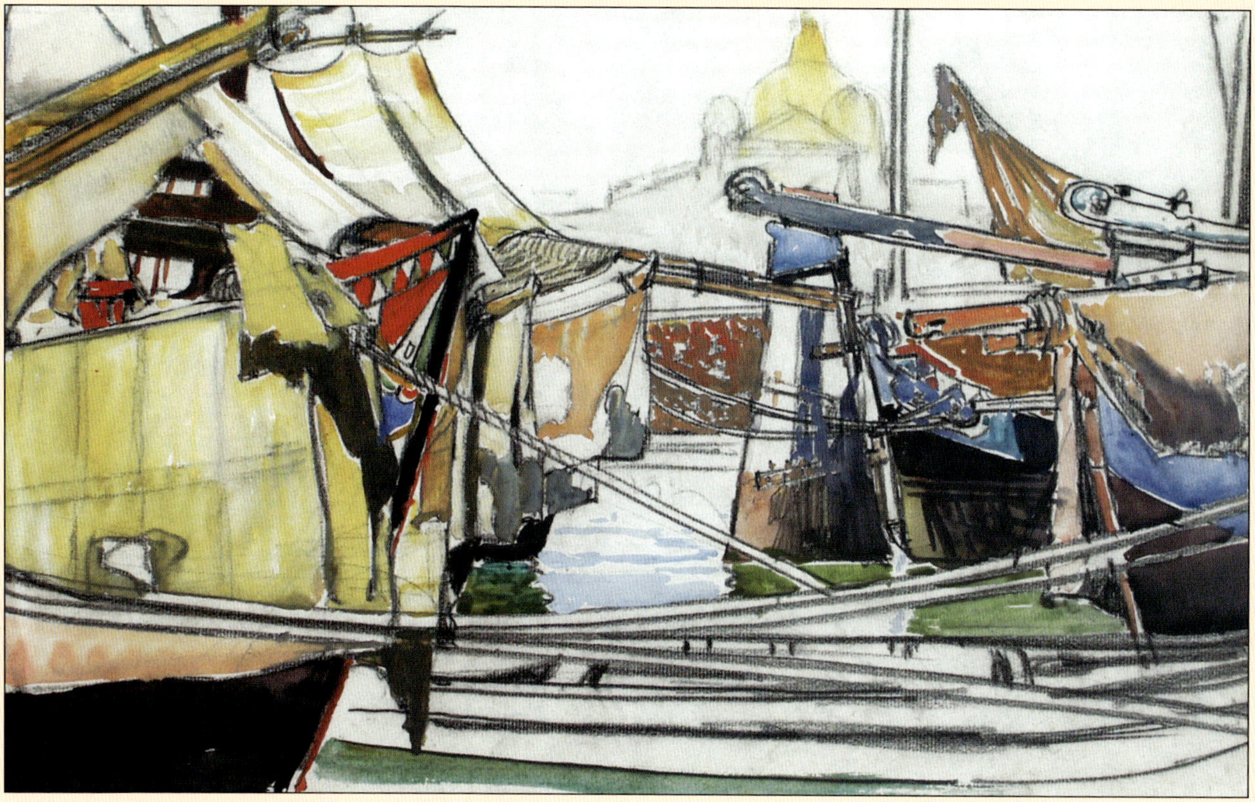

Anchored boats opposite St Mark's, Venice 1925.

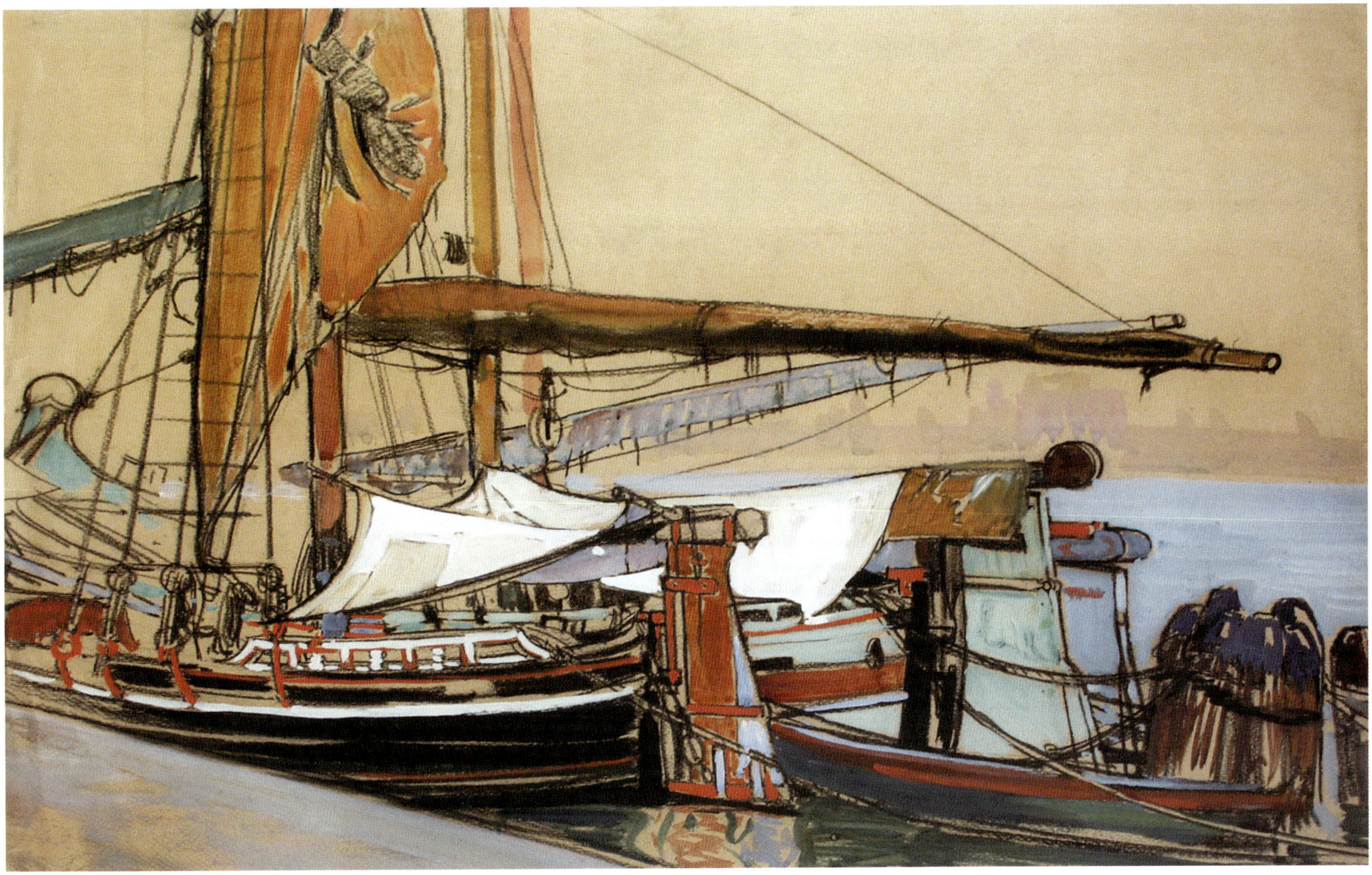

Lagoon trading vessels, Venice 1925.

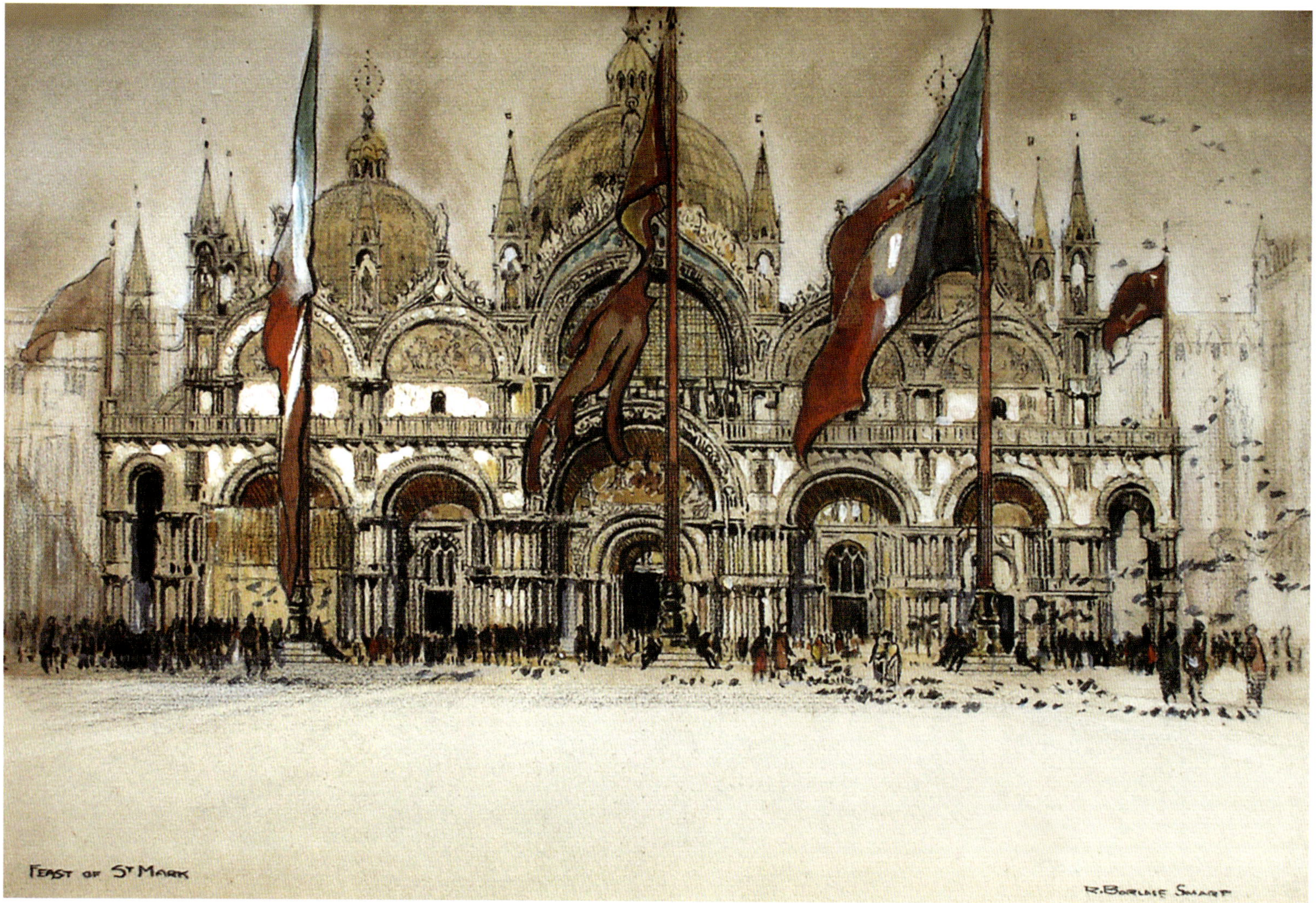

The Feast of St Mark, Venice 1925.

On returning to Cornwall the Smarts took up residence in The Cabin on Westcott's Quay, next to Ocean Wave studio

With the return of artists from the war and to recognize their sacrifice and ease them back to normal life, St Ives artists were invited to enter a friendly competition to design and provide a presentation certificate to those who had served in His Majesty's forces. The winning entry was by Borlase Smart who also designed the memorial plaque to four Arts Club members who had died during the war. It was made in copper by another remarkable seascape painter, Edmund Fuller, and mounted on a board by Lanham's.

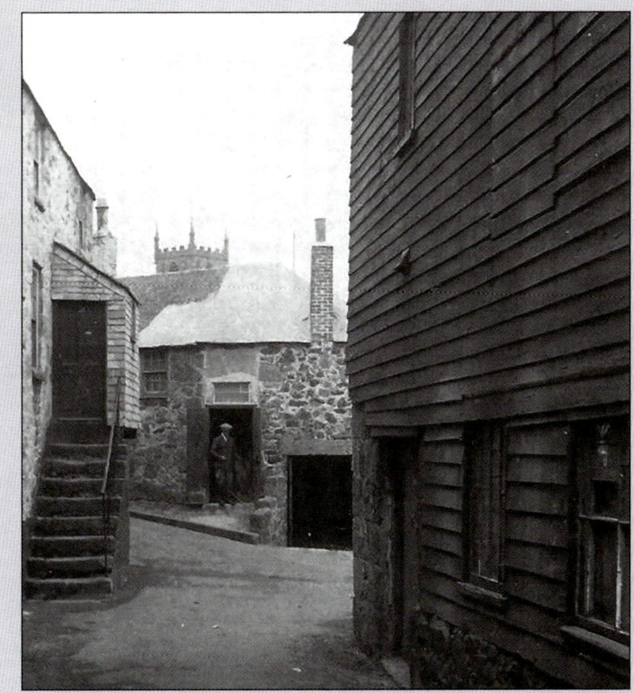

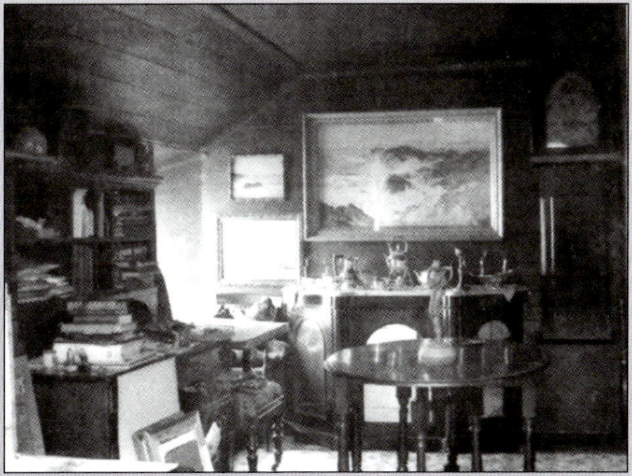

Left: *The Cabin with Borlase Smart. The Arts Club is on the right.*

Above: *Interior of the Ocean Wave Studio.*

Below: *Ocean Wave Studio balcony; beyond is the St Ives Arts Club.*

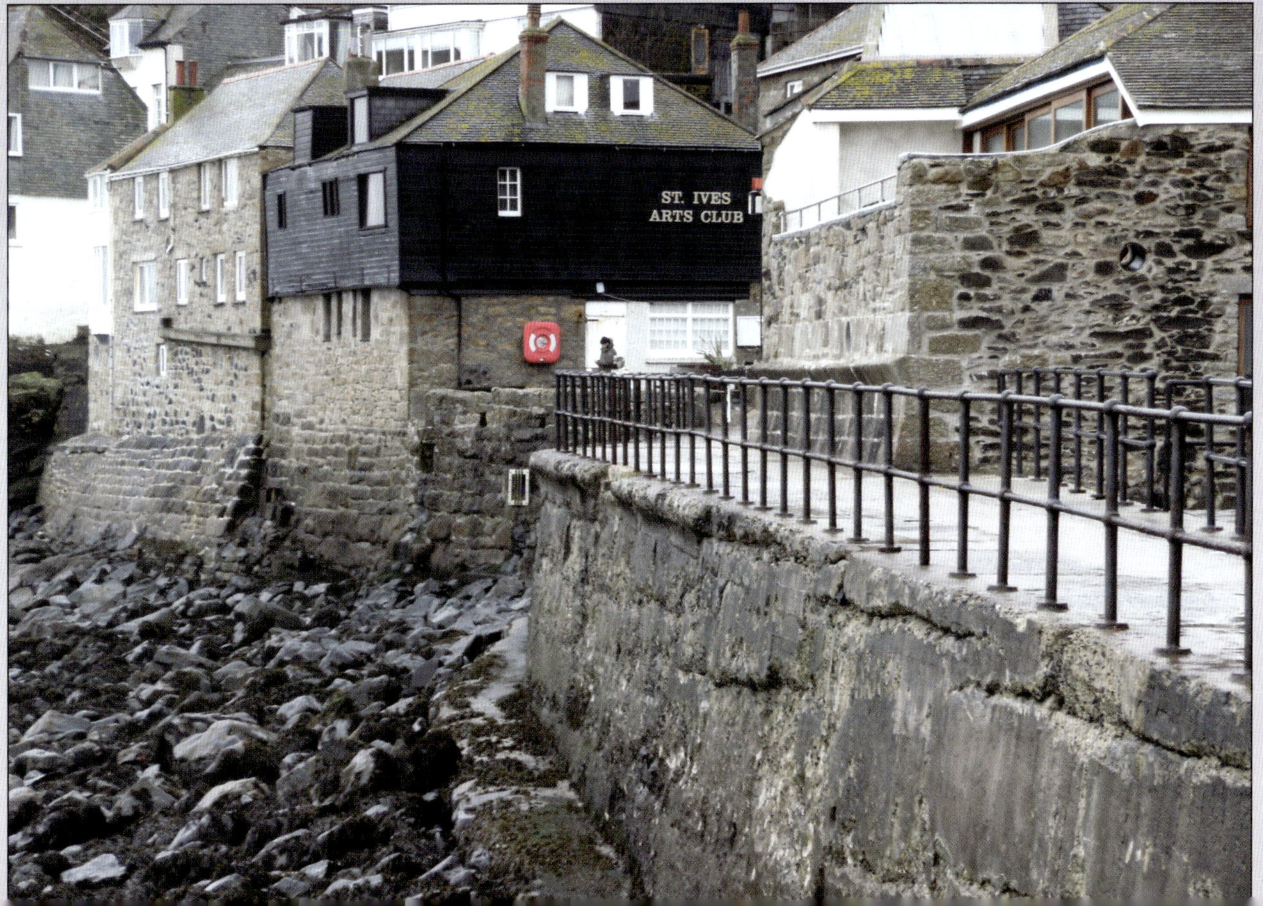

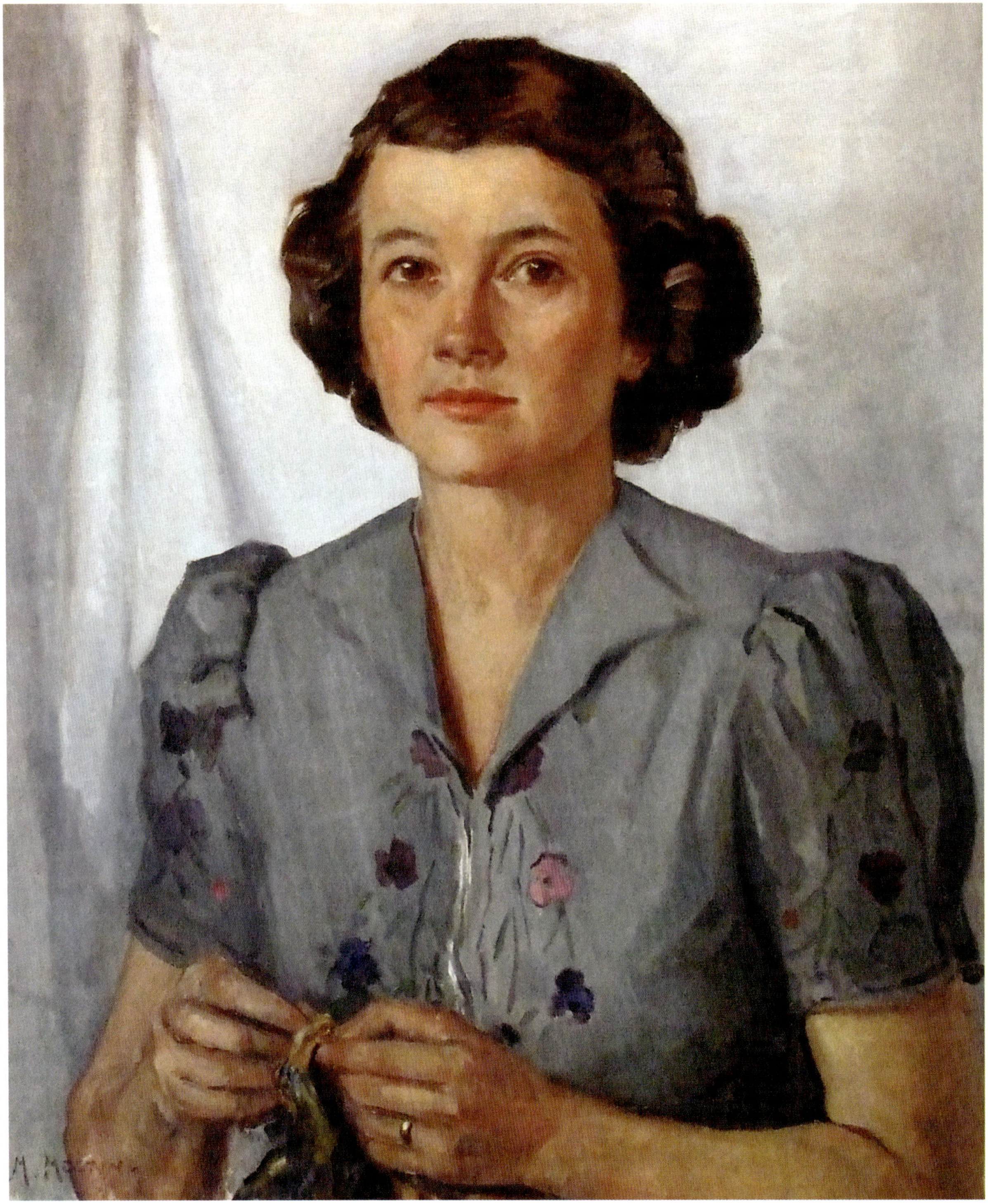

Irene Smart.
A painting by
Marjorie Mostyn.

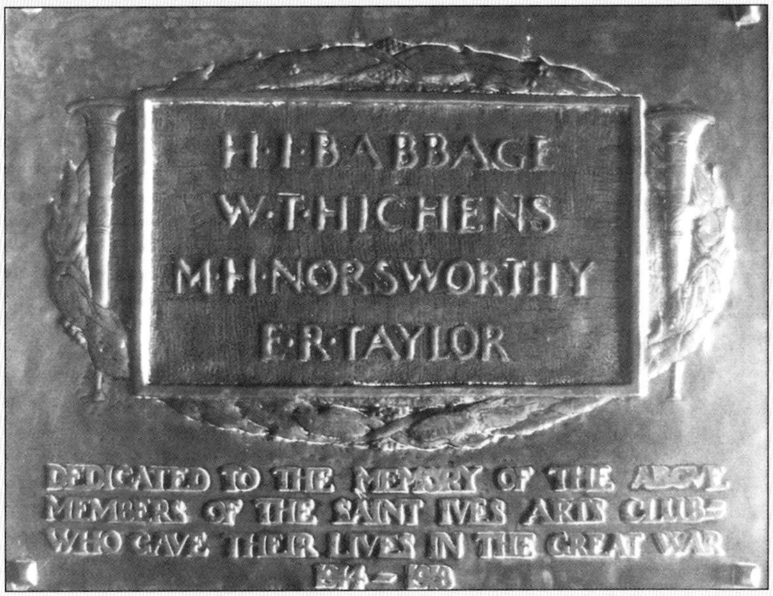

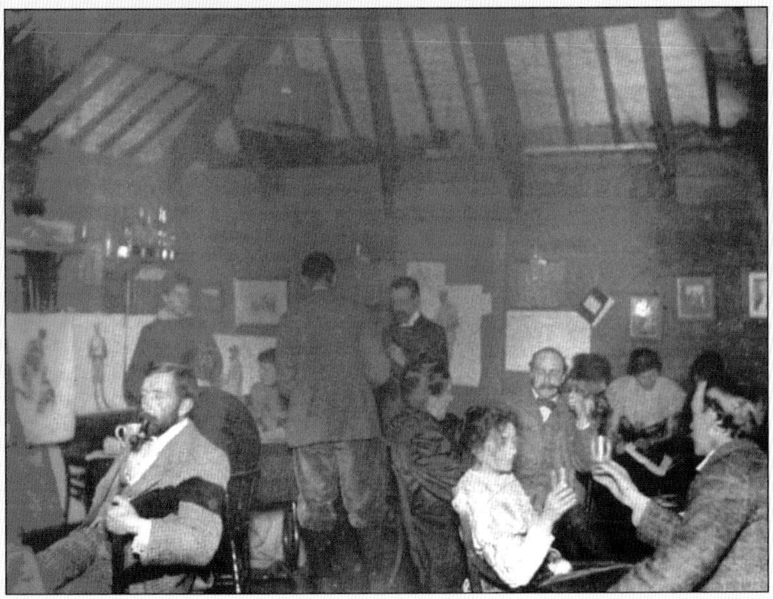

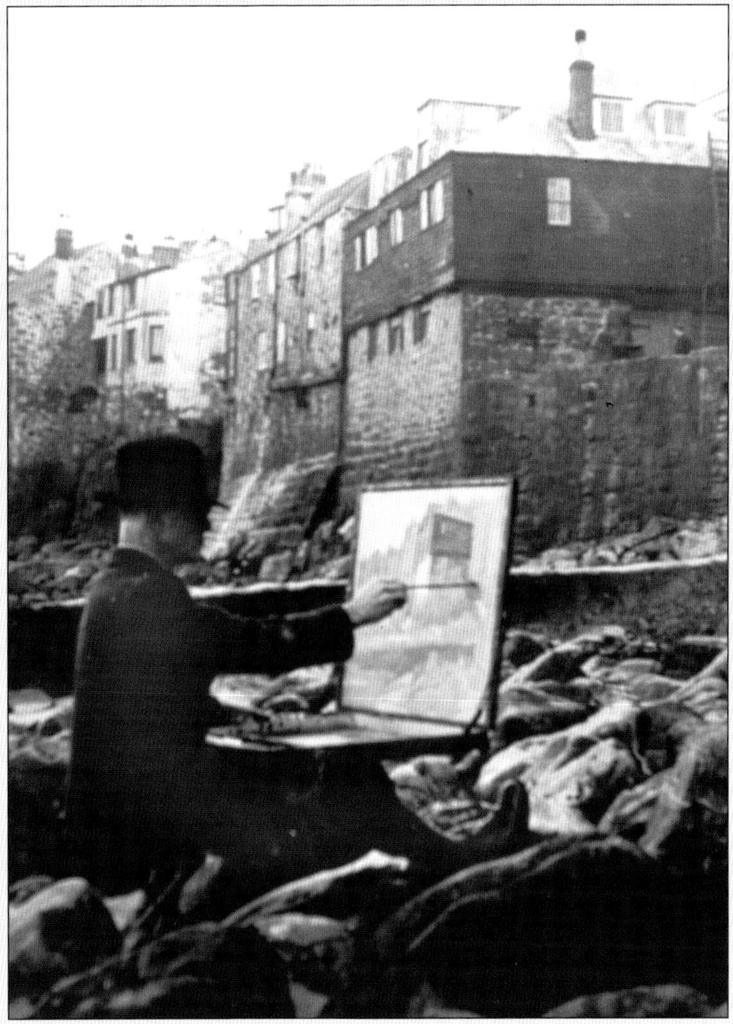

Above: *Borlase Smart painting the St Ives Arts Club.*

Top left: *Arts Club memorial plaque.*

Left: *Men and women painters in St Ives Arts Club, 1895. Louis Grier is seated far left.*

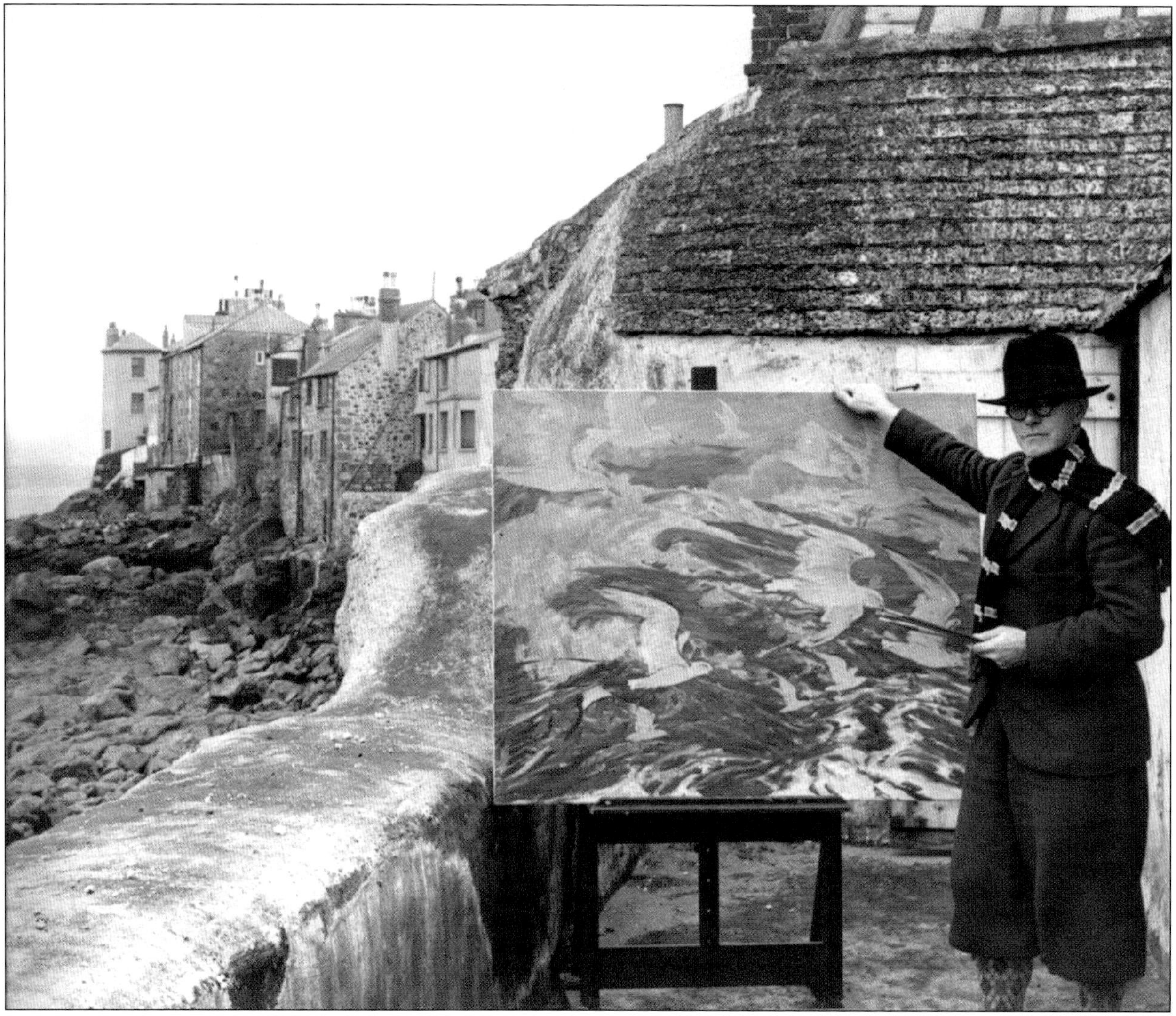

Borlase Smart on the Ocean Wave Studio balcony.

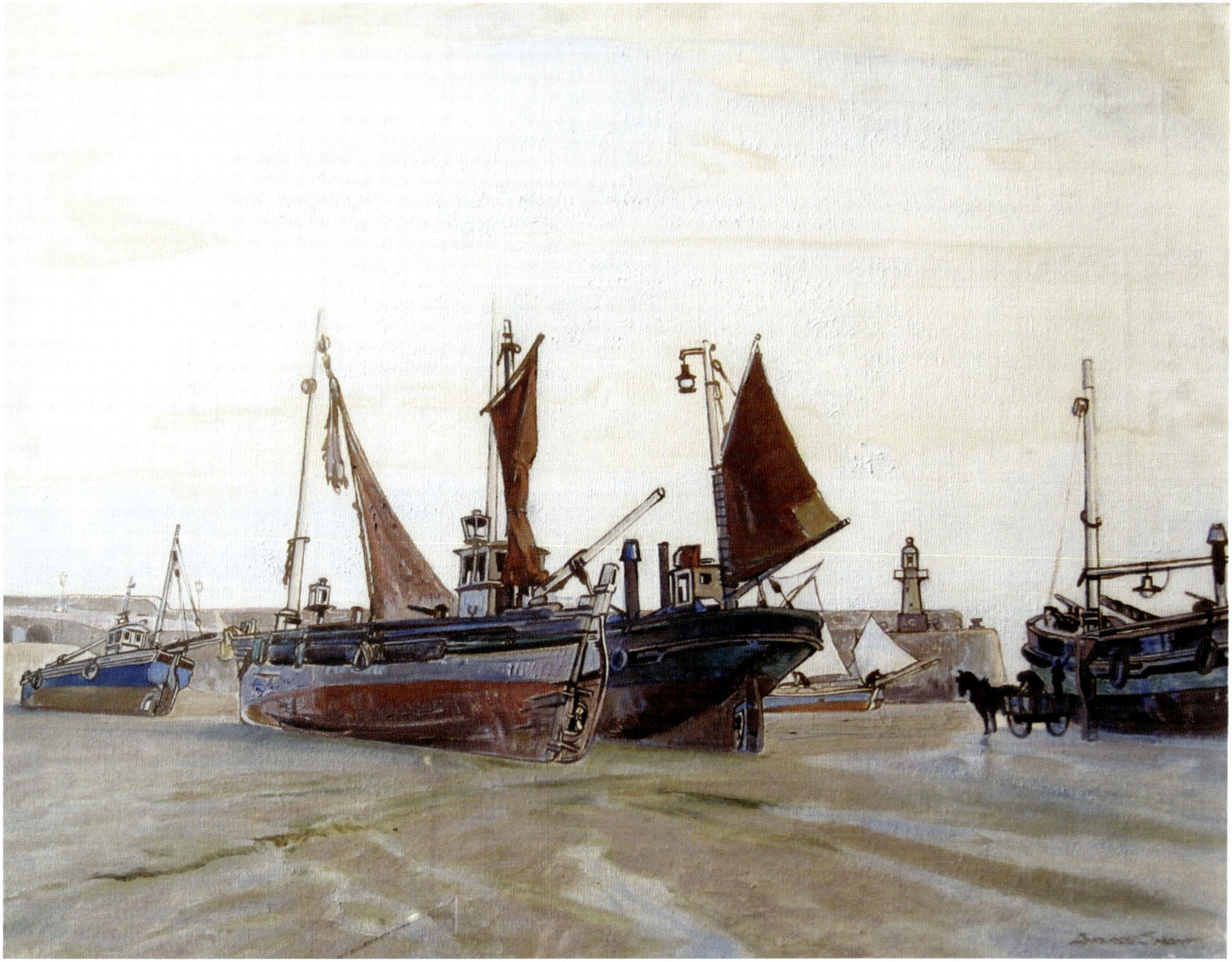

Fishing boats in St Ives harbour.

Hayle Bar.

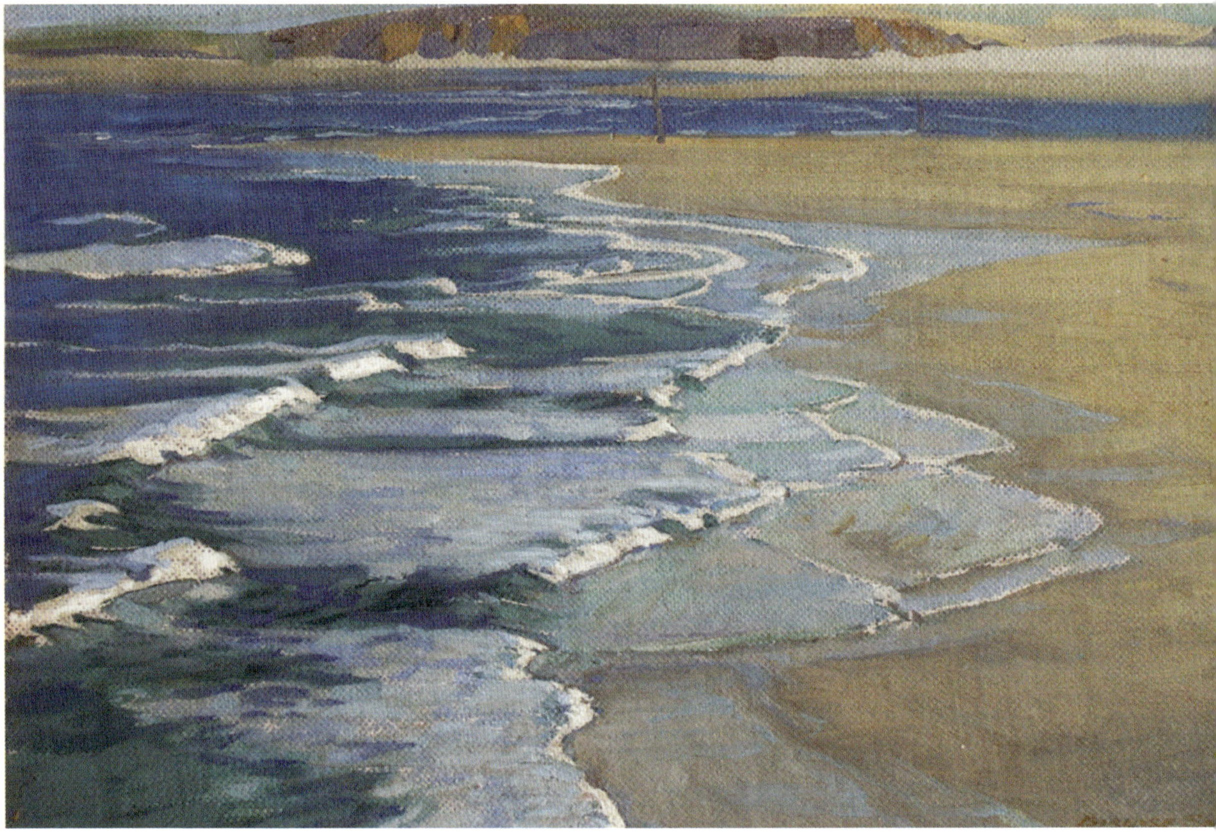

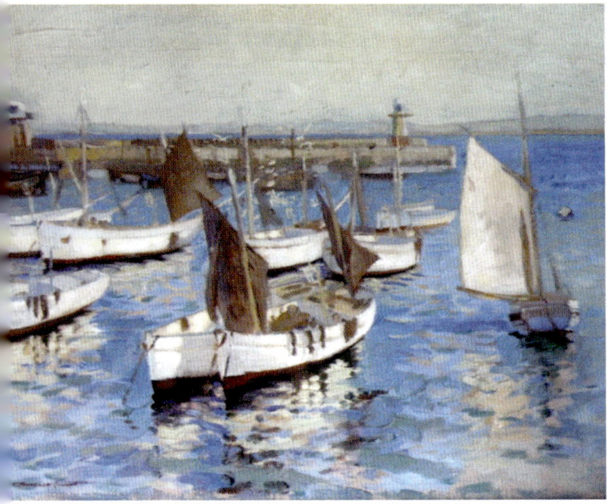

St Ives harbour.

St Ives Arts Club

St Ives Arts Club was the first artists' club in St Ives, established in 1890 by the founder member Louis Grier, who for two years previously had held meetings in his studio on the Wharf. The membership was increasing in numbers and Grier feared for his large painting 'The Night Watch' destined for an exhibition, so premises were secured over a carpenter's shop in the Warren on Westcott's Quay. The club was primarily a meeting place for 'professional painters, engravers, sculptors, architects, authors and musicians.' There were regular drawing classes and no shortage of models. Grier noted, *'We have a model twice a week, and it is no cheery place for the idler then, as there is little to disturb the monotony of silence save the grating of charcoal.'* [5]

The Arts Club members numbered around one hundred. Stanhope and Elizabeth Forbes from Newlyn were two of the first to join; their names are listed in the Arts Club Members book. Among many famous names is Leslie Stephen, father of the writer Virginia Woolf and Vanessa Bell the artist, who were children at the time, enjoying their annual summer residence at Talland House, where Leslie wrote and edited much of the *Dictionary of National Biography*.

In 1920 Louis Grier died and the committee, through the Suggestions Book, decided to ask Mrs Grier for the palette used by her husband, which would hang on the wall in the club room. Numbered among the signatories of this request, was Borlase Smart. There is also a photograph of Louis Reginald James Monro Grier (to give him his full title). Both these commemorative assets have hung in the club for over ninety years.

In 1920 Smart collaborated with Frank Emanuel, of the *Architectural Review*, in providing illustrations of the town for his article 'The Charm of the Country Town, St Ives'. The writer stated, '*Borlase Smart is one of the few members of the art colony who have ever set themselves to record the architectural features of the picturesque old town.*'[6]

The Community

There are those in a community who make a difference to the lives of its inhabitants and who create a respect for what they achieve for themselves and for their town, and leave a lasting memory in the minds of folk; such a town is St Ives and such a person was the artist, Borlase Smart. He was an icon for whom the local community of artists founded an art gallery in his honour, the Penwith Society of Arts in Cornwall, and in his memory, the Borlase Smart Memorial Trust, inaugurated with the aim of buying the Porthmeor Studios, a block of thirteen studios, which included the St Ives School of Painting. This was a primary aim of the Trust which would fulfill Smart's ambition to preserve the working conditions for fellow painters, potters and sculptors; to improve standards in presentation of art, to ensure publicity, reviews, criticism and promotion. Borlase had a great belief in the ongoing development of the Art Colony into the future.

He was no less enthusiastic in public affairs as he was in committing himself to the advancement of the aims of the artists. He was elected a Town Councillor, and was also secretary of the Chamber of Commerce. However, too much time discussing town affairs would take him away from his fellow artists and his primary aim was to promote their world.

With a great surge of interest in the art of print making The New Print Society was set up by Alfred Hartley in 1923, which included nine etchers and others working in colour printing, woodcuts and lithographs. They held their first exhibition of 65 works at Lanham's Gallery, where Borlase praised the fine etchings of Bernard Leach, the potter. Hartley had studied at the Royal College. His award-winning colour etching, 'A Wessex Valley', was purchased for the Los Angeles Museum.

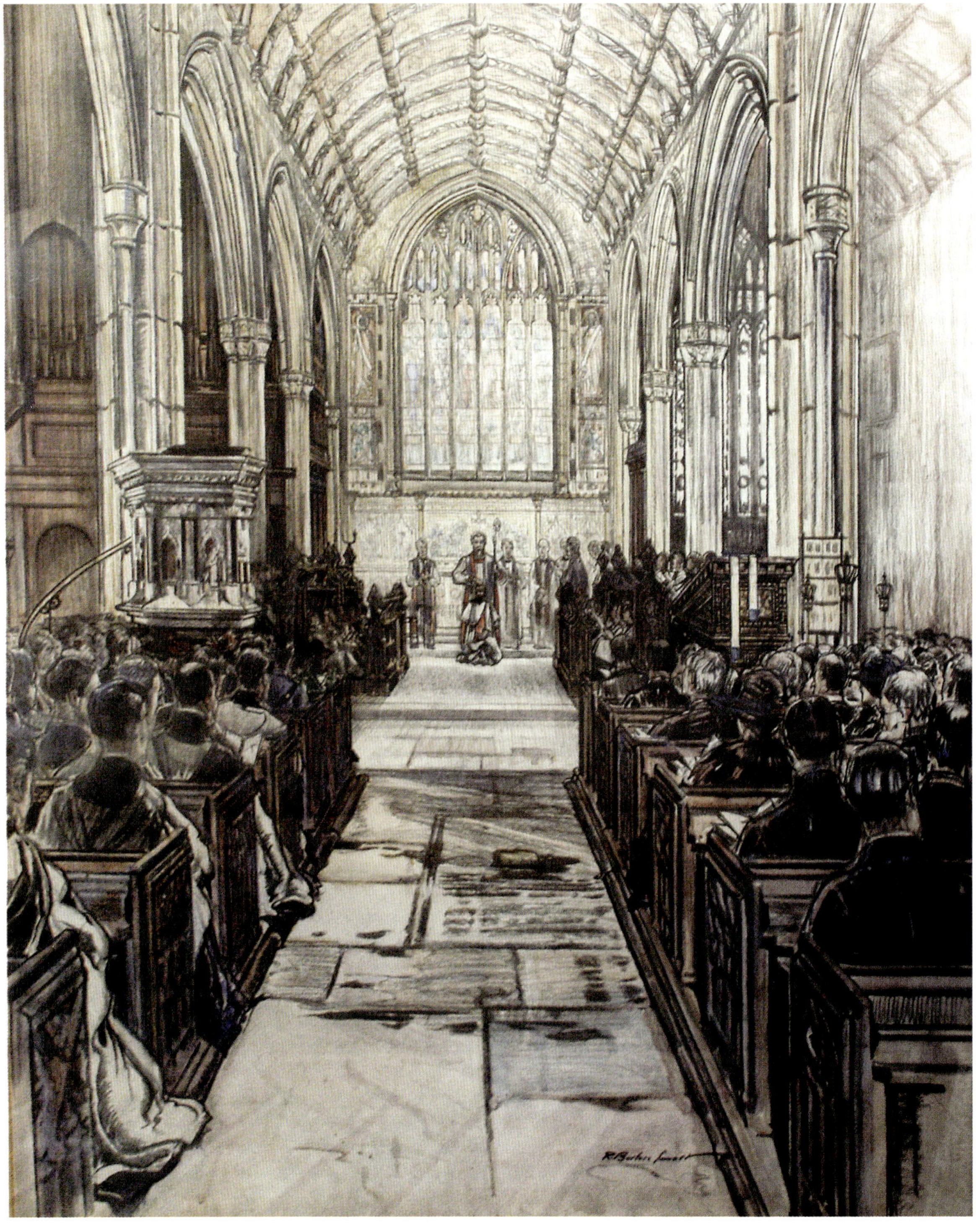

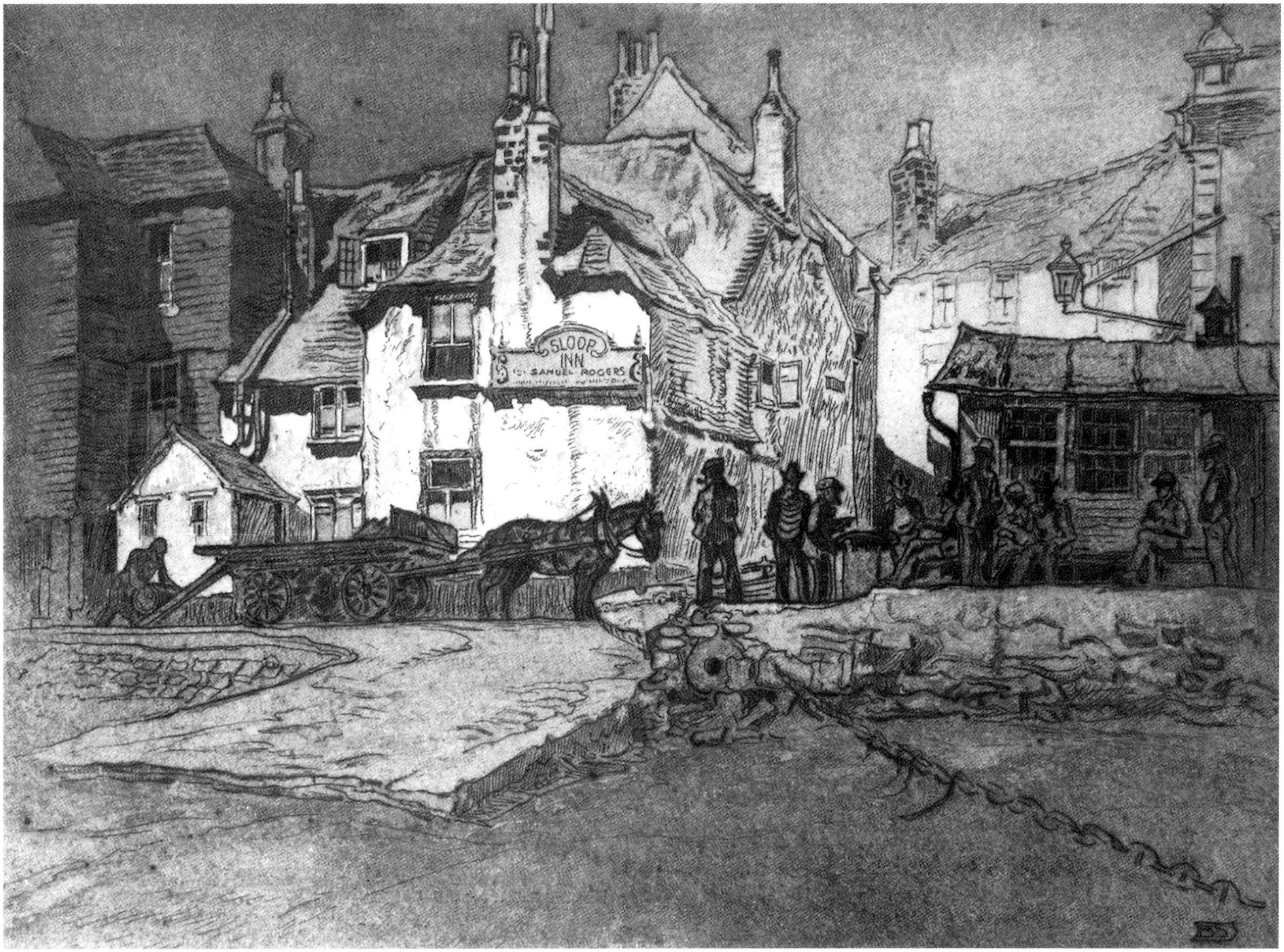

The Sloop Inn, etching.

Opposite: *St Ia Church interior, St Ives.*

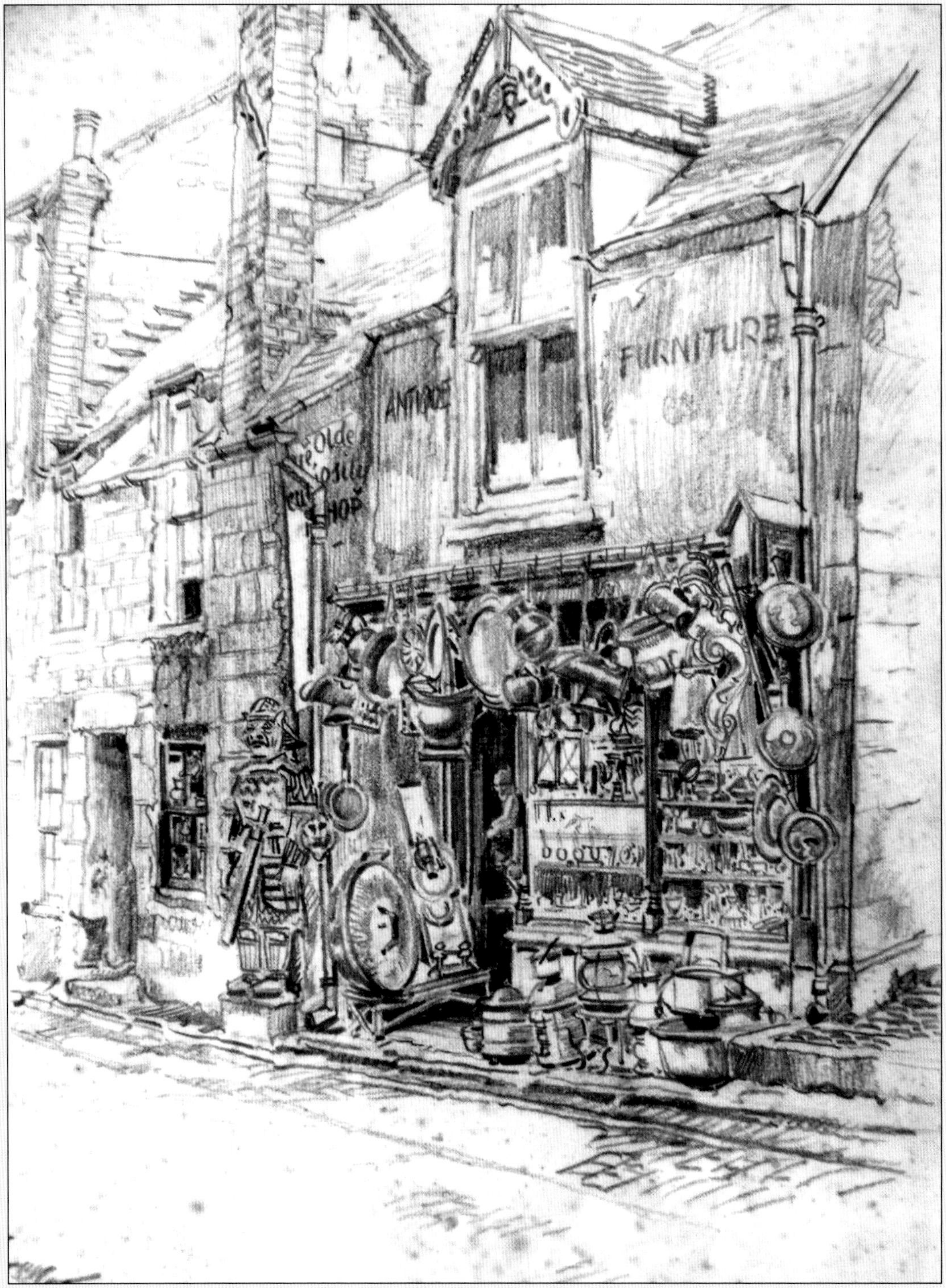

The Old Curiosity Shop, St Ives.

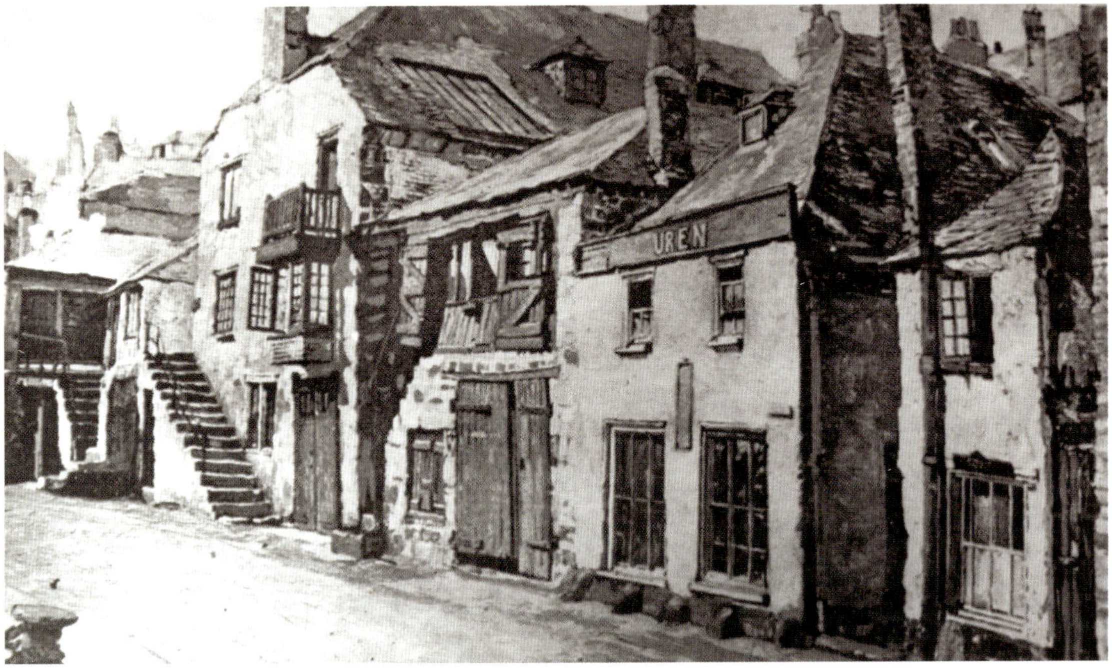

The Wharf, St Ives.

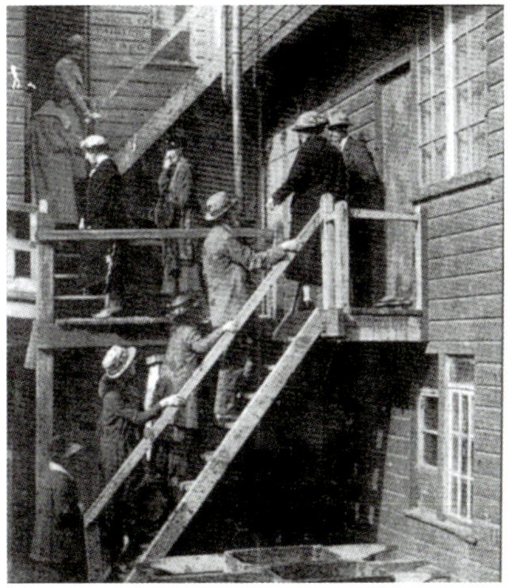

Visiting the Studios.

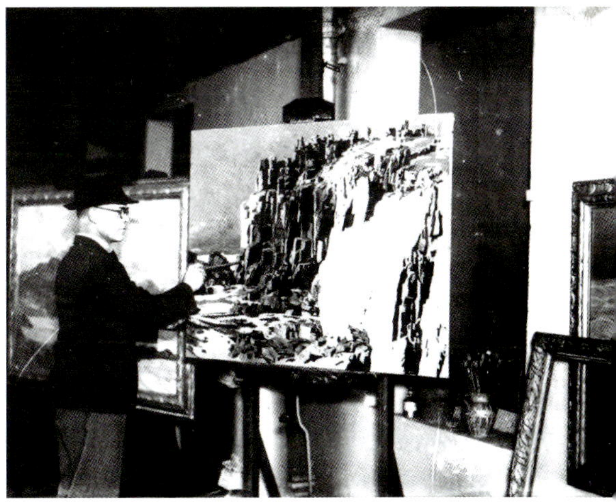

Borlase Smart in his Studio.

Show Days

It was the tradition in St Ives for artists to open their studios on one day in the year to show the work they were sending to the Royal Academy in London for inclusion in the Summer Exhibition. After the war this custom was re-established. The St Ives train brought in large numbers of people, who flooded into the town for this annual event. Schools closed and the pupils, accompanied by their teachers, walked along to Back Road West to view the paintings in the Porthmeor and Piazza Studios whose enormous windows fronted the rolling Atlantic ocean and whose foundations were built on the copious sands of Porthmeor beach. There were various studios all over Downalong, the fishing quarter of the town, where many a net loft, once housing fishing gear, had been turned into an artist's workplace, and skylights appeared on the old ochre lichen-covered roofs. The Wharf had its studios around the harbour with its constant activity of boats, fishermen on the quay landing a catch, holding fish auctions, handling barrels of pressed fish, mending nets and the general activity of men and women engaged in their livelihood.

It was noted that St Ives every year, had large numbers of works of art hung in the Royal Academy Summer Exhibitions. One critic observed, that the percentage of St Ives pictures was higher than any other town in Cornwall. In one year 80 works of art were accepted and of these 48 were hung on the line, the most favoured spot for work to be shown; meaning that the public viewed the paintings at eye level.

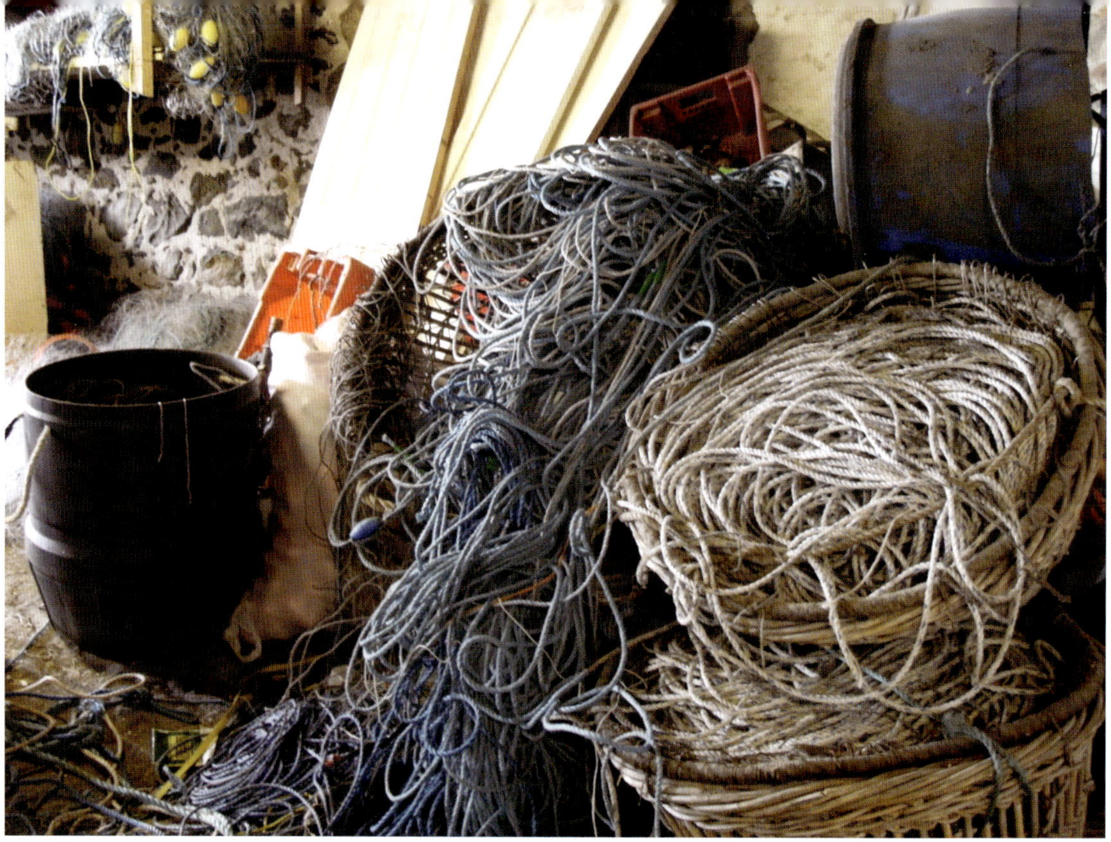

Fishermen's gear in St Ives.

Artists and Fishermen

In the Porthmeor complex the artists and the fishermen worked in close proximity, as had been the tradition since the arrival of artists in the 1880s. Fishing was already in decline and fishermen could gain additional money from letting their largely unused net lofts to the artists, who had also provided local families with jobs as housekeepers, maids, servants, nannies, artists' models, and were spending money in the town shops. It was a case of refloating the economy, when mining and fishing were on the wane. Artists occupied the spacious top floors of the buildings, some of which had been built as studios. They were flooded with light and the artists welcomed visitors and the chance to show their work and discuss their art.

The fishermen stored their gear and made their nets in the basement below, which contained tanks for salting the pilchard and for the salt in which the fish were cured; also the cooperage workshop for making barrels for transport of the pressed fish. Behind the doors of these premises the processing of fish was carried out on an industrial scale. The fishermen kept their working environment very private and open only to other fishermen. However, toleration of each other's world was respected by the artists and fishermen. The men of the sea were considered to be good models and the Sloop Inn, where artists and fishermen gathered, was the venue for many portraits and caricatures of local familiar faces. Harry Rountree and later, Hyman Segal, exhibited their drawings of St Ives characters for many years in the Sloop Inn by the harbour.

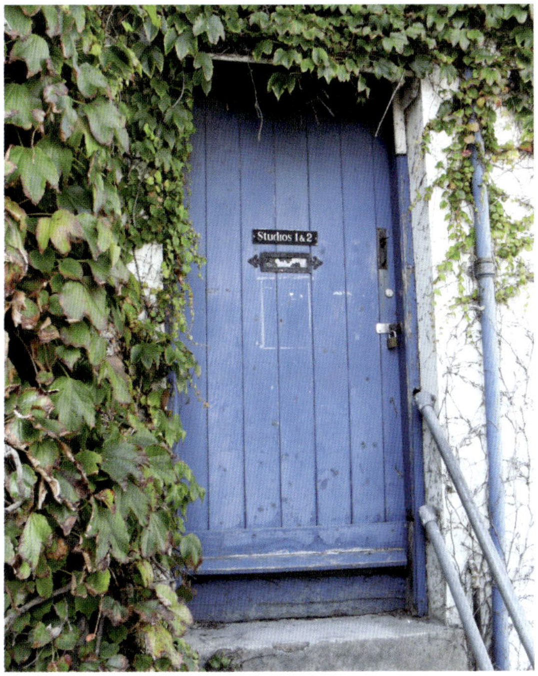

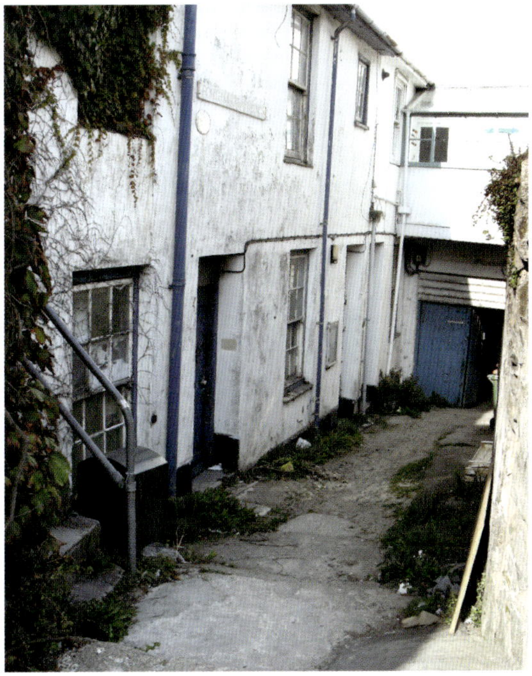

Left: *Entrance to 1 and 2 Porthmeor Studios before renovation.*

Right: *Entrance 3 to 9 Porthmeor Studios before renovation.*

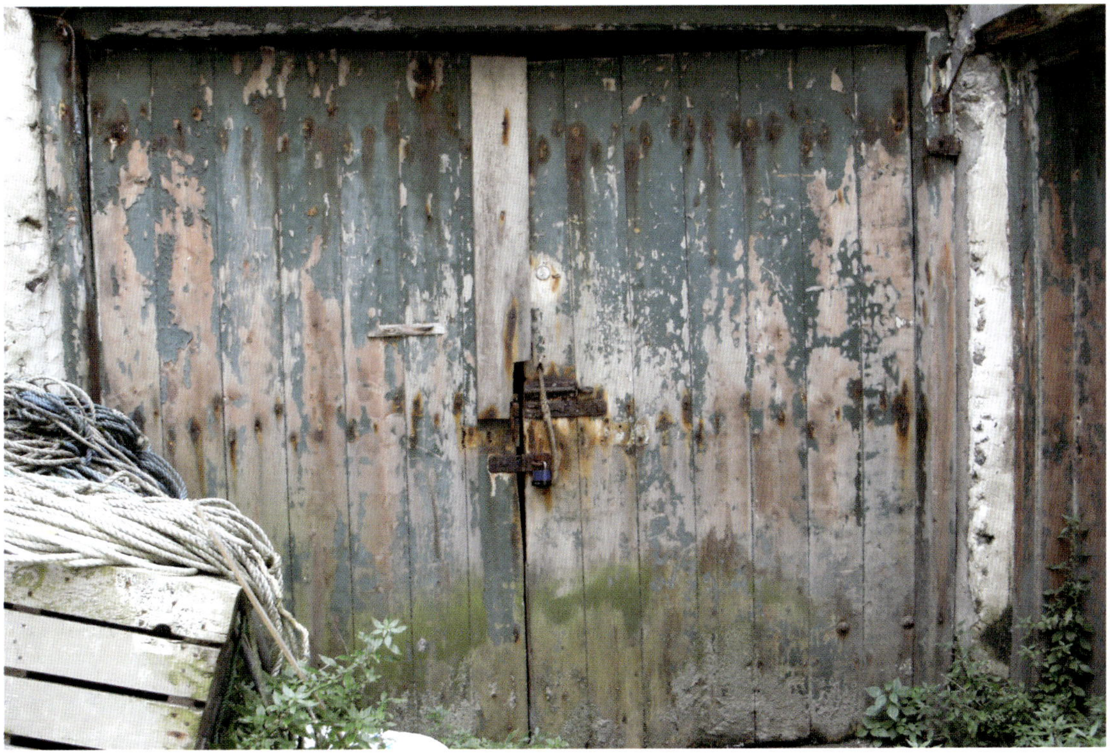

Entrance to cellars under the studios, Porthmeor.

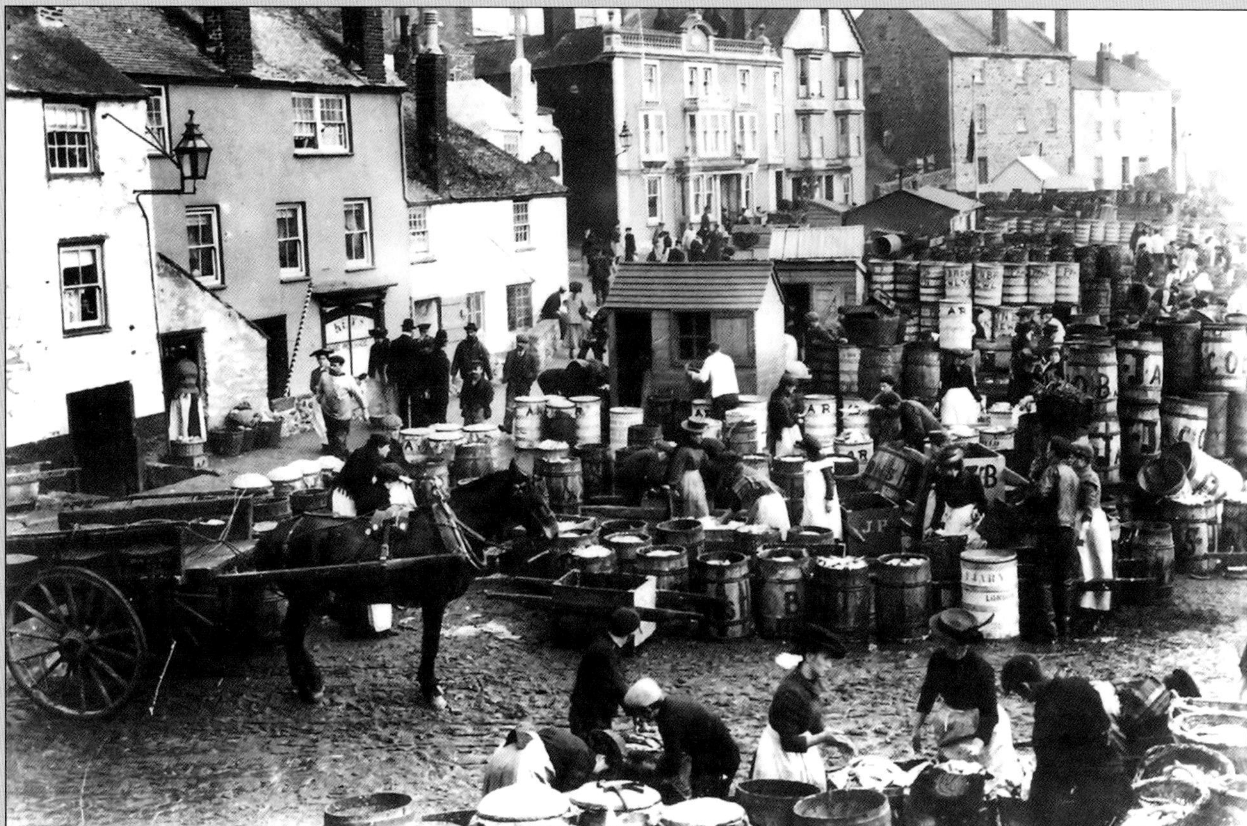

The harbour, St Ives, c.1920.

Lanham's Gallery

In 1922 Smart, along with his friend, John Park, were serving on the Hanging Committee of Lanham's Gallery in the High Street. James Lanham Limited, the general merchants store in town, was established in 1869. They advertised themselves as, Artists' Colourmen, Printers, Stationers, Wine, Spirit and General Merchants, Art Galleries, Fine Art Packers, Frame Makers, Auctioneers, Valuers, House and Estate Agents. Their premises remain and they are still trading as letting agents.

At that date Lanham's was the only art gallery in town. The selection and display of works in their gallery was carried out by St Ives Arts Club members who endeavoured to exhibit their paintings to their best effect.

Members of the committee were entirely responsible for hanging the exhibits and James Lanham was completely happy with this arrangement. It was a symbiotic relationship. Lanham's rented

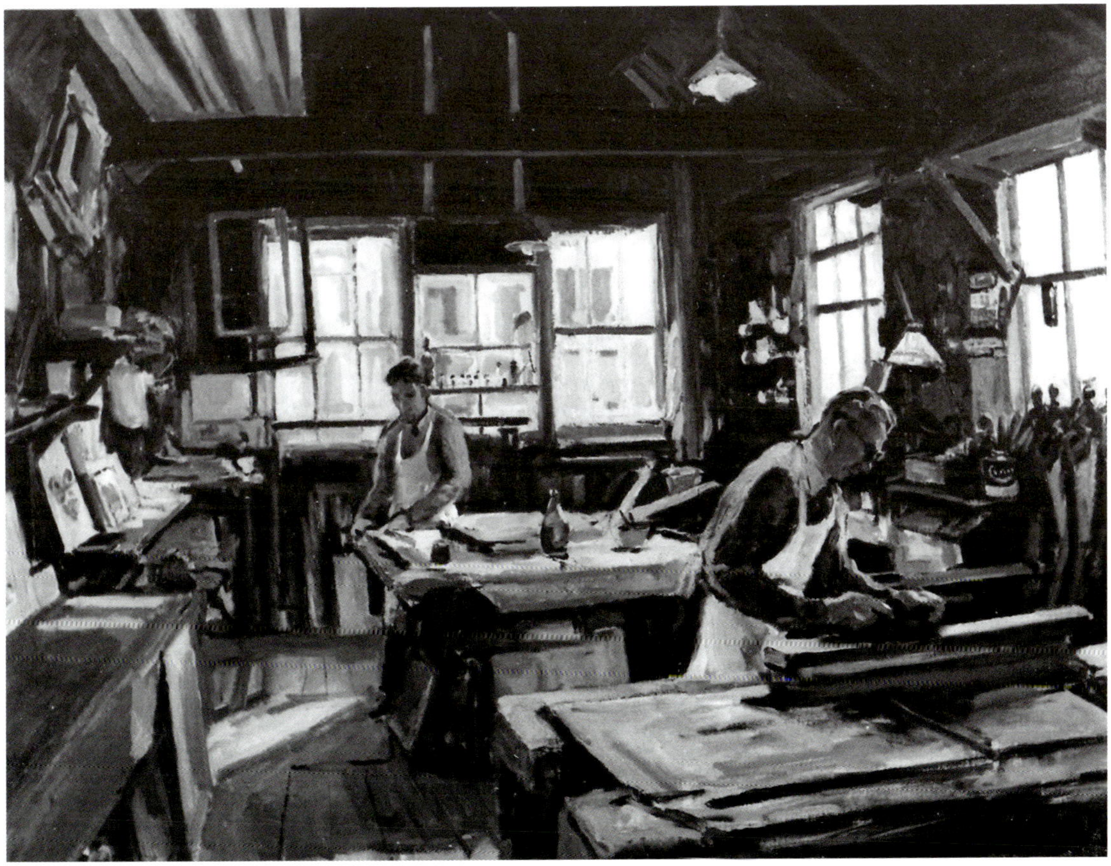

A painting of Lanham's framing workshop.

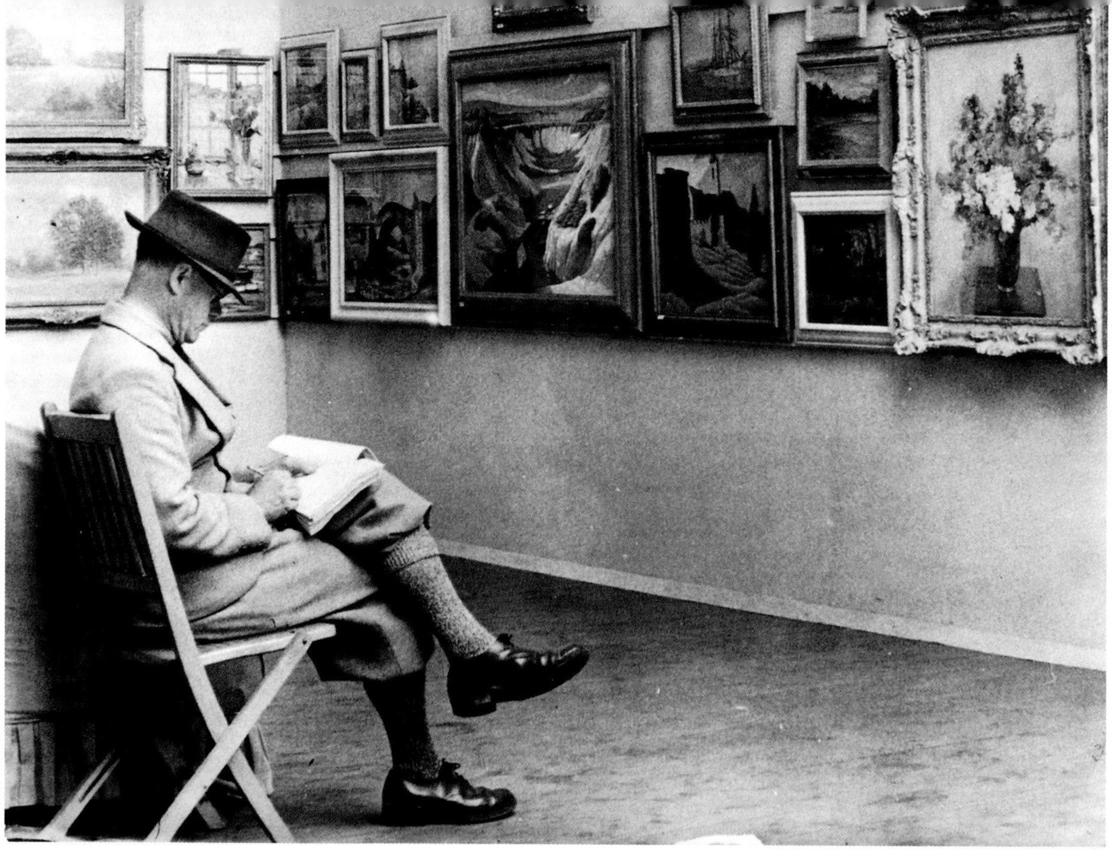

Borlase Smart writing a review.

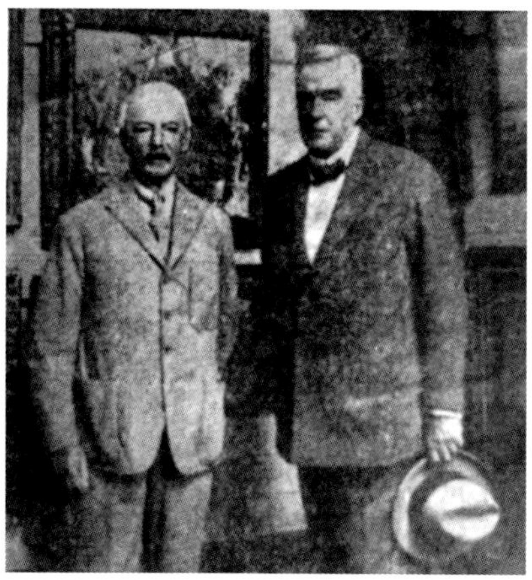

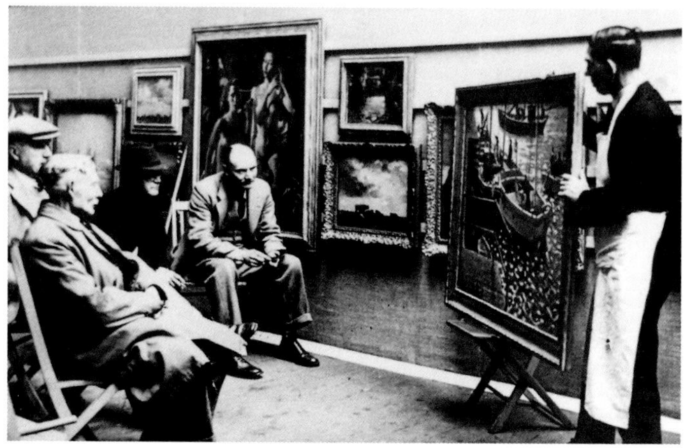

Left: *Moffat Lindner and Julius Olsson, 1928.*

Right: *The Hanging Committee. Maidment, Bradshaw, Smart, Fuller, Tonkin Prynne, and the picture framer.*

houses and studios to the artists; they bought their art materials from his shop; they required his services for framing, packing and transport to galleries throughout the country and abroad; especially the all-important shipment of canvases to the Royal Academy each year, for which a special railway carriage was hired. Even so, Julius Olsson had to attend the RA to repair his painting, 'The Moonlit Bay' when paintings and fish were travelling in a carriage together and fish oil had leaked from a barrel on to his canvas. It was thought to be beyond repair but Olsson worked on it and the painting was hung on the line, no doubt bringing a whiff of St Ives to enhance the exhibits.

Visit of the Hon. H. Herbert Asquith

A historic moment for the town of St Ives was recorded when the Right Honourable Herbert Asquith, former Liberal Prime Minister, visited the town in 1922. Martin Cock of Lanham's closed the High Street Galleries in order to introduce his distinguished guest to some of the one hundred artists working in the town and show his visitor their studios.

Asquith declared himself an old friend of artist Alfred Hartley and from there he was taken to the School of Painting at the Shore Studio, Piazza, run by Charles and Ruth Simpson from 1920 to 1924. Ruth tutored in portrait painting and Charles, an ardent naturalist, in wildlife studies. He also painted a series of 22 paintings depicting the working lives of the St Ives fishermen, showing the process of landing the fish to the packing in barrels. The couple met at the Stanhope Forbes School of Painting in Newlyn and married in 1913, moving to St Ives in 1916.

Asquith also visited Borlase Smart's studio, having heard that he had some interesting pictures of the battlefields in Flanders. *'The Rt Hon. gentleman paid a short visit. The artist, being absent, the visitor was shown around by Mrs Irene Smart. He was deeply impressed, not only with the war pictures, but the many representations of Captain Smart's artistic ability.'* [7]

Mr Asquith was also impressed with the old world buildings in the lower part of the town, and the narrow streets. *'He only hoped the Town Council of St Ives was progressive, but they should remember that if they did away with the old buildings and tried to make the town too modern they would spoil the attractiveness of the town.'* [8]

These comments were great encouragement to those people trying to preserve the cobbled streets and cottages fronting the harbour and lanes in Downalong; and indeed this warning is even more vital today.

The Fairy Queen's Palace

In 1922 St Ives artists were asked to submit miniature specimens of their paintings to Princess Louise, giving a size of one-and-a-half inches by one inch for inclusion in the famous Fairy Queen's Palace, designed by the renowned architect Sir Edwin Lutyens. Those contributing were Moffat Lindner, Edmund Fuller, Borlase Smart, Marcella Smith, Alfred Hartley, James Lynn Pitt, W. Cave Day, W. B. Fortescue and W. S. Parkyn. A letter from Buckingham Palace dated April 1924 thanks the contributors. *'It is with the greatest pleasure that I say "thank you" to all the very kind people who have helped to make the Dolls House the most perfect present that anyone could receive; and I hope through*

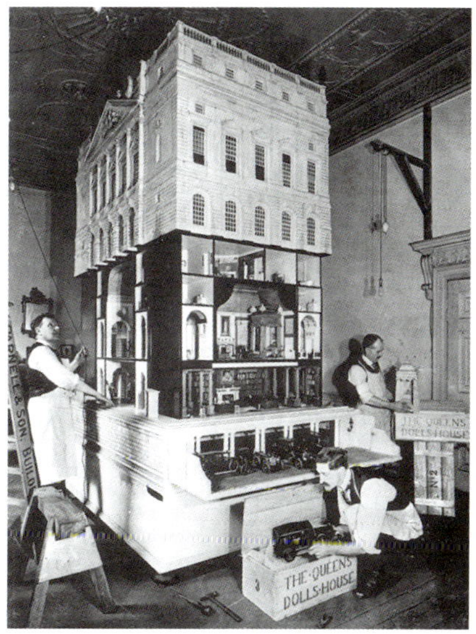

Workmen putting finishing touches to the Queen's Doll's House in 1924.

having it at the British Empire Exhibition, that it will be the means of raising funds for the many charitable schemes that I have at heart.' Signed Mary R. [9]

Those selected were granted free access to the Palace of Arts at Wembley.

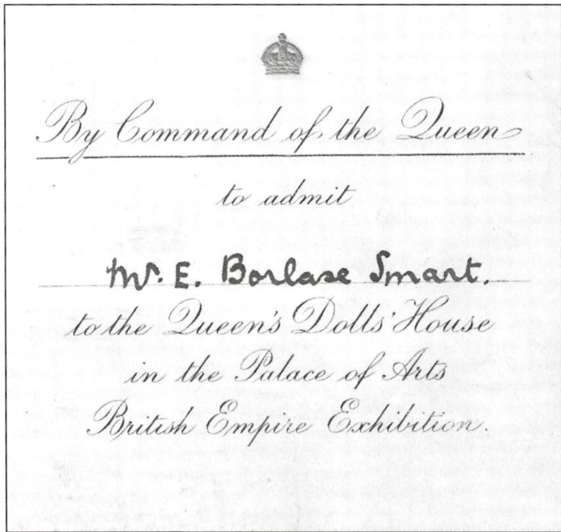

By Command of the Queen

to admit

Mr. E. Borlase Smart.

to the Queen's Dolls' House
in the Palace of Arts
British Empire Exhibition.

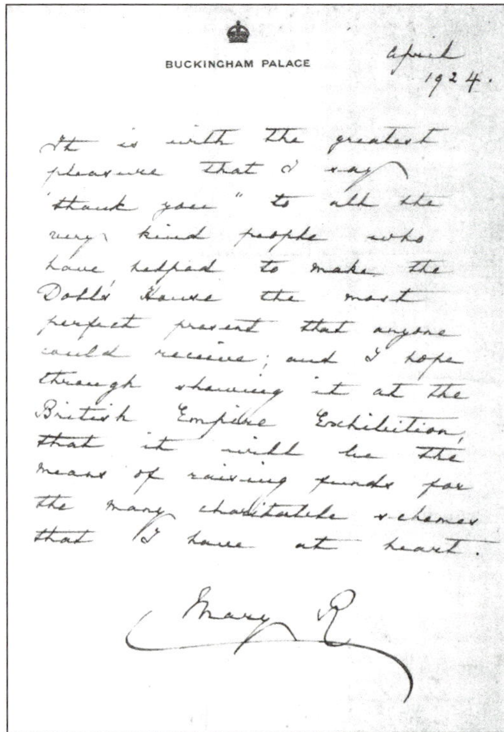

BUCKINGHAM PALACE

April
1924.

It is with the greatest pleasure that I say "thank you" to all the very kind people who have helped to make the Dolls' House the most perfect present that anyone could receive; and I hope through showing it at the British Empire Exhibition, that it will be the means of raising funds for the many charitable schemes that I have at heart.

Mary R.

Invitation and letter from Buckingham Palace.

Posters

A poster designed by Smart in 1922 and commissioned by The Great Western Railway was 'The Cornish Riviera for Golden Sands and Sunshine.' Another design was 'St Ives, Carbis Bay and Lelant'. He was also responsible for providing a map of St Ives town as a guide for visitors. This was on display at the Malakoff, a high point overlooking the harbour and bay. Herbert Truman and Leonard Richmond were also involved in poster design, and in making prints and postcards advertising St Ives as a holiday resort.

Smart made a poster for Crysede, the manufacturer in St Ives making hand block- printed fashionable dresses. The catalogue stated, *'The models which are being displayed are created from our exclusive materials, hand printed Crepe-de-Chine, Silks, Linens and Woollens.'* Chief designer was Alec

Walker, whose designs were inspired by the flora of West Penwith. These dresses, costumes and other garments were for a discerning market, although many a St Ives woman working at the factory would save her wages to buy a dress. The Managing Director of the firm was Tom Heron, father of the painter, Patrick Heron. Smart organized a visit to the firm on the Island, where many men and women of the town worked, and he prepared the Society's new gallery at Porthmeor studios to allow a mannequin parade to take place.

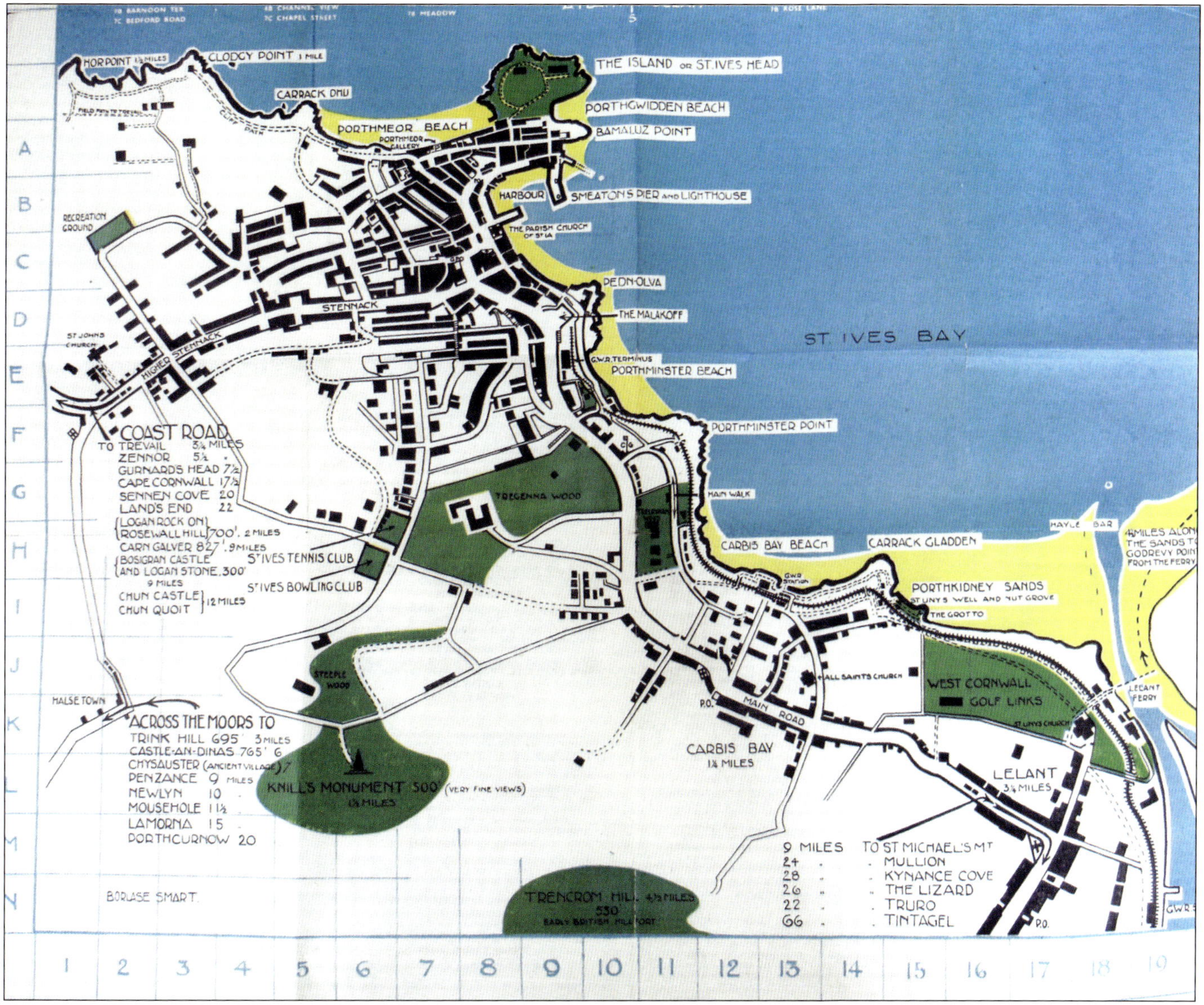

The Town Map of St Ives designed by Borlase Smart.

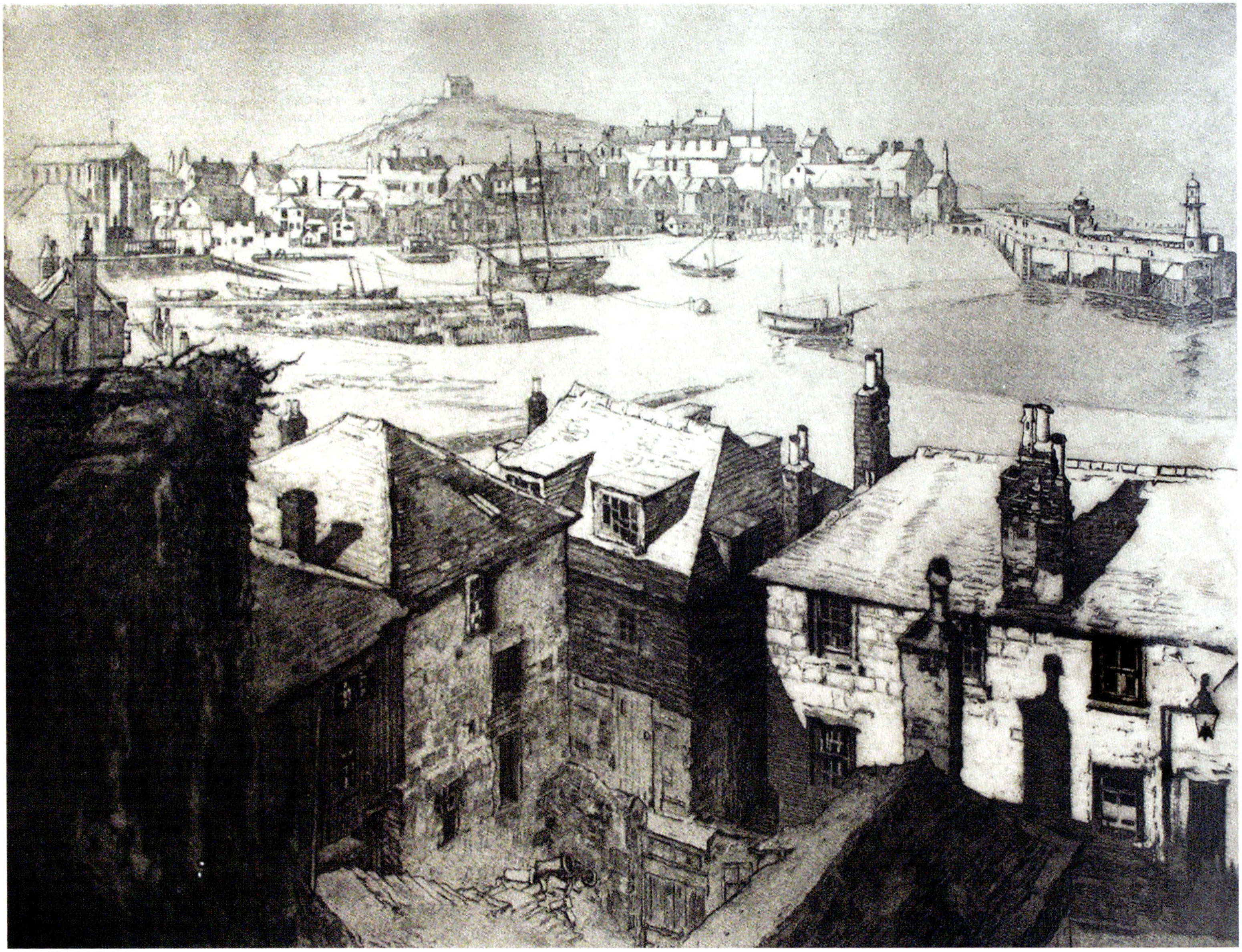

The illustration used on the poster for Crysede.

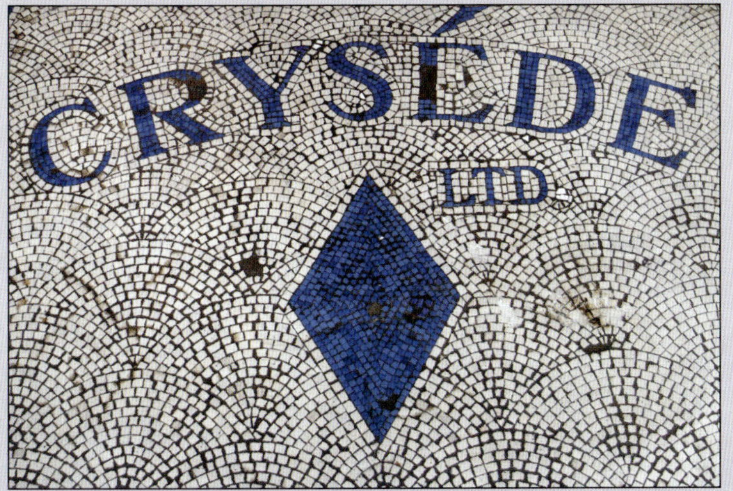

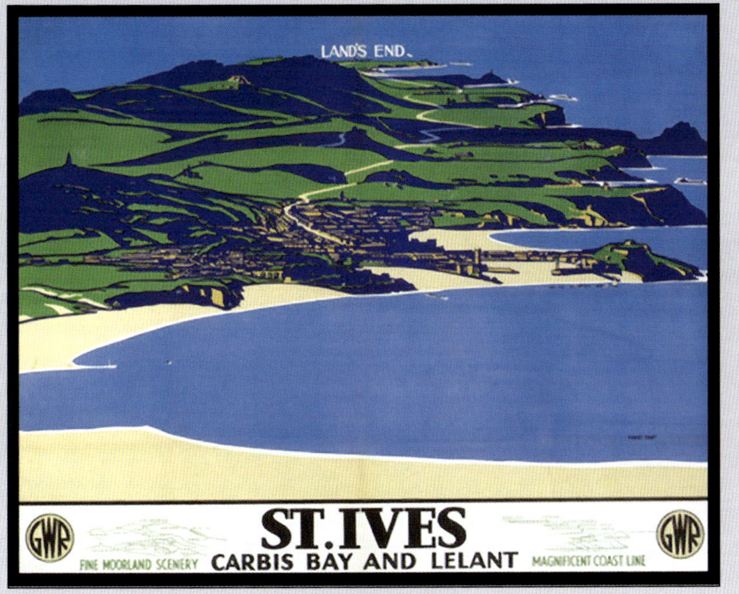

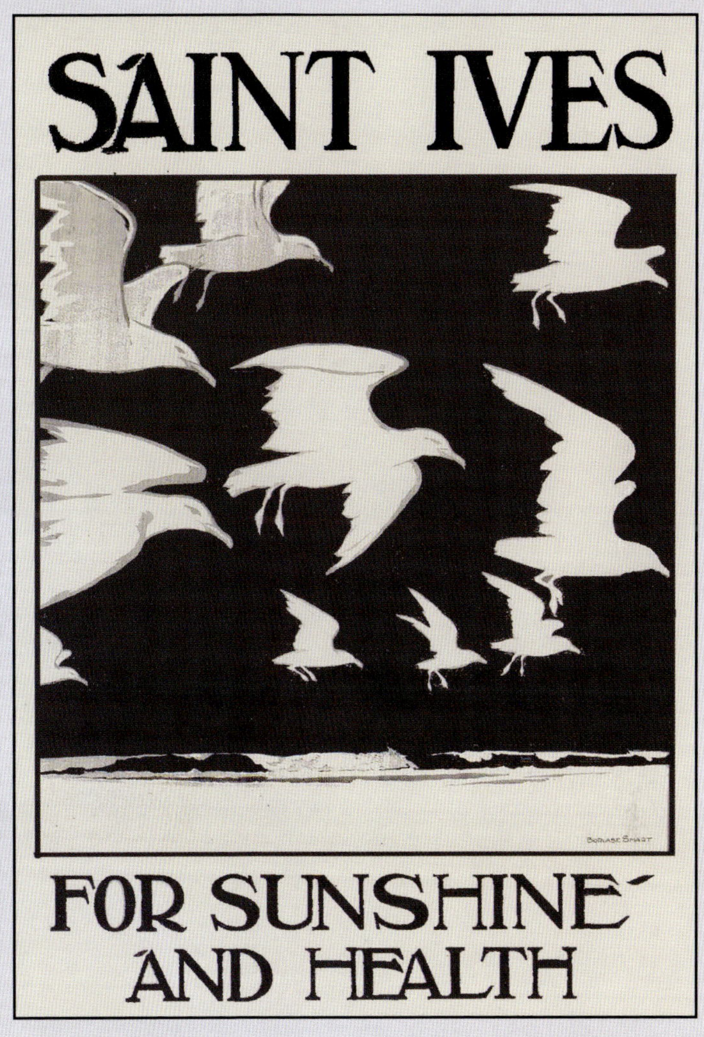

Above left: *Mosaic entrance to shop at 68 Chapel Street.*

Left and above: *Posters designed for the Great Western Railway.*

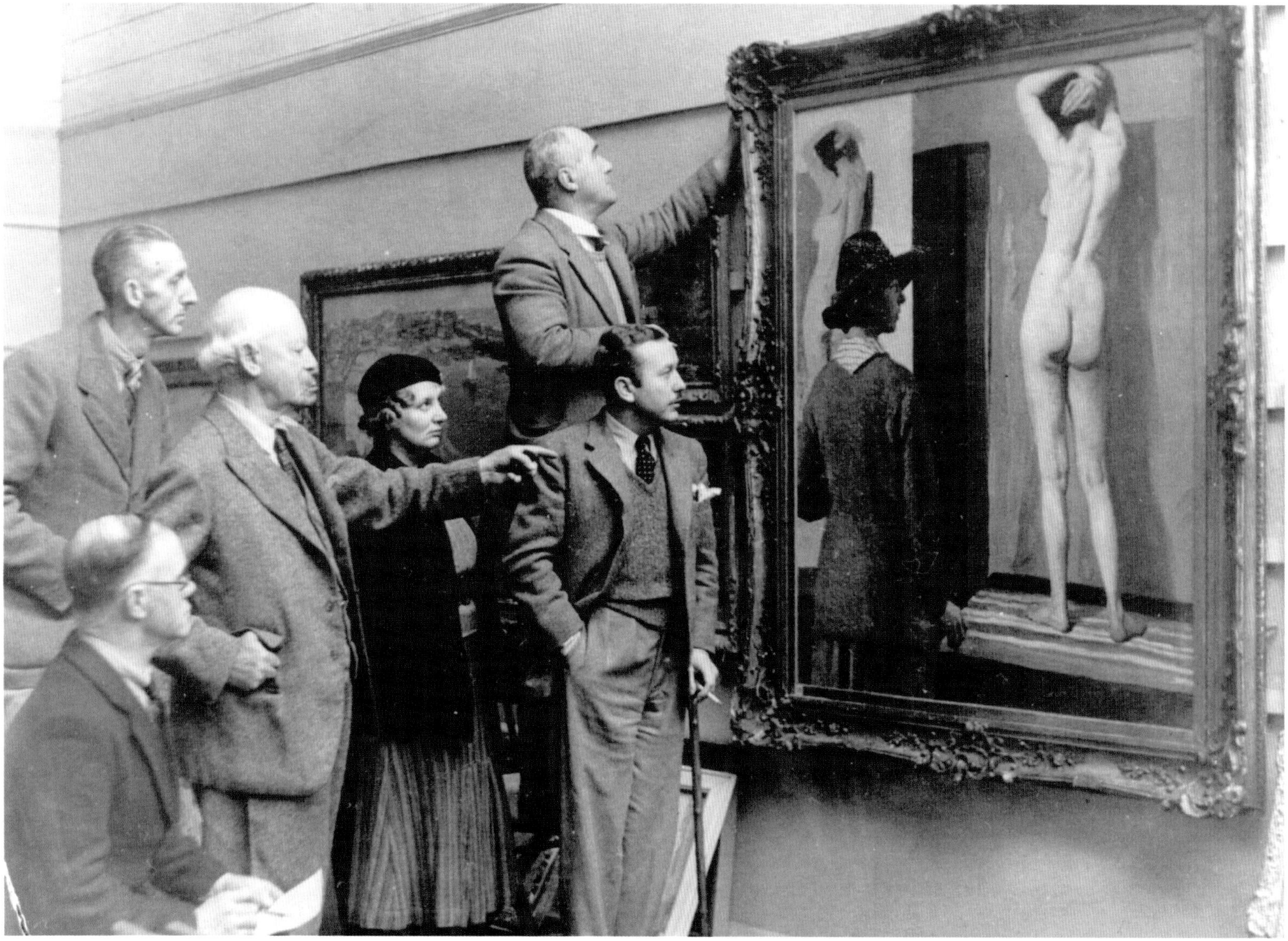

Porthmeor Gallery. Painting by Dame Laura Knight. 'Self Portrait and Model'. Left Borlase Smart, J Millar-Watt, Moffat Lindner, Shearer Armstrong, Bernard Ninnes and George Bradshaw.

St Ives Society of Artists

After a great many years of exhibiting at Lanham's Gallery, the artists desired an independent art gallery to show the work of the St Ives Society of Artists, newly created in 1927, with Moffat Lindner as President, a breakaway from the Arts Club, although entirely made up of members of the Club. Lindner was to remain a staunch supporter of both the Arts Club and the St Ives Society of Artists. He was the elder statesman, a stable and reliable figurehead of these organizations. He retired from painting and active life at the age of 94 and was often seen sitting in the window of his home at Chy-an-Porth, a large granite house overlooking Porthminster beach.

This new society was exclusively for artists, rather than the more general run of the Arts Club, which operated on a broader base and included drama, music and social activities. Before obtaining their own premises, the first exhibition of their work was shown at Lanham's Gallery. It included work by artists who were living, or had lived in St Ives, and other artists associated with the town, including Borlase Smart, Louis Grier, Adrian Stokes, Marianne Stokes, Thomas Millie Dow, William Holt Yates Titcomb, Julius Olsson and John Park.

Through the newly created St Ives Society of Artists, the members were becoming independent of Lanham's and the Arts Club and seeking their own premises for exhibitions of their work. In 1928 the Smarts returned to St Ives from a period of living in Salcombe, Devon, where in 1926 their first son Michael, was born. Their second son, Brian, who was born in St Ives, arrived three years later. Though not a founder member of the Society, Borlase was elected to the committee in 1928 realizing that he, as a former reporter with the *Western Morning News* and familiar with the world of the arts, would be a suitable spokesman for advertising the Society and promoting its accomplishments. Hyman Segal drew a caricature of Borlase as the upright, efficient, man of action, the 'painter organiser' of the affairs of the society.

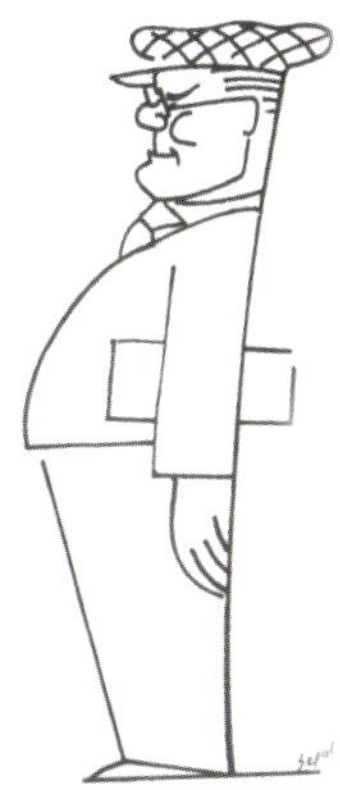

Caricature of Borlase by Hyman Segal.

Borlase enthusiastically set about arranging lectures on art, given by the members themselves, exploiting their own particular expertise, whether in drawing, etching, painting in oils and water colour, preparation of canvases and advice on framing their pictures. Borlase spoke of the history of the art colony and the importance of upholding its traditions. He organized exhibitions in Studio Four, Porthmeor. It was a home for their paintings and a place where the professionals could discuss their work and feel that the constructive criticism of other artists was of vital importance. The aim was to raise the status and quality of art and artists in St Ives.

This first show in the new gallery was opened by Julius Olsson, the much admired seascape painter of the time. Such was the success of the exhibitions of the Society that the adjoining Studio

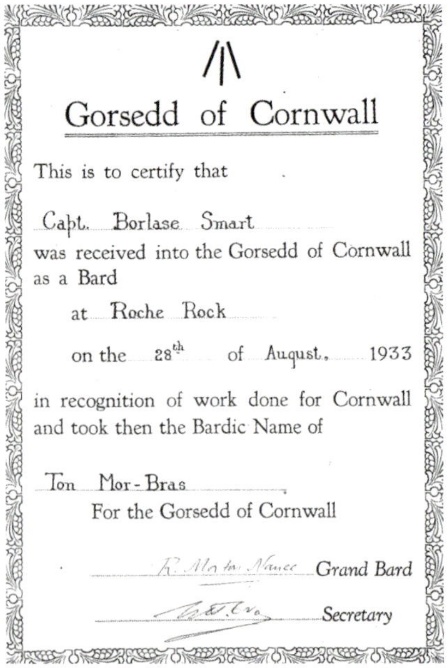

Gorsedd of Cornwall

This is to certify that

Capt. Borlase Smart

was received into the Gorsedd of Cornwall as a Bard

at Roche Rock

on the 28th of August, 1933

in recognition of work done for Cornwall and took then the Bardic Name of

Ton Mor-Bras

For the Gorsedd of Cornwall

[illegible] Grand Bard

[illegible] Secretary

Certificate confirming Borlase Smart's election as a Bard.

Five, previously occupied by Olsson, was incorporated into the complex, allowing more artists to showcase their work.

In 1933 Borlase Smart became secretary of the Society of Artists, enabling him to organize exhibitions outside of St Ives and spread the work of his contemporaries more widely. He was greatly helped in the organization by his friend and fellow seascape painter, Commander Bradshaw.

'Borlase Smart is, I think, one of the busiest men in St Ives. Anything that will help to add to the artistic reputation of the town is certain of his help and support. His studio is on the harbour front, and on my first visit (early one morning) I found the door left open; I could have helped myself to the choicest of his paintings easily. Doors are seldom locked in St Ives.' [10]

In this same year he was honoured for his services to art and made a Bard of the Cornish Gorsedd. His Bardic name being Ton Mor-Bras, or Ocean Wave, perhaps named after his studio, or because of his majestic seascape paintings.

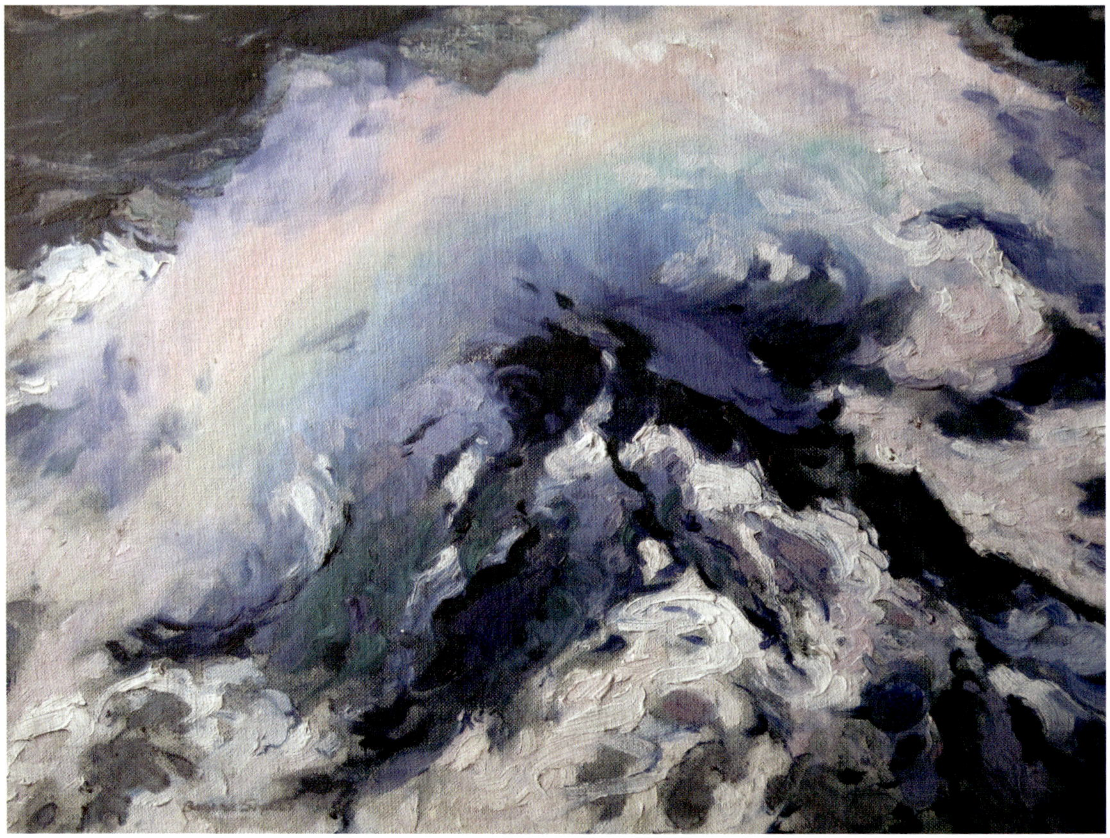

Bow wash from the liner Otranto.

Opposite: *Moonlit Sea.*

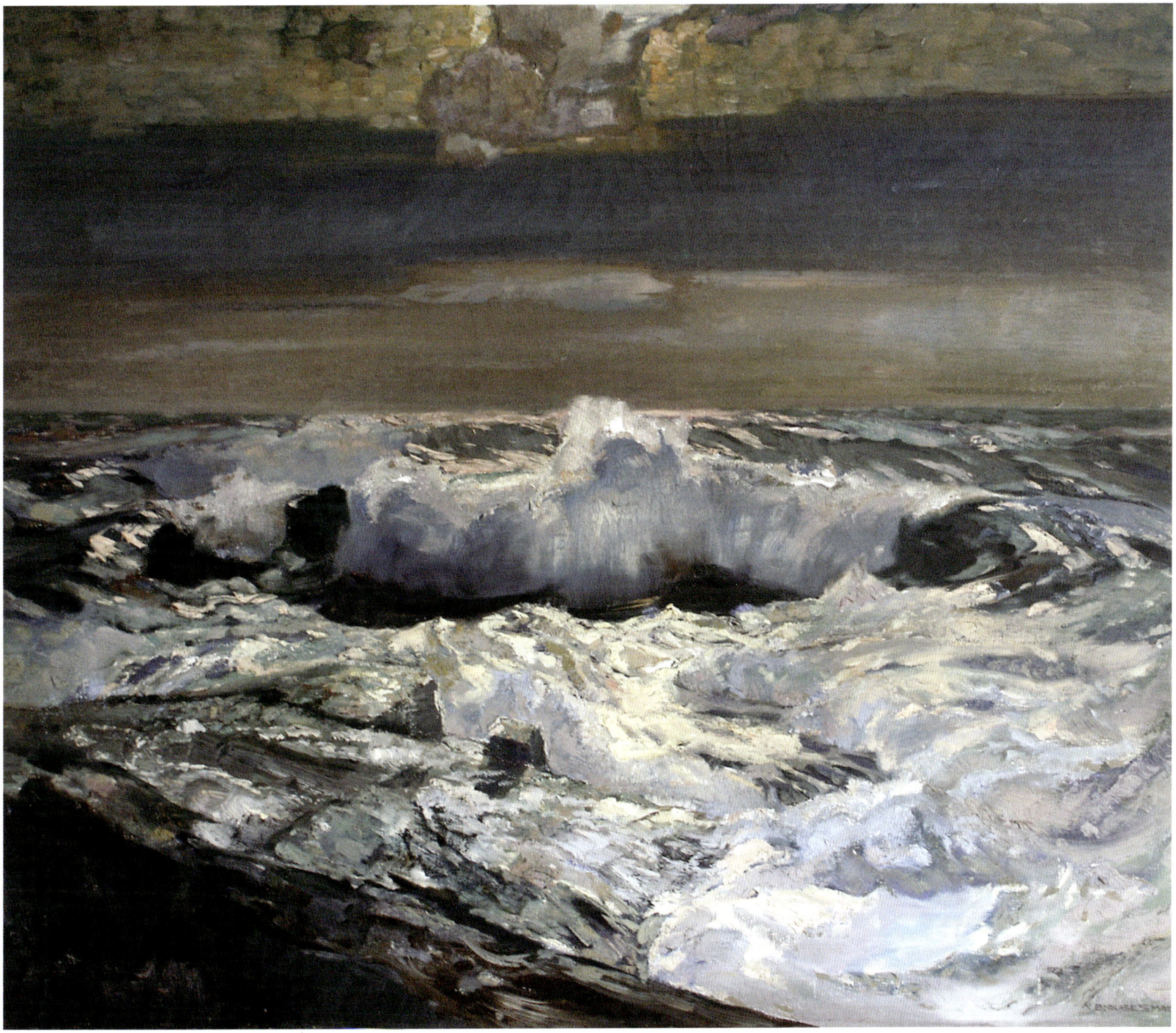

The Paintings, Drawings and Recording of Events

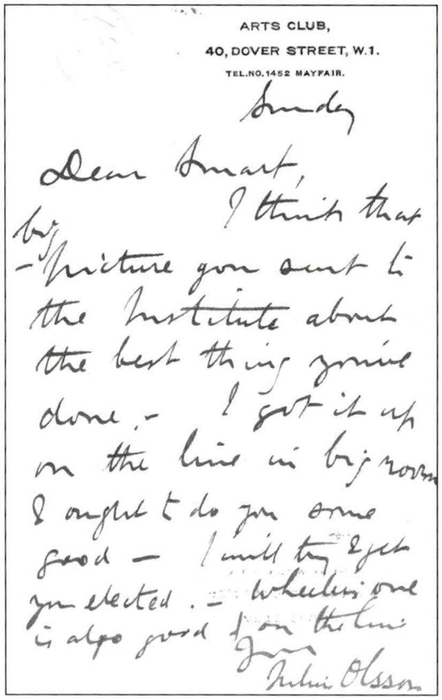

ARTS CLUB,
40, DOVER STREET, W.1.
TEL.NO.1452 MAYFAIR.

Sunday

Dear Smart,
I think that big picture you sent to the Institute about the best thing you've done. – I got it up on the line in big room I ought to do you some good – I will try & get you elected. – Wheelers one is also good & on the line

Yours
Julius Olsson

Letter from Julius Olsson.

Whilst undoubtedly occupied in promoting St Ives and its artists, Borlase Smart was engaged in producing his seascape paintings to which he devoted study and gained an expertise of the movement and wave variations of this elemental force. It was a difficult subject to tame and to capture in paint because of its lack of stillness and impermanence of structure. However, he allowed nothing to defeat his endeavours and produced some wonderful paintings, portraying the ocean in all its moods and weather changes and the effects of sunlight, moonlight and variations of the seasons on his subject. His confidence was never eroded; his ability never questioned. His mentor and former master class tutor, Julius Olsson, recognized his extraordinary talent, as testified in an undated letter from the London Arts Club.

Not only was Borlase Smart renowned by St Ives artists for his skill as a painter but also for his dexterity in detailed drawings of gigantic cliff faces, of buildings and of portraits of local people. As far back as WW1 the War Office had recalled Smart from France to provide drawings and to work on the component parts of the development of the Lewis gun. One wonders if this had come about because of the sketches he had made of the conditions of the buildings of towns and villages devastated by the war, and the situation of soldiers serving in the trenches overseas.

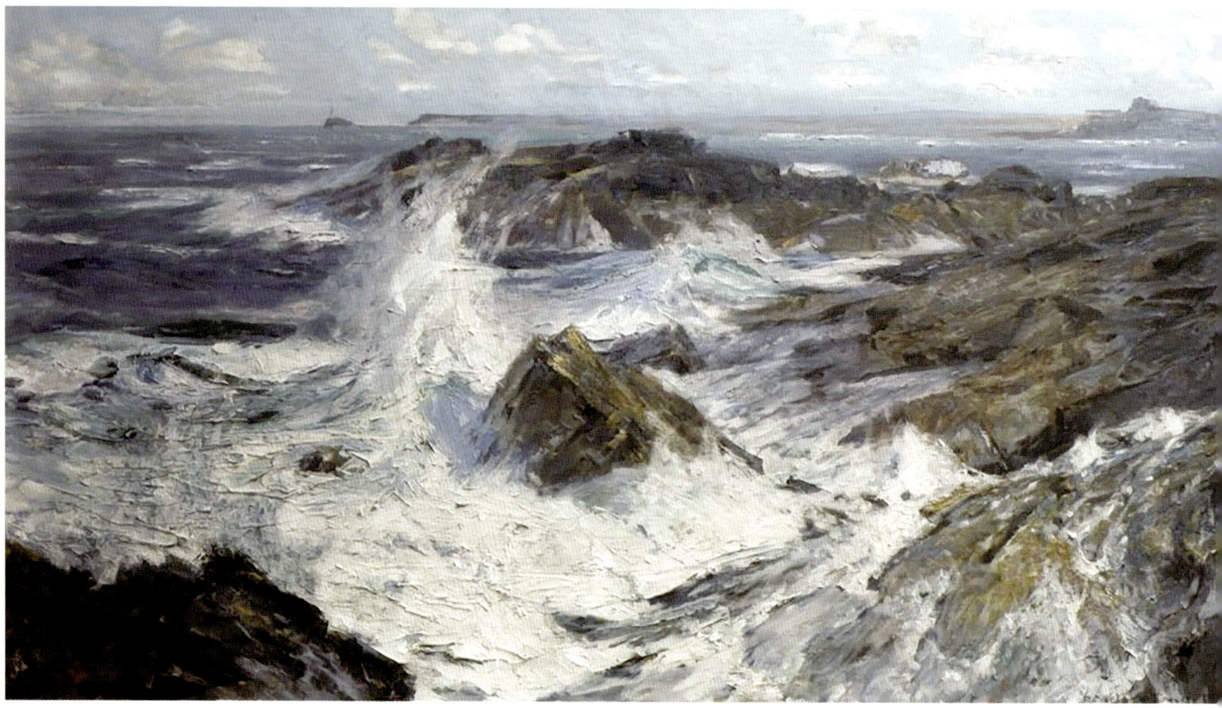

St Ives Bay from Clodgy, with Godrevy Lighthouse far distant.

Heavy Seas Breaking at Land's End.

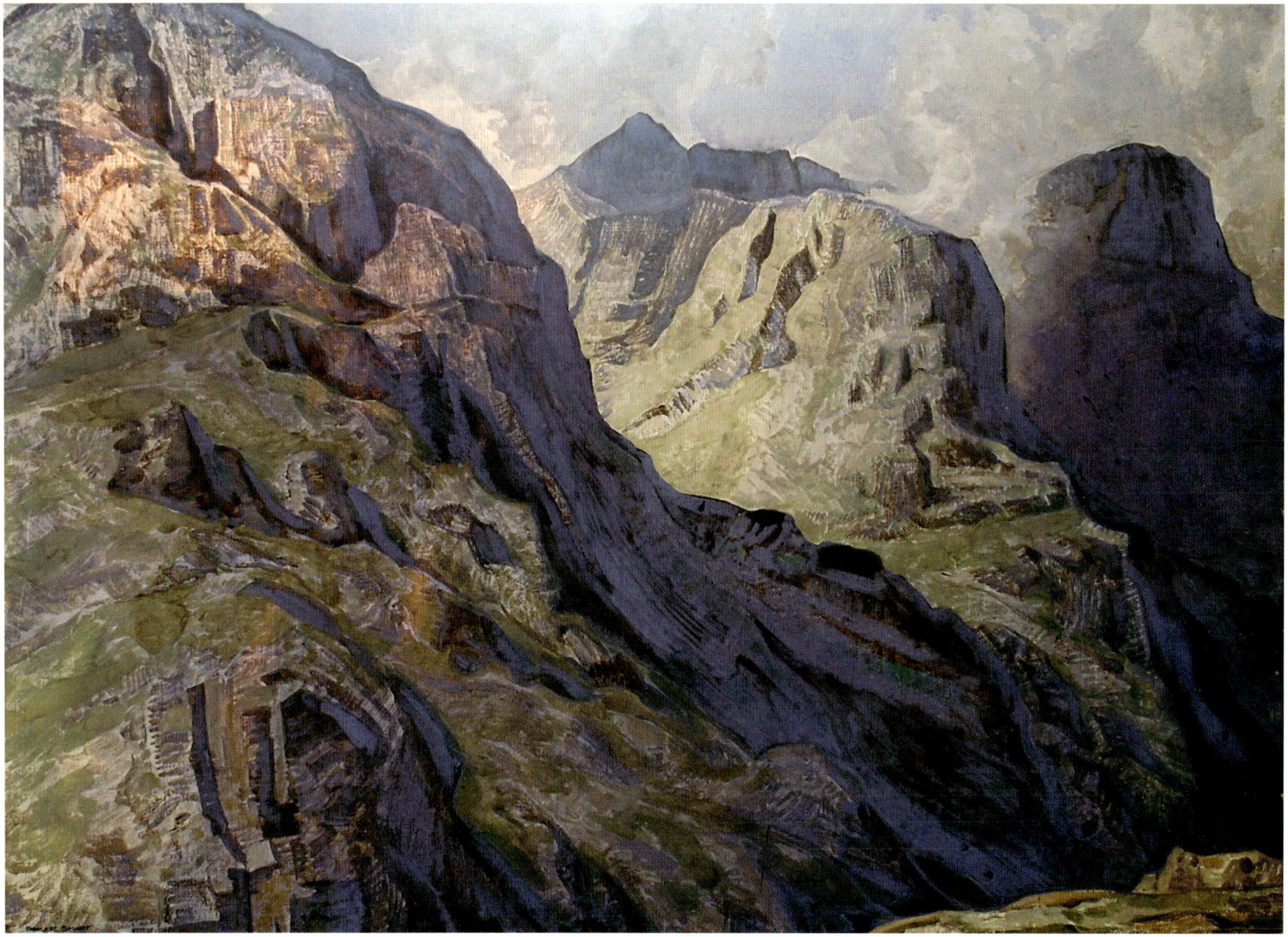

Three Sisters, Glencoe.

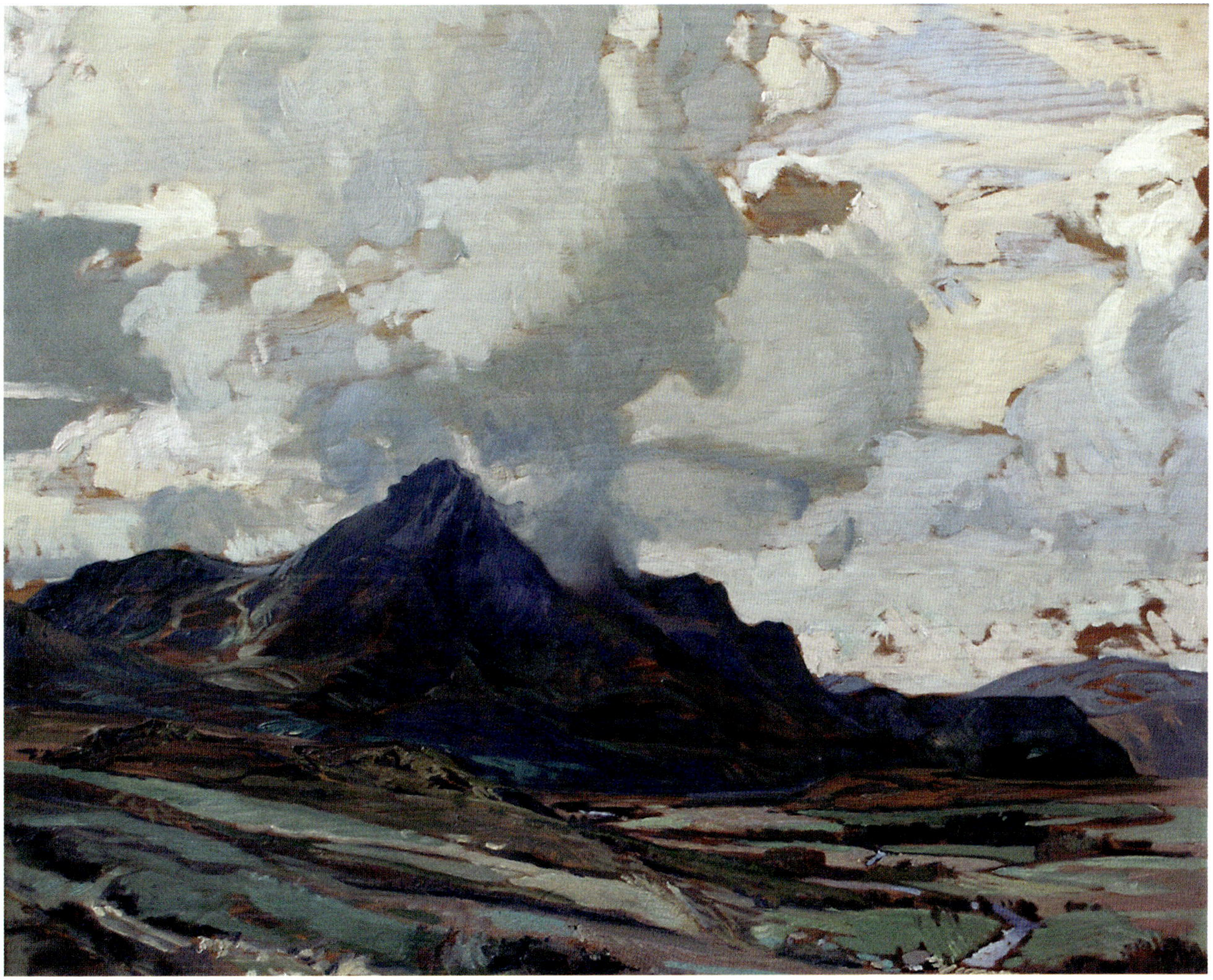

Mountains and Clouds Scotland.

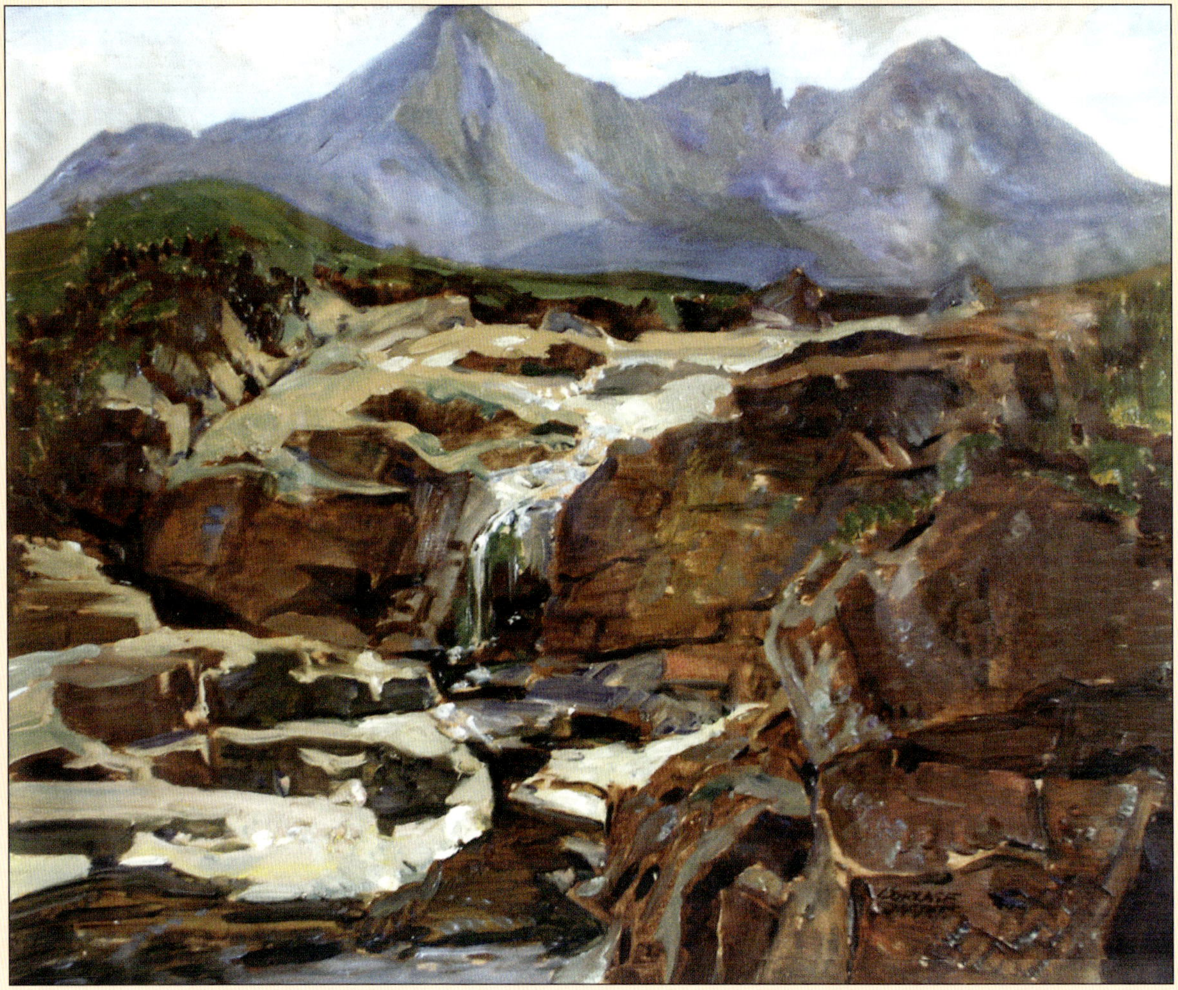

Mountain Stream.

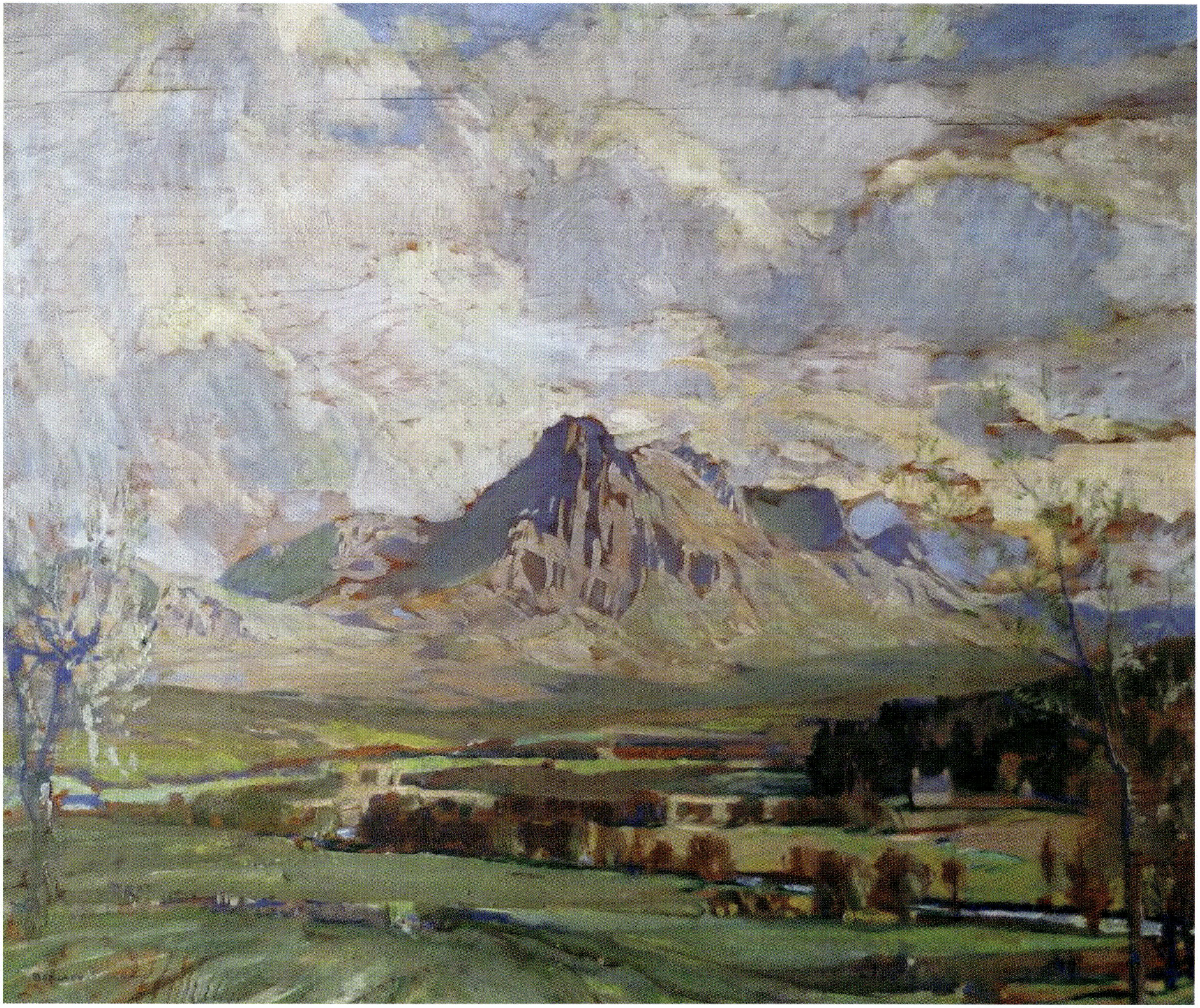

Ben Loyal, Scotland.

In the Second World War Smart had designed and drawn posters to alert the population of St Ives to the importance of supporting the war effort in helping to raise funds to provide equipment for the armed forces in their battle against the German offensive in the air and at sea.

The painting 'Ben Loyal' was bought from the Royal Academy by the Duke of Sutherland in 1933. It subsequently found its way to St Ives via an art dealer and is today in the private collection of a local artist.

The Technique of Seascape Painting

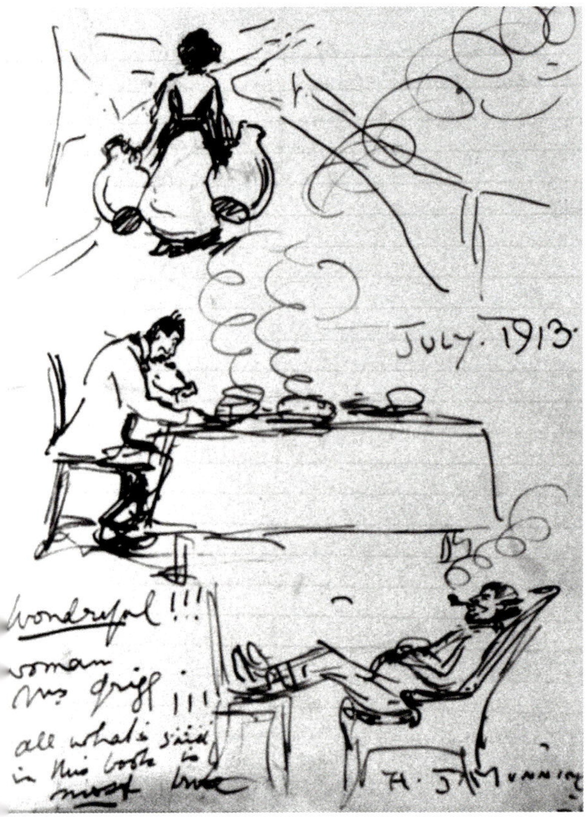

Alfred Munnings' sketch from Mrs Griggs' visitors' book.

1934 saw the publication of Borlase Smart's book, *The Technique of Seascape Painting*, with a foreword by his mentor, Royal Academician, Julius Olsson, who wrote, '*.. no one can be more fitted for this task of love and labour than Borlase Smart.*' [11]

Smart loved the tremendous surging seas of the Cornish coastline and captured the spirit and strength of the natural tidal activity of the ocean. He admired and charted the geological structure of the rugged cliffs on the seashore, capturing their majesty in both paint and detailed drawings.

In his book there are beautifully illustrated colour plates of studies of the sea in all its moods and as affected by moonlight, sunlight and the seasons. Many of these pictures feature works painted in Zennor and the coves and cliffs leading from St Ives to Land's End. It is interesting to note that he stayed at Mrs Griggs house, next to the Tinners Arms, in Zennor during this time. It was near to his subject matter and the area in which he loved to paint. He could leave his paints and canvas ready to continue the next day, rather than transport them from St Ives. Mrs Griggs house was a favourite guest house of many of the artists, as testified in the drawing by Alfred Munnings in her visitors' book.

July 1913. Wonderful woman Mrs Griggs !!! all what's said in this book is most true

The colour plates in *The Technique of Seascape Painting* also features work from Scotland, where he ventured on frequent trips in the thirties, always seeking the majesty of rock formations, sea and coastline.

Borlase counselled his readers, '*Realize you are not a photographer, but one who is striving to be an artist. A photographer gives you every detail. You will find with experience there is no merit in painting this detail... The merit lies in knowing what to leave out in painting the sea.*' [12]

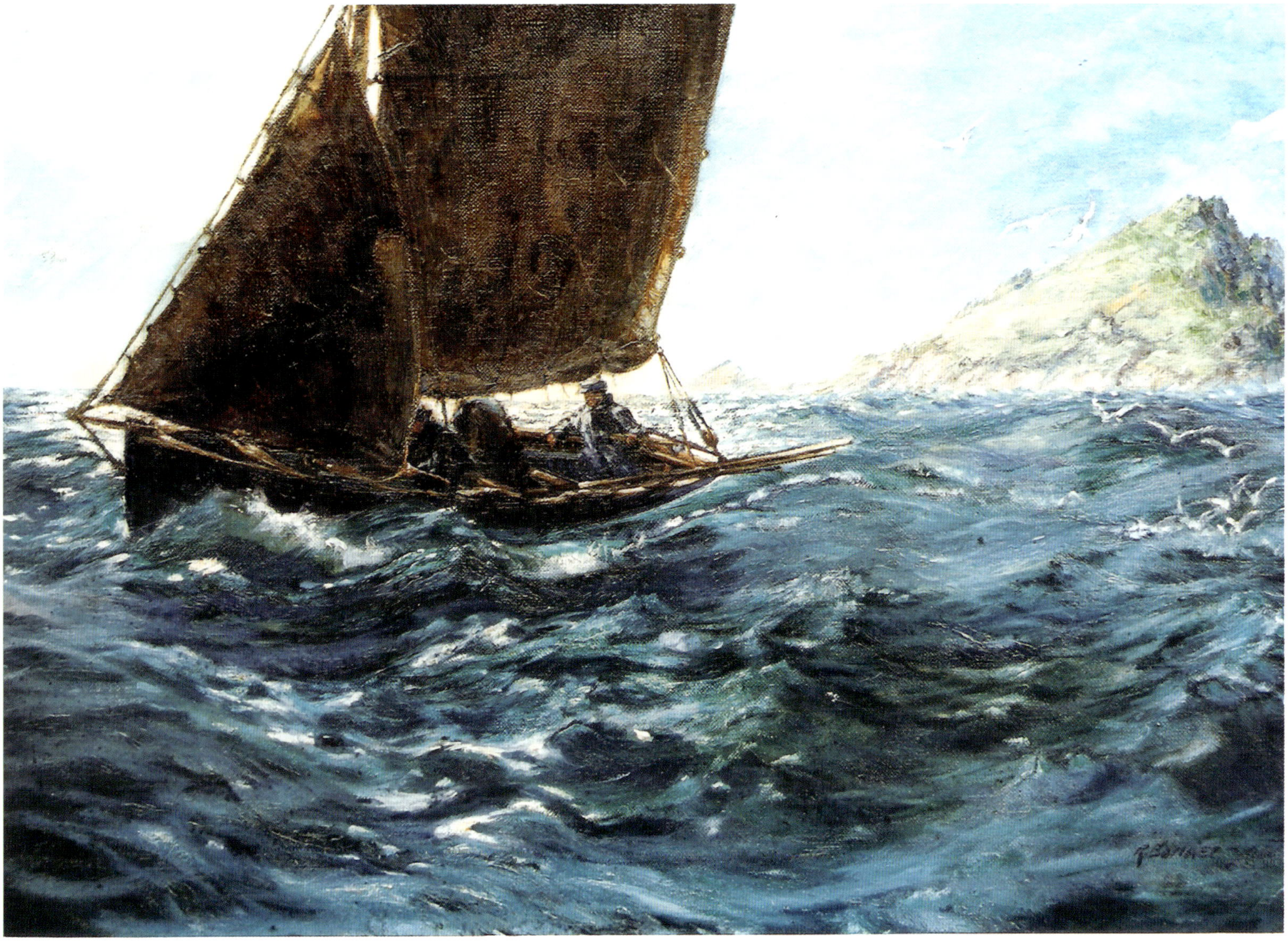

A Stiff Breeze.

Borlase had the temerity to analyse a wave. Consider a wave, he wrote, and described it in five stages as it rolled in towards the shore and ended its movement on the beach. He obviously spent some time in intensive study and tried to organize this natural phenomenon into quantifiable matter. *'The lines of the sea and foam are examples of the finest elements of design, and a successful picture embraces balance, symmetry, growth, movement, massing, and spacing. Above all occurs a centre of interest or focus-point of attraction.'* [13]

He also considered that marine painting, in which ships featured, or other incidents became the focal point, were not as dynamic as pure seascapes. This comment must have offended his friend and fellow artist, George Fagin Bradshaw who, having been a commander in the British Navy saw ships as the major subject of his paintings. However, ships do appear in Smart's paintings, as a necessity, when he was illustrating ships at sea, or boats in the harbour.

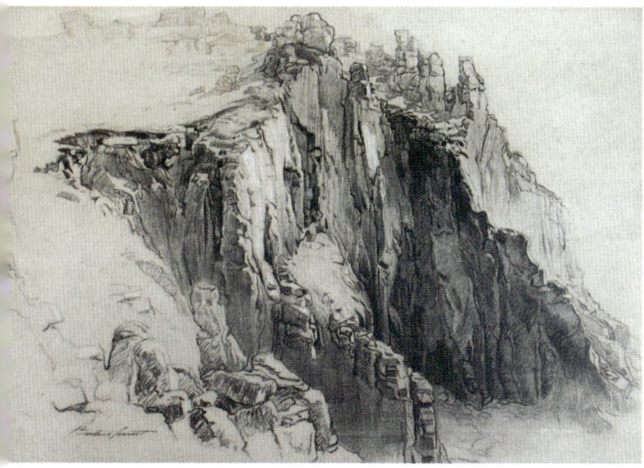

Drawing of Cathedral Cliffs, Land's End.

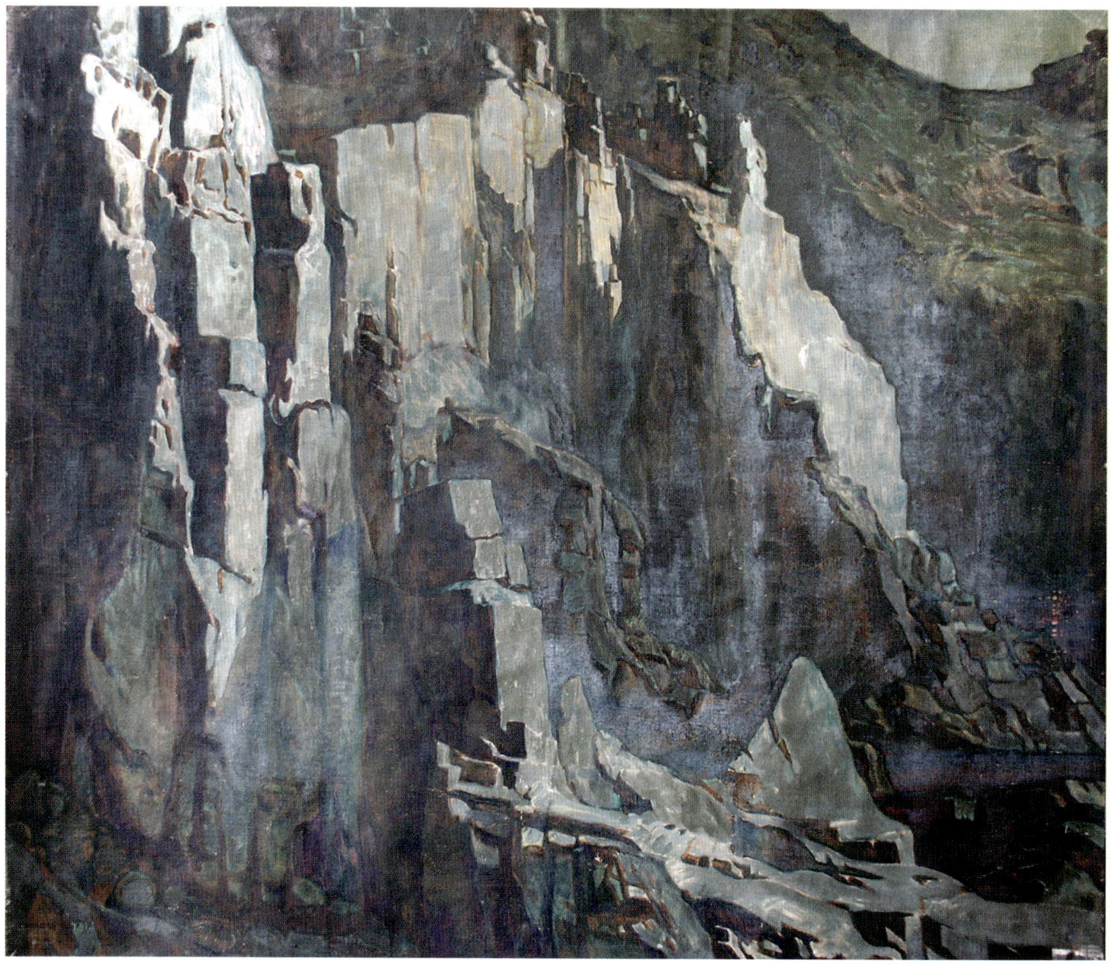

Cliffs at Land's End.

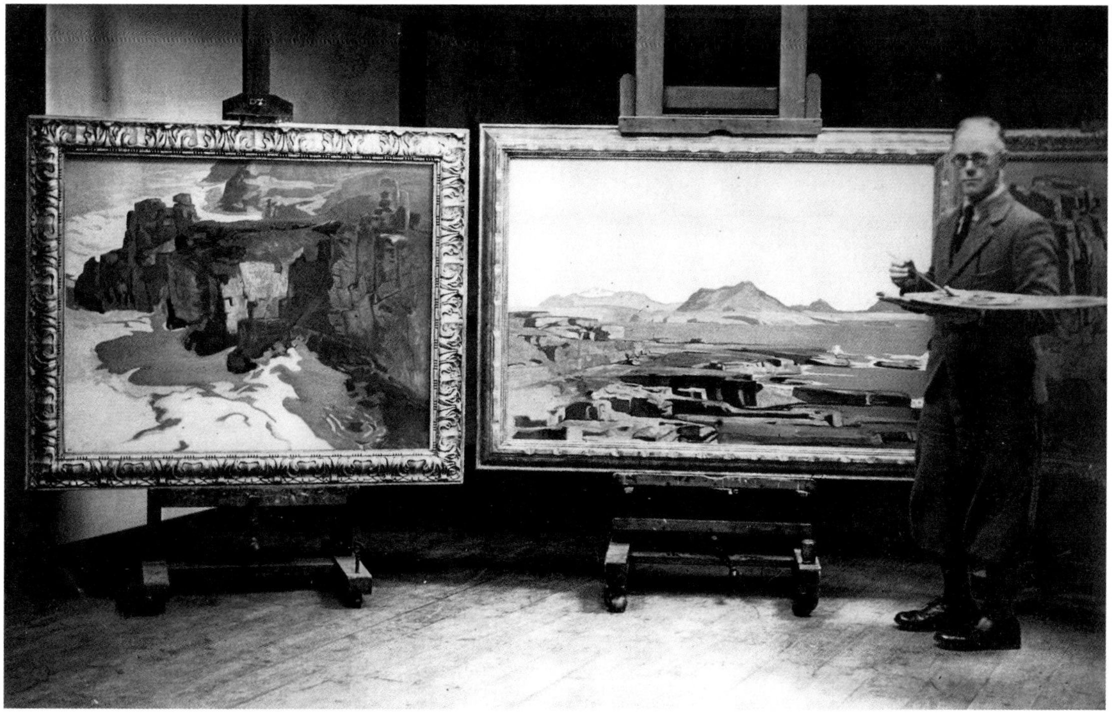

Borlase in his studio.

In 1938 Borlase Smart was delighted to receive a letter from America asking for his signature to paste in the book. He replied, *'It is good of you to buy a copy and I do hope you will enjoy it. I am flattered to find that your country has been the book's best buyer.'*

And always on the look-out for promoting the artists, he added to his note that it would a great opportunity if the St Ives Society of Artists could find a gallery in New York in which to exhibit their work. This became a prime objective but was never to be realized.

The book was still selling well in 1941 when the publisher, Sir Isaac Pitman & Sons Limited, wrote to Borlase Smart, giving him the figures for overseas and UK sales up-to- date, which were 1504. The editor writes, 'I *am glad that you are pleased with the sales. It is certainly encouraging to see continued interest in any of the arts.'* [14]

The book was reprinted four times, including a new edition in 1965, and the book continues to be a valuable resource for today's seascape painters and its quality is confirmed by its republication in 2011.

Pitmans also published Leonard Fuller's book on *The Technique of the Poster.*

The Threat to Downalong

Over a period of years the town folk were engaged in controversy over cottages in the traditional fishermen's area of Downalong. The Town Council in their enthusiasm to propel St Ives into the twentieth century proposed to demolish a great number of properties in a plan to modernize and improve the health and lives of the inhabitants by building council houses in their place. It seemed a very worthy cause, but the artists, as well as the locals, whose traditional cottages had been passed down through families for generations in Downalong, were appalled by this lack of consideration for those involved in this destruction. They were offended to hear their cottages described

Typical Cornish Cottages in Downalong, Back Road West.

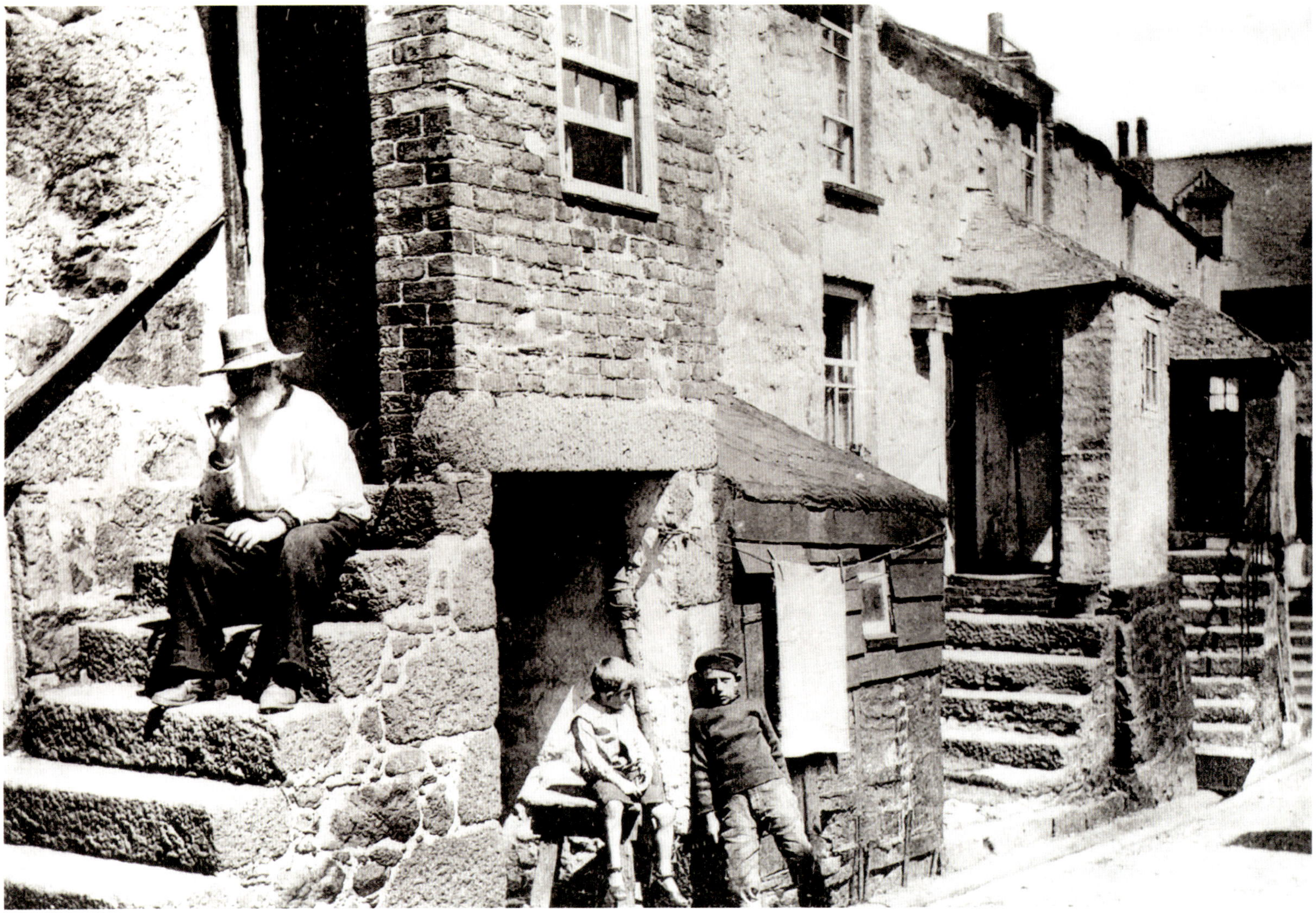

as 'hovels' and 'slums.' Commander Bradshaw and family lived in Ship Studio in the centre of Downalong, so he was particularly opposed to the Council's proposals.

The artists, spearheaded by Borlase Smart, set themselves in opposition to the spoliation of the old fishing quarter. They proposed that the cottages should be modernized rather than demolished. He challenged the Council not to interfere with the liberty of the local people of St Ives and their right to live in the homes they loved and which were near their life's work, the sea.

A letter dated September 1934, composed by Borlase Smart and sent to the local MP, The Right Hon. Walter Runciman, was co-signed by Moffat Lindner, President of the St Ives Society, Fred Bottomley, President of the Arts Club, and Morton Nance for the Old Cornwall Society.

'The members of the above Societies view with grave concern the Town Council's "five year plan" to demolish hundreds of scheduled houses in the old part of the town in the vicinity of the harbour. ...Are the Medical Officer of Health and the Borough Surveyor absolutely agreed that these properties should be demolished, and not reconditioned whilst at the same time preserving their character?' [15]

The reply from Walter Runciman said he had made enquiries of the Minister of Health and according to the Housing Act 1930, it required a local authority to have regard to the beauty of the landscape or countryside and other amenities and the desirability of preserving existing works of architectural, historic or artistic interest. He hoped that the valuable publicity in the Press would remind the Town Council of these provisions.

Bitter arguments rumbled on for several years with objections made to fishermen's cottages described as being 'unfit for human habitation'. Meanwhile, houses were built on the upper slopes of the town with bathrooms, kitchens and gardens and were enjoyed by many St Ives people, who moved from Downalong and were delighted to have these facilities. At the same time, the cottages in Downalong were also being upgraded by incomers buying these dwellings and moving into the area, thus everybody's wishes seemed to be satisfied.

In a last letter on the subject Borlase Smart wrote to the *St Ives Times.*

'I personally have been attacked in certain open, and committee meetings, for the stand I have consistently taken in regard to the preservation of the amenities of this town, and have often fought a lone hand. This has been considered damaging to the town's interests. In other words no one outside any official quarter must open their mouth.' [16]

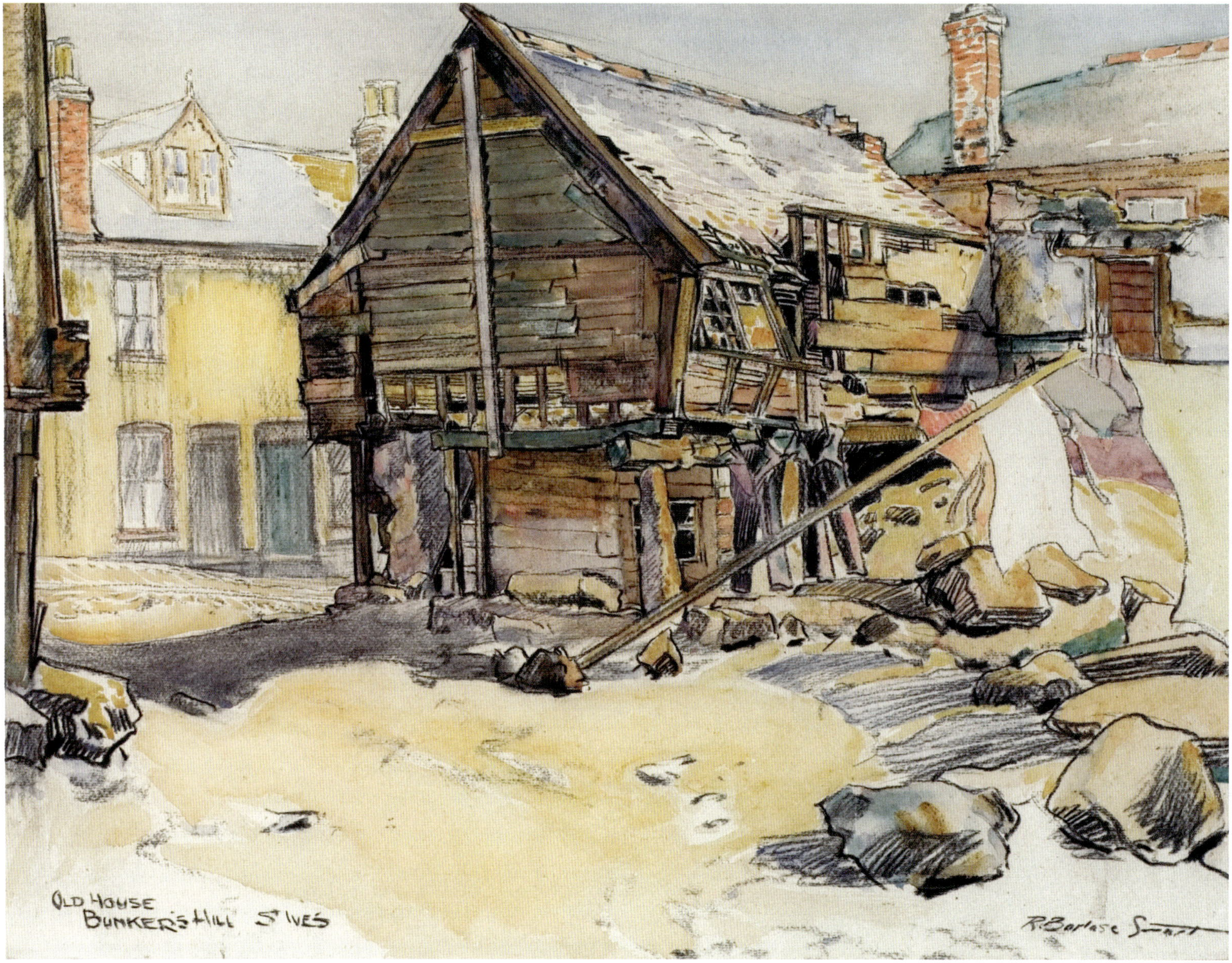

Old House, Bunker's Hill, St Ives.

However, although the major area of Downalong was saved from destruction, such areas as Pudding Bag Lane were demolished. What grew in its place were not houses, but a car park. What faith could the population place in its Town Council? Smart made a number of drawings of partly demolished buildings in Downalong reminding the inhabitants of what was happening under their noses.

A number of drawings were shown in the 1949 exhibition of Smart's work after his death, and Misome Peile writing of the show and thinking of Borlase Smart wrote,

'...that Mr Smart keenly felt the passing of old buildings is clear from the way he slashed in under the pathos of the moment, Demolition St Ives - *is a shuddering huddle of cottages fronted by debris and timbers and bricks – all that was left of Pudding Bag Lane.'* [17]

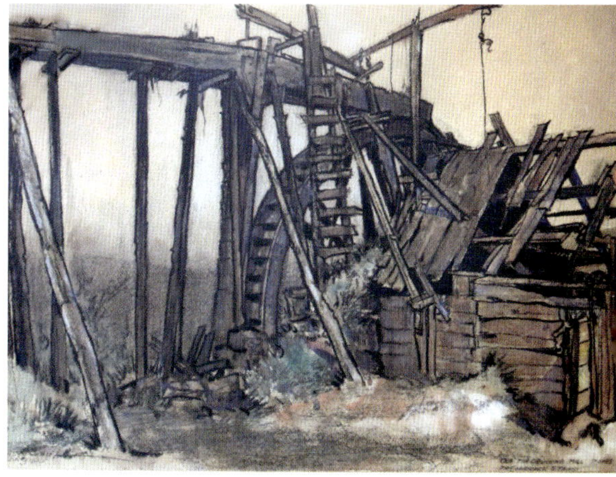

Old Tin Stamps, St Ives.

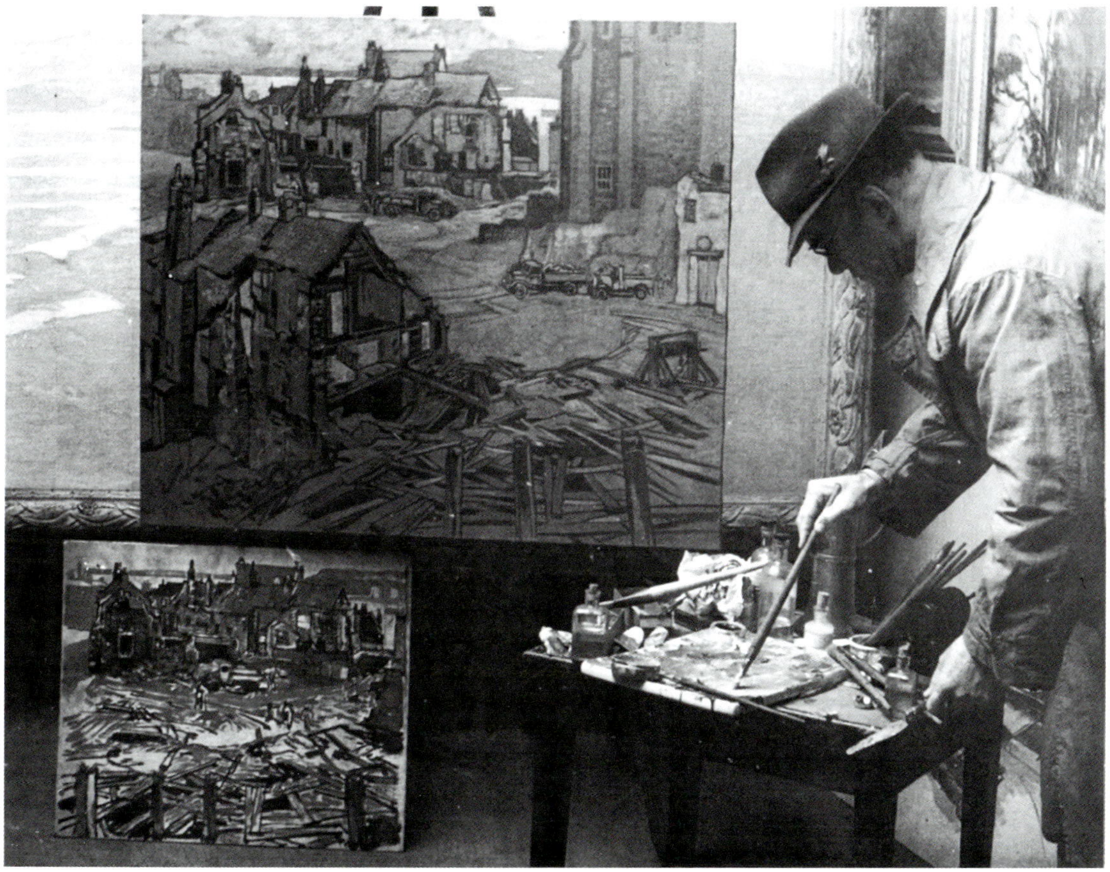

Borlase painting the Demolition of Pudding Bag Lane

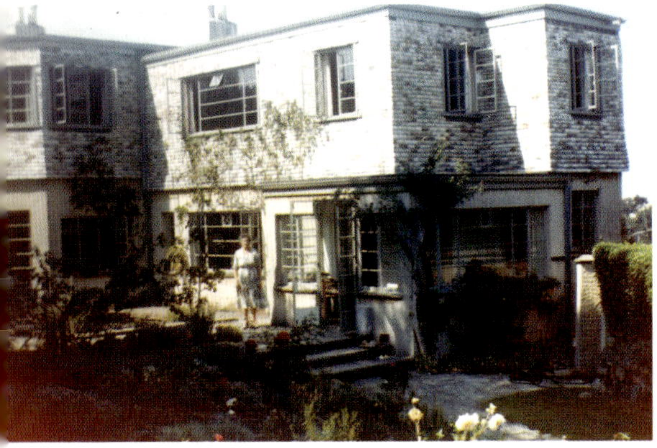

Ty Bryn, St Ives home of the Smarts.

Peter Lanyon

Peter was born to Herbert and Lilian Lanyon at the Red House in St Ives, named because of its red tiled roof at that time, an unusual feature in St Ives. Both parents were connected with Cornish mining. The Smarts lived nearby at Ty Bryn and the families were friends. The Lanyons were great entertainers and many artists came to gatherings to perform, and to enjoy a concert given by Herbert Lanyon, on the piano. The Red House is now part of the Chy Morvah hotel.

In 1936 Borlase introduced the young eighteen year old, Peter Lanyon, to painting out-of-doors. They traipsed the Penwith countryside and roamed the rocky cliffs to find their subjects. Peter Lanyon remembered Borlase Smart as a really marvellous person, a wonderful draughtsman and a very interesting painter. Peter Lanyon's son, Andrew, confirmed the importance of the Smart/Lanyon association.

'He had been taught in his teens by that great afficionado of moving water, Borlase Smart.' [18]

Borlase produced an oil painting of Carn Galva, Zennor, which was given to the City Museum and Art Gallery in Plymouth in 1935. Peter also painted this same subject in 1938. It was a favourite spot and probably found in their ramblings during their search for good places to paint. They worked on seascapes and landscapes and also poster design. Borlase Smart invited Peter to exhibit his work in number One Porthmeor Studios, which he was occupying at the time.

Borlase was insistent that a seascape should be just that; the sea, with all its dignity and power, could best be expressed through the medium of oil paint. Lanyon seemed to agree with this

Below left: *Borlase painting out of doors.*

Below right: *Completing his painting of the Pilot's Boathouse.*

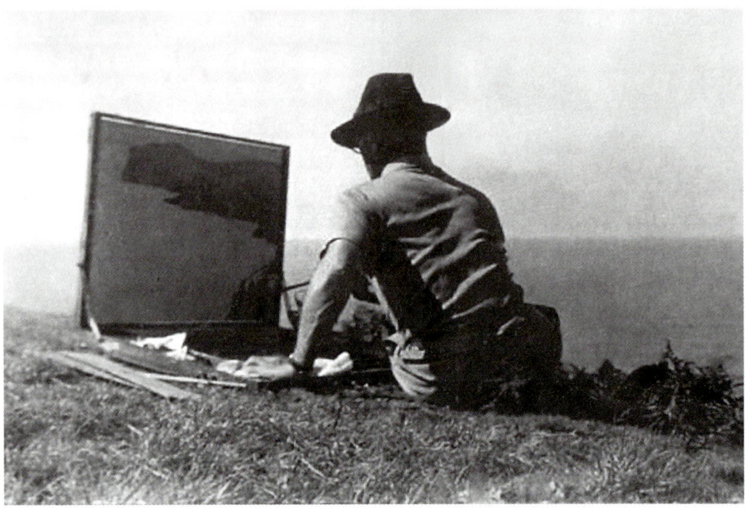

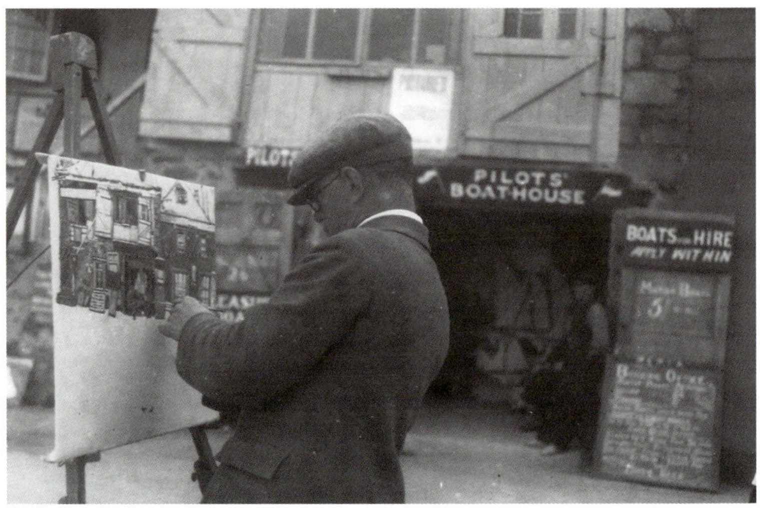

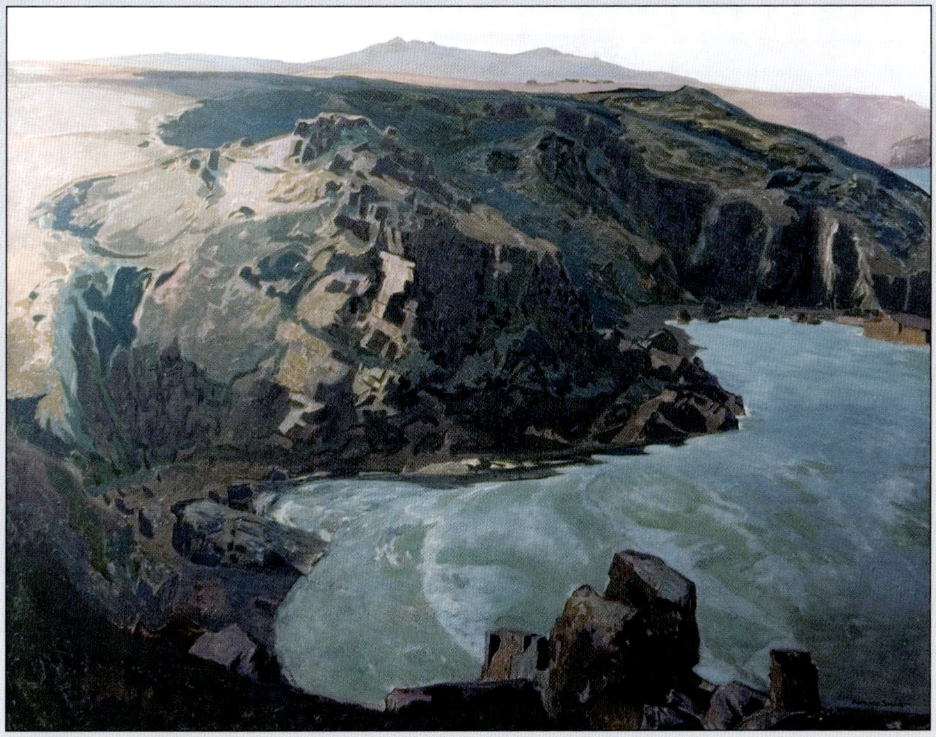

Carn Galva.

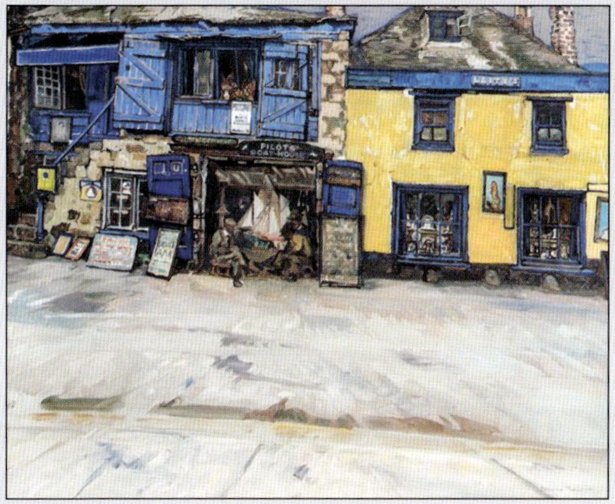

The Pilot's Boathouse.

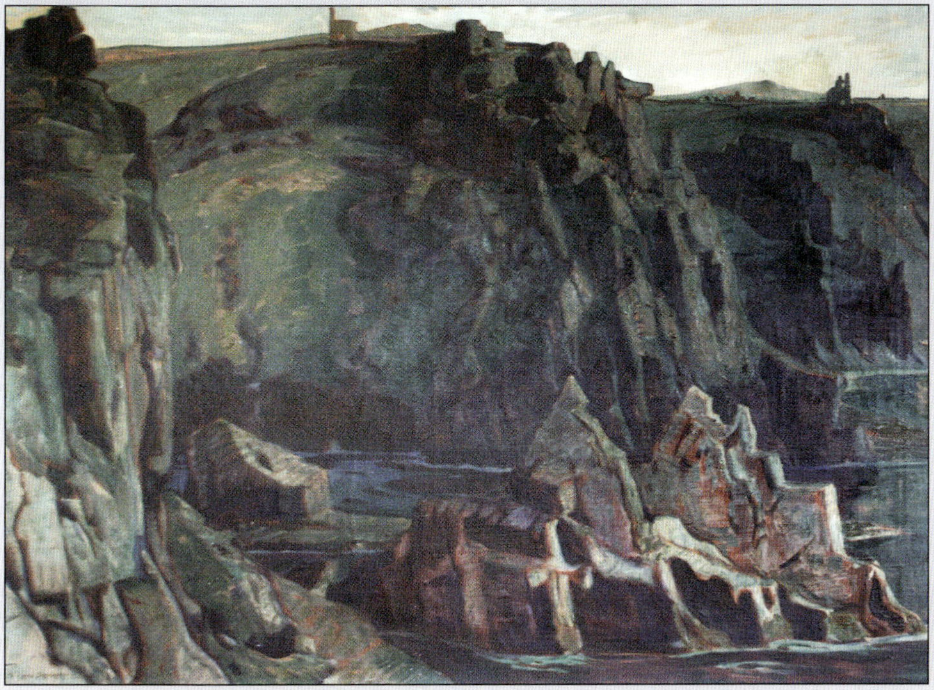

Cliff Top Mines.

statement, his own work being thick with the pigment of oils. He also favoured the idea of the immediacy of his subject and continued observational studies and painting out-of-doors. The area of West Penwith with its mines and ancient history was important to a young man born in Cornwall and a native of St Ives. *'It is impossible for me to make a painting which has no reference to the very powerful environment in which I live.'* [19]

Lanyon always identified himself with the traditional painters and indeed admitted that if it hadn't been for Borlase Smart's willing and enthusiastic desire to introduce him to all that area of West Penwith, and the challenge that sea and coastline had to offer, he may not have taken up painting at all.

The Borlase Family

The house Ty Bryn was designed by Borlase in 1936 and built with Irene's inheritance on the death of her father. They had moved into the Chy Carne Hotel, near by, while their home was being built. At first they had first bought Pendennis, where Brian Smart was born in 1929. Both properties were above the town and meant a daily trip of 110 steep steps to town, to and from Borlase Smart's Porthmeor studio in Downalong

Borlase was a fond and loving father and concerned himself with all aspects of the boys', characters, their upbringing and their education at private schools, but mother 'ruled the roost' at home. Although the parents did attend school sports days and events, Borlase wished that his responsibilities had allowed him more time to support the boys during their boarding school years. However, according to his two sons, their father was always kind and attentive and full of fun and good spirits and their mother delighted to see them when they came home for school holidays.

From the left : *Brian Smart age 7, a drawing by Borlase. Michael Smart age 9, a drawing by Borlase. Irene Smart with Brian and Michael.*

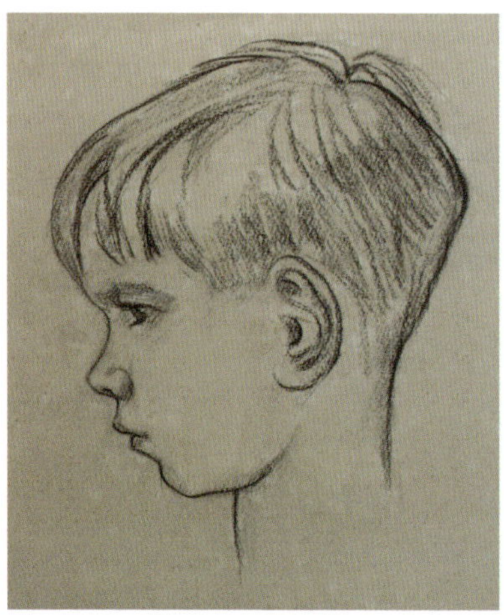

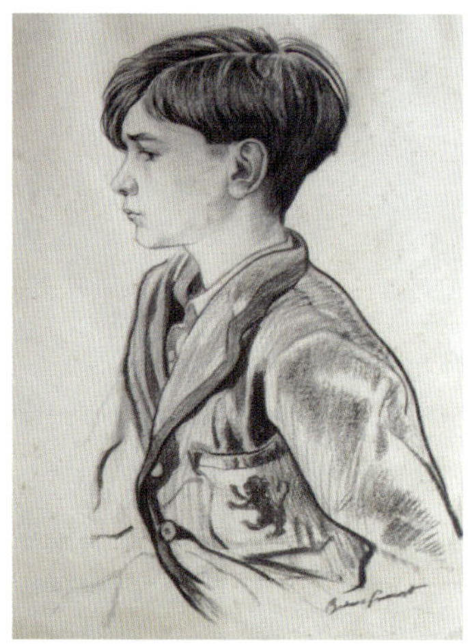

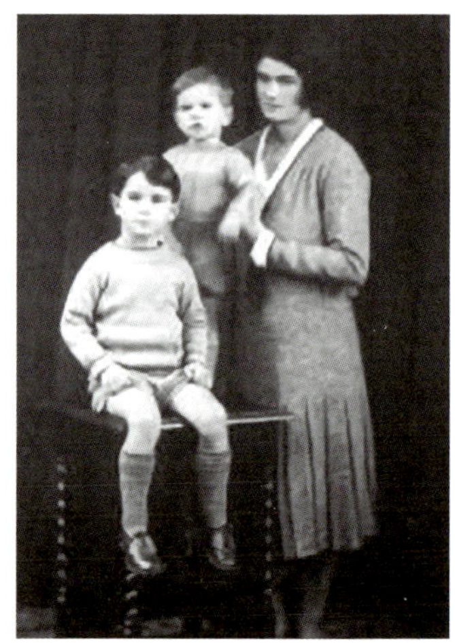

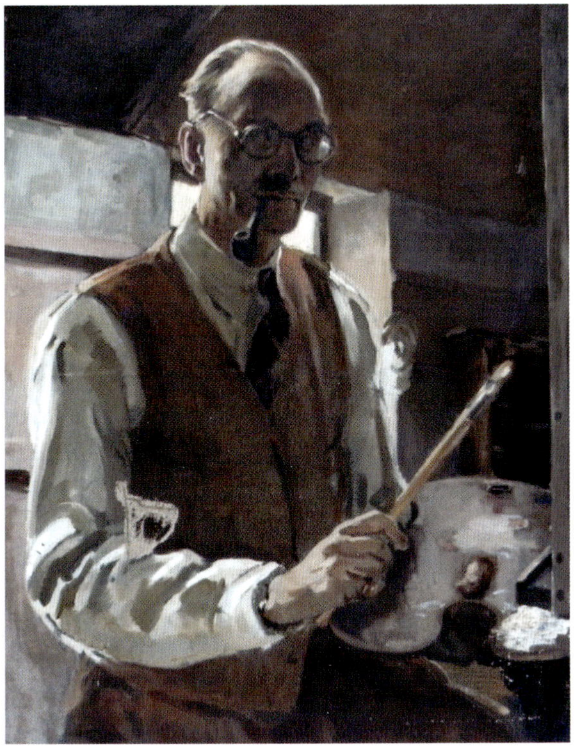

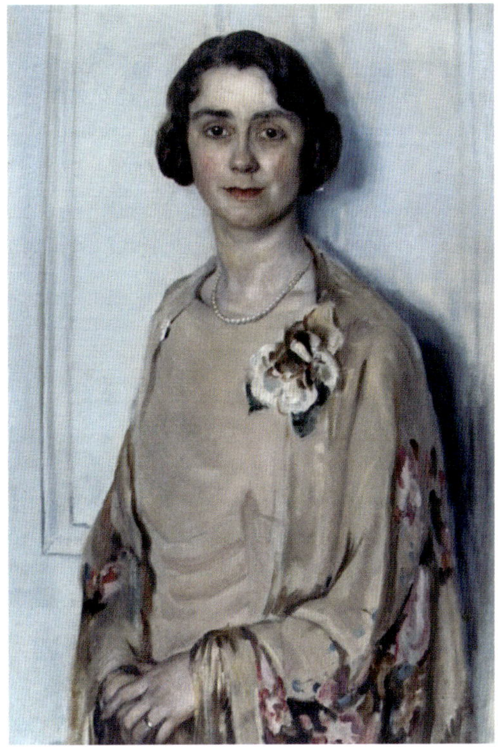

Leonard Fuller painted by Margery Mostyn.

Margery Mostyn painted by Leonard Fuller.

St Ives School of Painting

At last, in 1938, Leonard Fuller and his wife Marjorie Mostyn, arrived in St Ives to set up the School of Painting, planned years ago with Borlase Smart and finally coming to fruition. Borlase and Leonard first met in the summer of 1915 in the Instructors' Mess at Harrowby Camp, Grantham, Lincolnshire. Smart was recalled from active service to join the Machine Gun Training Centre, where they were desperate for good draughtsmen to work on the new Lewis Machine Gun. As artists, Fuller and Smart fulfilled this requirement in their ability to draw.

The gun was developed in America and named after its inventor Colonel Lewis. Lewis had been working with a British Arms manufacturer to overcome some of the initial problems. The gun was officially adopted by the British Army for land and aircraft use in 1915.

Smart was later recalled to serve at the front, where he was again engaged in fighting and trying to capture through his drawings the appalling conditions of the men thrown into fruitless attack after attack in a pitiful waste of life. Most of Smart's drawings were of the battlefields of Belgium and France in 1918.

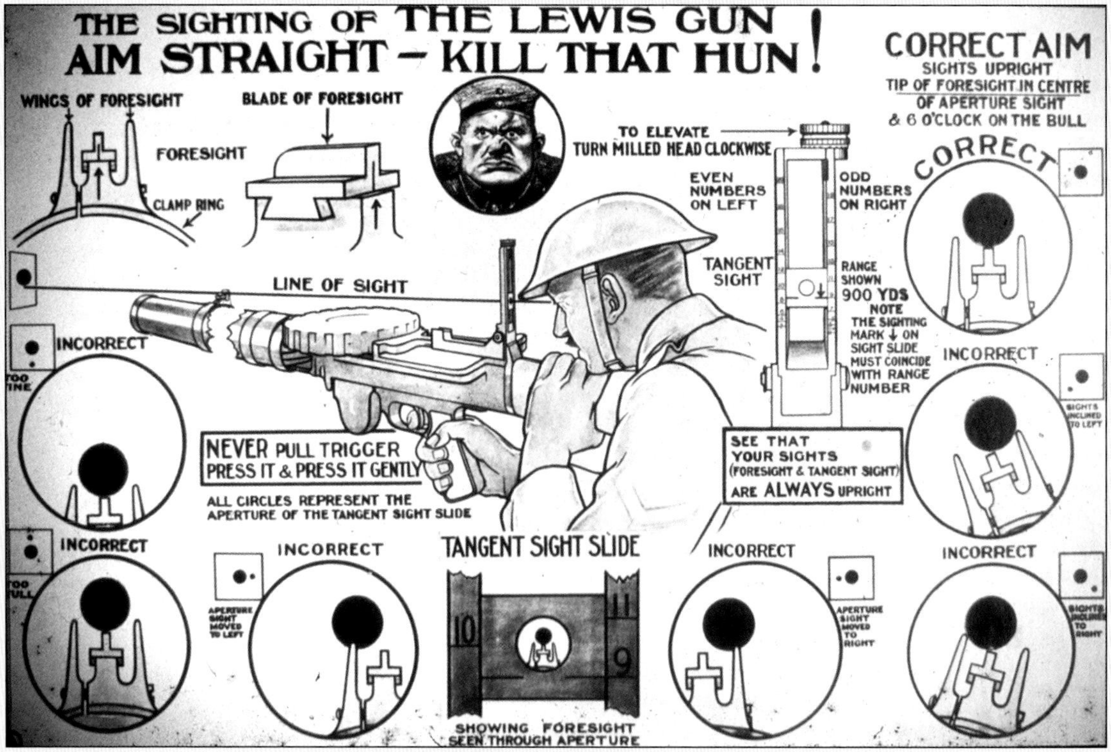

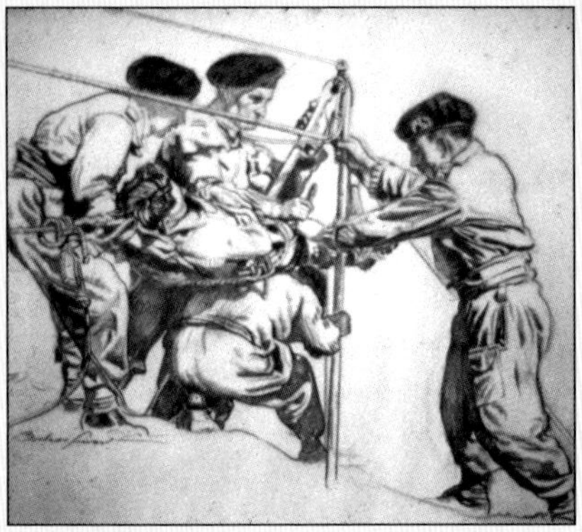

Technical drawings completed on behalf of the Machine Gun Training Centre.

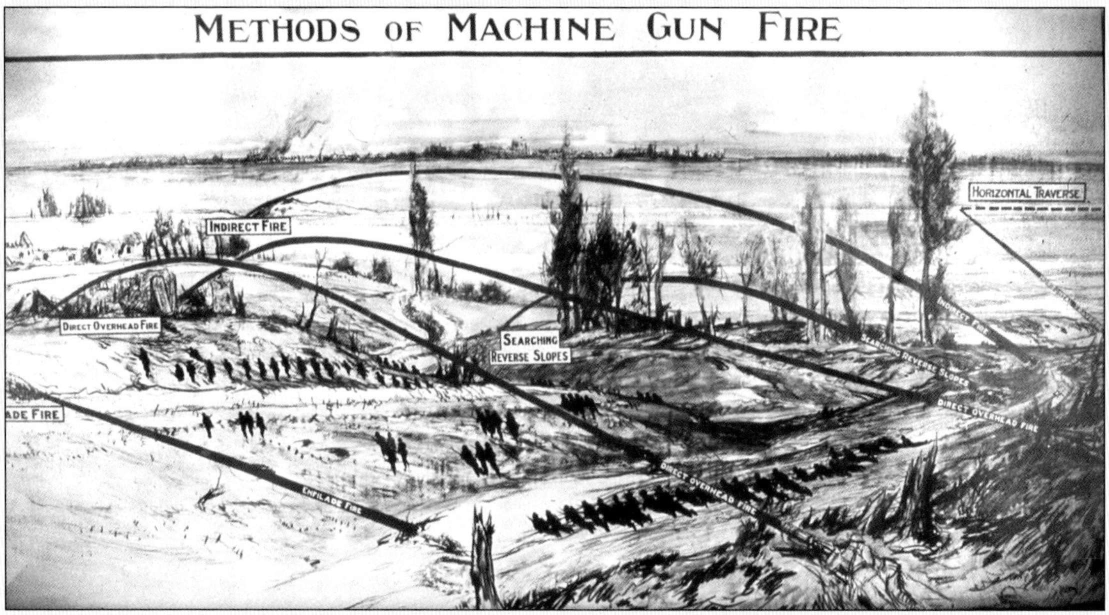

During their experience of working together and sharing ideas Smart and Fuller became firm and lifelong friends and talked of their ambition to go to St Ives and study art and establish a school of painting. Only Borlase and his young wife Irene, were brave enough to fulfil this ambition as early as 1919.

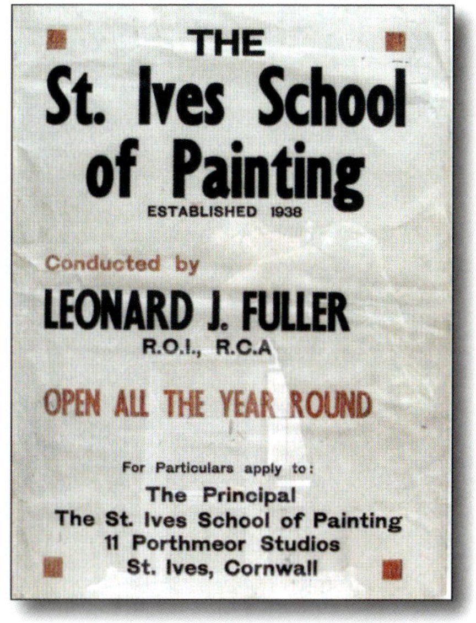

However, twenty two years later, Smart was delighted that his friends had finally made it to St Ives. He and Fuller were heavily engaged in promoting the art colony and the school. It was on one of his painting trips to Scotland that Borlase met fourteen year old Morwenna Thistlethwaite, who told him that she wanted to be a painter and took lessons from him at that time. He advised her to go to the St Ives School of Painting when she was seventeen, but it wasn't until the mid-seventies, when she was an established artist that she came to live in St Ives, where generations of her family were born.

The school provided a very scholarly and broad style of training. The advertised aims were, *'To assist the many resident and visiting students in attaining the requisite proficiency to enable them to express themselves adequately in the various mediums; especially to enable them to combine their studies in landscape with figure and portrait work, carried on simultaneously.'* [20]

Leonard Fuller was a portrait, figure and still life painter. He taught at St John's Wood School of Art from 1922-1932 and at Dulwich College until 1938. He was an academic painter of great integrity and an understanding teacher. Marjorie Mostyn, was an accomplished painter of portraits, children, interiors and still-life. She had won silver and bronze medals for life and composition. She studied at the Royal Academy Schools under John Singer Sargent, George Clausen and Sir William Orpen. As well as teaching at the school she put an advertisement in the *St Ives Times* in 1942. *'Mrs Leonard Fuller will take a few children for lessons in drawing and painting. Apply Scot's Craig, St Ives.'*

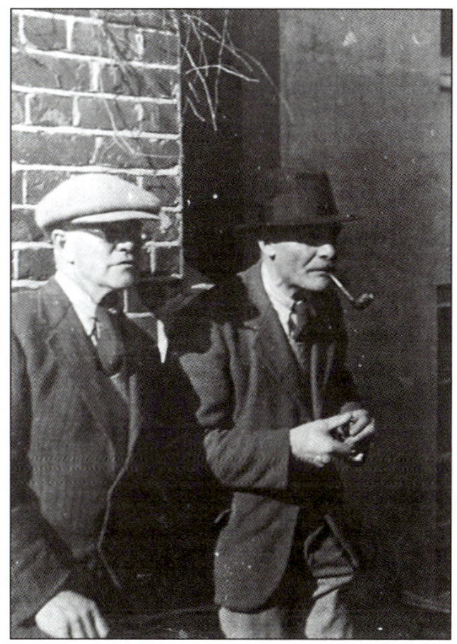

Borlase Smart and Leonard Fuller

Sir Terry Frost said, *'We young painters used to go to the painting school. It was the cheapest way we could get a model. There was Peter Lanyon and Sven Berlin. We were some of the early pupils who went along to draw'*. Later, two young St Ives lads, Eric Ward and Stuart Peters, took advantage of their local art school and both became painters but, unlike some of the more privileged artists who arrived in the town, they had families to support and for many years combined painting with a need to earn a wage. Eric Ward was a fisherman and became Coxswain of the St Ives lifeboat and Harbour Master. Stuart Peters was a teacher and became Head of Art at St Ives School. *'I remember, as a young lad, working with Denis Mitchell on Barbara Hepworth's 'Winged Figure' which was commissioned by John Lewis for their Oxford Street store.'*

The painting school premises in Back Road West, are opposite Norway Square, up a flight of stairs; below are the offices and studios. Following tradition, there are fish cellars in the basement; all part of the Porthmeor Studio complex. The school continued until the death of Leonard Fuller in 1973, it was then carried on by his wife, Marjorie, and when she felt incapable of managing the school on her own, she invited the artist, Roy Ray, to assist in running the school. On her death in 1986 Roy became the Principal. After 23 years Roy handed over the administration of the school in the year 2000 to an Educational Charity and became a Trustee/Acting Principal of the school.

In 1938 Leonard Fuller, Dod Procter, Stanhope Forbes, Gertrude and Harold Harvey and Borlase Smart were featured in the magazine Picture Post under the title, 'Great British Artists.' Borlase was also a member of the Newlyn Society of Artists and at one time was secretary. In spite of a busy schedule as secretary of the St Ives Society of Artists, he always found time for friends, both in Newlyn and St Ives, among them were Lamorna Birch and Stanhope Forbes. Brian Smart said, "Stanhope used to ring father and regular talks took place between them. Bernard Leach and father were very much in touch. They had ideas in common." Bernard was well-known for his thoughts on Zen and his discussions on philosophy and the making of craftsman pottery.

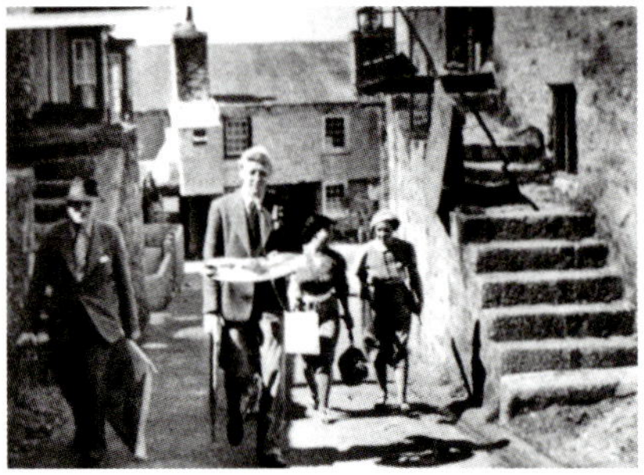

Leonard Fuller, centre, with students.

Loading Borlase paintings from Porthmeor studio.

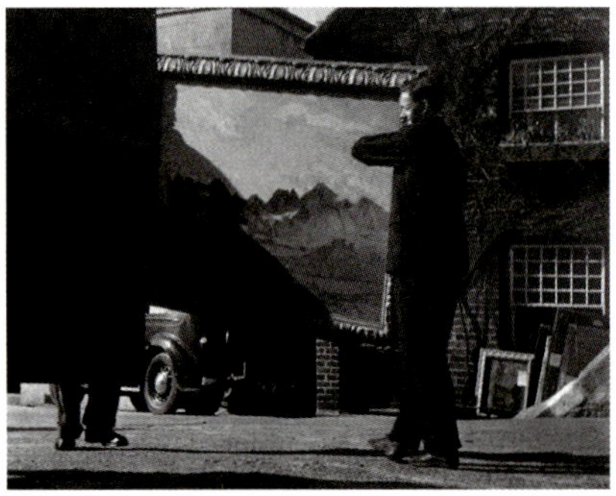

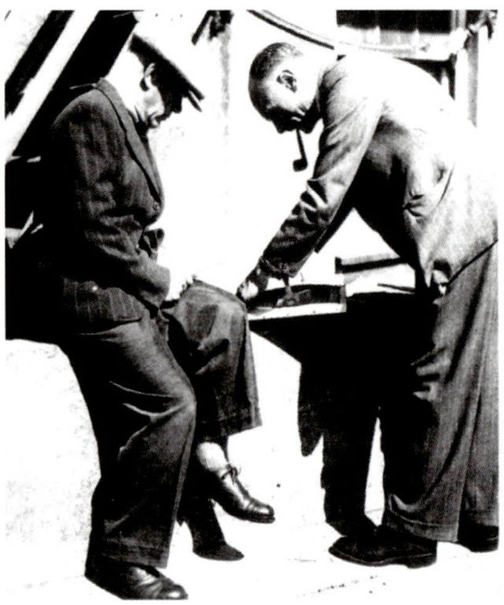

Borlase and Leonard outside the School of Painting.

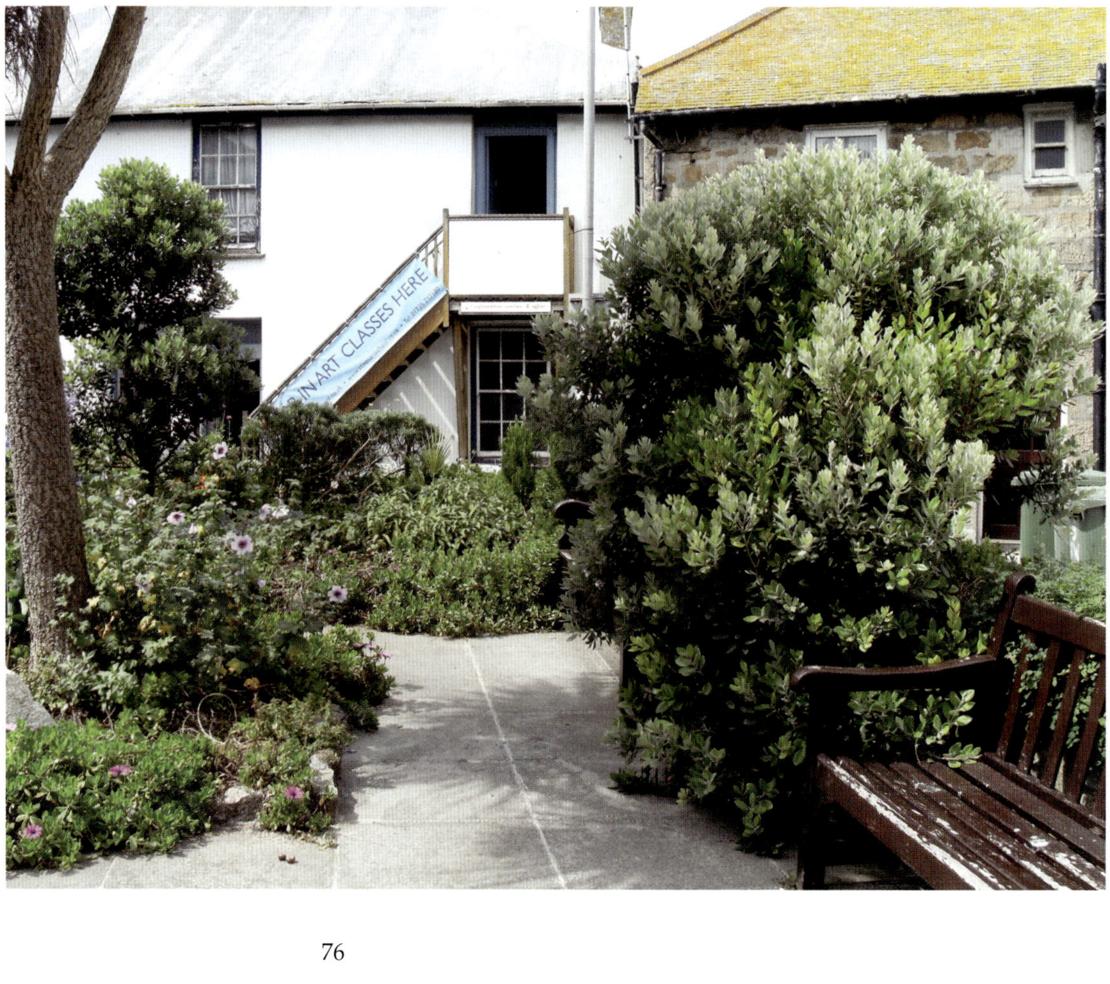

Norway Square with the St Ives School of Painting and the Borlase Smart bench.

The Society of Marine Artists

In 1938 using his initiative and the advantage of his newspaper experience, Borlase Smart wrote to the *Daily Telegraph* and proposed that seascape painters should get together and form a Society of Marine Artists. Although there was some opposition because of hard times for artists, Smart, having once thought of an idea, pursued it with dogged determination. A group of like-minded local artists and others established the first committee, on which Smart served as Treasurer. His friend, George, Fagin Bradshaw also joined, seeing a greater market for his work.

However, the Second World War threatened the function of the new group. Art materials were in short supply and they were forbidden to paint or sketch the seashore, which placed restrictions on their ability to portray their subject and to exhibit their work. After the war the Society of Marine Artists began to flourish and the public to appreciate the traditional skills of the painters of seas and ships, from artists of a seagoing nation.

It was also towards the end of the war that Borlase became a founder member of the Plymouth Society of Artists, eventually its Vice President.

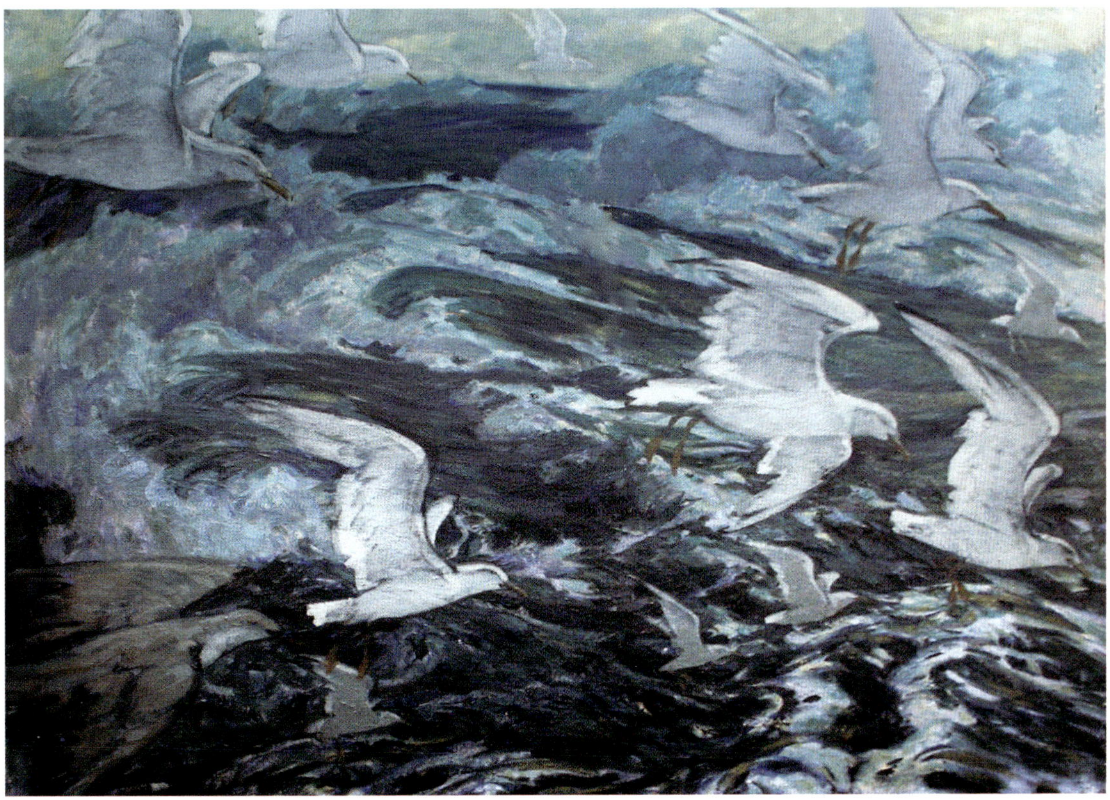

Seabirds.

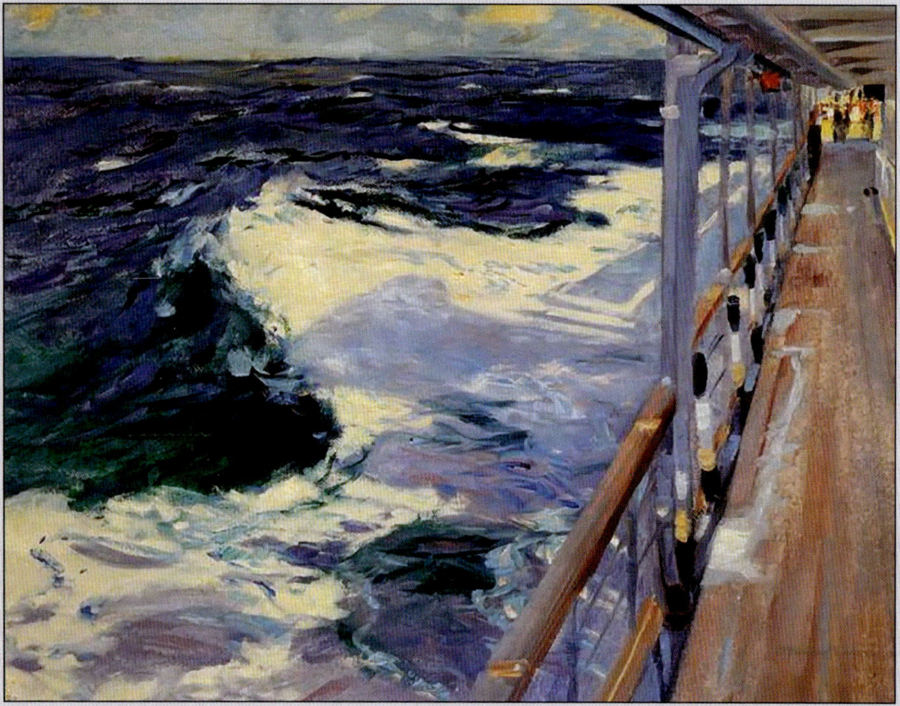

On the deck of the liner Otranto.

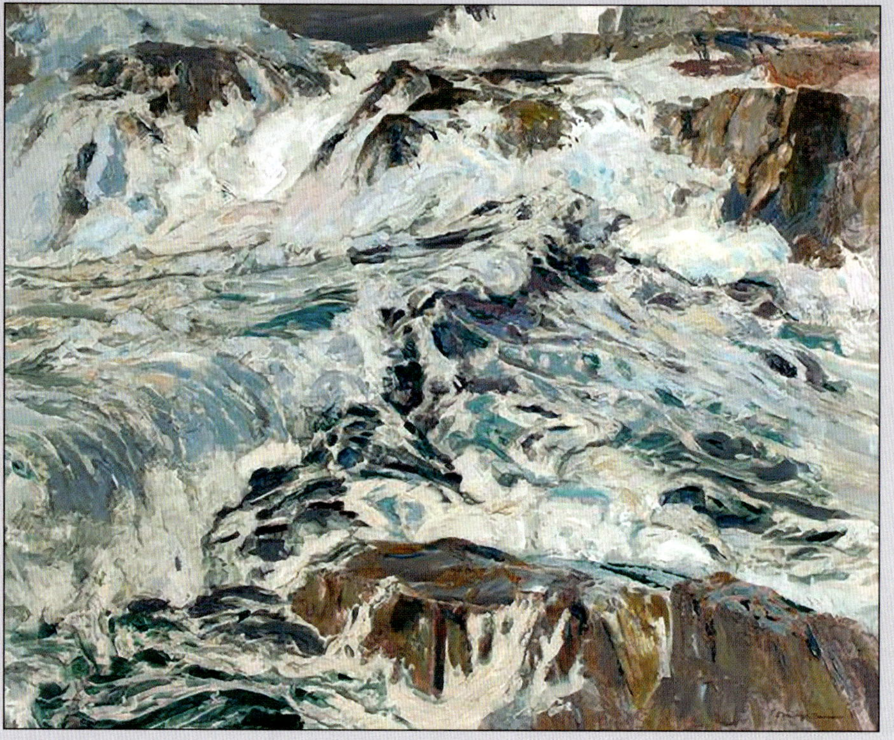

Ebb tide on the Reef.

Meeting the Moderns

In 1939, not only was there a tremendous upheaval by the outbreak of the Second World War, but St Ives was to experience a change to its traditional style of painting by the influx of artists with a more cosmopolitan outlook, a broader, varied breadth of experience of art. They had travelled to Europe and were familiar with the work of Matisse, Picasso, Braque, Mondrian, Cezanne and were influenced in their modernist approach to painting and sculpture. Ben Nicholson and Barbara Hepworth were already working in a style beyond the understanding of their St Ives contemporaries. They were making names for themselves in the wider art world and must have been distressed by artists in this small town who could not accept or recognize their work. On the other hand this more progressive, younger group, were probably equally disparaging of the painters producing the age old scenes of boats in the harbour, a sunset over Porthmeor, fishermens' cottages in a cobbled lane, studies of the local inhabitants; all drawn from nature and the environment.

Barbara Hepworth and Ben Nicholson arrived from London with their young family of triplets, Sarah, Rachel and Simon and took up temporary residence at Little Parc Owles, Carbis Bay, by invitation of artists Adrian Stokes and Margaret Mellis.

'Borlase Smart 1881-1947 and Leonard Fuller 1891-1973 were the leading painters there when BN and Hepworth arrived; they were respectively secretary and chairman of the St Ives Society of Artists founded in 1927.' [21]

Borlase Smart, especially, was aware of the arrival of new artists with their philosophies and was interested in their innovative ideas. He was a man with an eye to the future. He saw St Ives as the pivotal centre of the art world, seeing in the young modern painters the means of achieving his dream. He promoted their work in the face of fierce opposition from the traditional painters who reigned supreme in the world of the scenic and picturesque. Borlase admitted to being a painter who inherited these academic qualities, but he also cultivated ideas. Captain Borlase Smart, who painted seascapes, embraced the mindset of the new art and artists.

He had already met Wilhelmina Barns-Graham with whom he shared a belief in the art of drawing. Willie was a friend of Margaret Mellis and Borlase asked her to introduce him to her friends. Barns-Graham was indebted to Smart, who had found her a studio at number 3 Porthmeor, formerly occupied by Commander Bradshaw, painter of sea and ships, who was away on war service in the navy.

Barns-Graham duly performed the introductions and Borlase Smart was delighted. Smart was anxious for Nicholson and Hepworth to join the St Ives Society of Artists and exhibit with them, recognizing that they were artists with a growing reputation in modernist ideas. He also invited Naum Gabo, the Russian constructivist, who had also moved to Carbis Bay from London. He declined on the grounds that he always refrained from joining groups of artists; meanwhile Smart allowed them to display their paintings and sculpture in his Porthmeor studio on Show Day.

Unlike the traditional painters, the Moderns were not in the least interested in showing their work in the Royal Academy, knowing they would find acceptance difficult because of their more enlightened view of the direction in which they were guiding their art, and also because they were not keen to be associated with a regressive and stagnant Royal Academy ideology. The RA now encompasses all styles of art and design.

'In 1943 BN and Hepworth were sought out by Smart … Borlase Smart was 15 years older than BN and never ceased being an enthusiastic painter, but he was eager to bring new life and new art into the society, unlike many of his fellow members.' [22]

As well as being introduced to Borlase, his wife Irene and Ben Nicholson got to know each other. Both were keen and competitive tennis players. Irene played golf, and played tennis for Cornwall. She was secretary of the Tennis Association and through that office was able to obtain tickets for Wimbledon, which at various times she shared with Ben and they sat together at Centre Court. Borlase was no games player, unlike Ben, but was proud of his wife's involvement in sport. He produced several amusing drawings of the members of the tennis club, which suggested that at least he was interested enough to watch her play.

Below left: *The Tennis Club.*

Below right: *Cornwall Bowlers on Tour, 1939.*

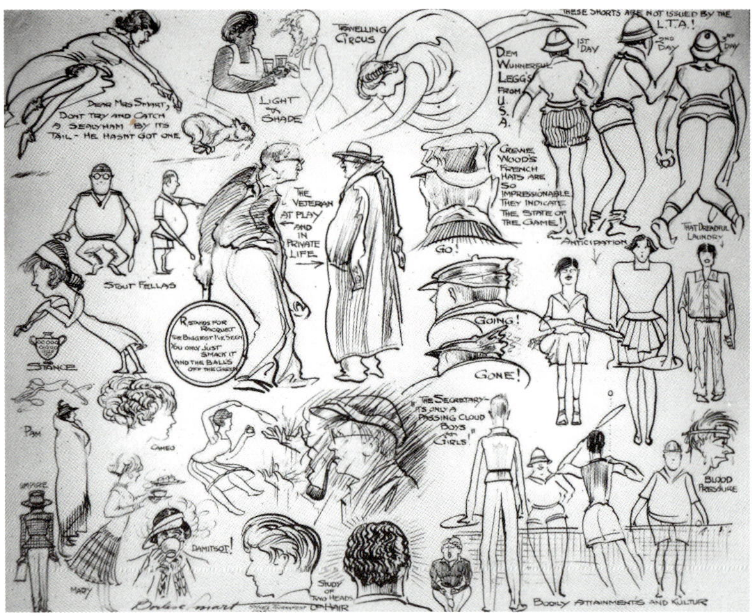

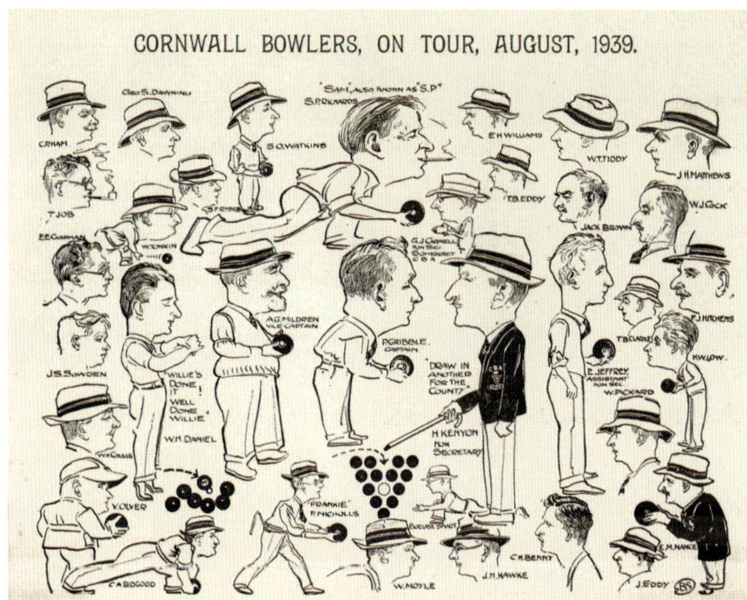

The Sea Scouts

Writing about Show Day in March 1940, the journalist was *'taken up with the work of L J Fuller with his fine portrait of a Sea Scoutmaster with its aura of National Service.'*

The Sea Scouts were an offshoot of the Scouts. I understand from many of my contacts that it was started before the war. An advertisement in the *St Ives Times* of 11 September 1942 reads, *'Junior Sea Scouts. Boys between 11 and 14 can now join the St Ives Sea Scouts. Meeting every Wednesday 7 to 8pm, The Battery, The Island, St Ives. Borlase Smart, District Commissioner.'*

I was fortunate to have conversations with many older men of St Ives who still remember, with affection, the time they spent with the Sea Scouts.

Cyril Bennetts
"I joined the Sea Scouts when I left school at 14. Borlase Smart was a great leader. We had two boats, the whaler and the gig. We went out in the whaler with Borlase Smart and we started to take in water. We had no life jackets at that time. We used our hats to bail out the water, but we made it back to harbour. Another time, after I had passed my test as a first class signalman, Borlase Smart said the Coastguard had complained to him that the boys were trying to get in touch with a warship in the Bay. 'You will refrain from doing that,' he said. Nevertheless, he was proud of the boy's expertise and his own teaching."

David Daniel
"The Sea Scouts used to meet up at The Battery on the Island. My career as a sea scout was short lived. I was about 13 or 14 at the time and this particular day I was up at the island and saw my friend making his way up the hill. For a joke, I fixed a bucket of water over the door. I stood behind the door and waited, then I heard him say, 'after you, Sir.' Borlase Smart walked through the door and was soaked. That was the end of my career as a sea scout. 'Get out and don't come back,' he said. But, he was a very nice chap."

Harding Laity
"Borlase Smart used to teach art at the Grammar School in Hayle so I attended his classes. I was also a Sea Scout. I remember there was an old whaler in the harbour and one of my jobs was to scrape the hull with a piece of glass, when that wore out it was replaced with another piece of glass."

Jack Murt's daughter, Sarah
"Dad said Borlase Smart painted a picture of a battleship with lights. These lights were shown

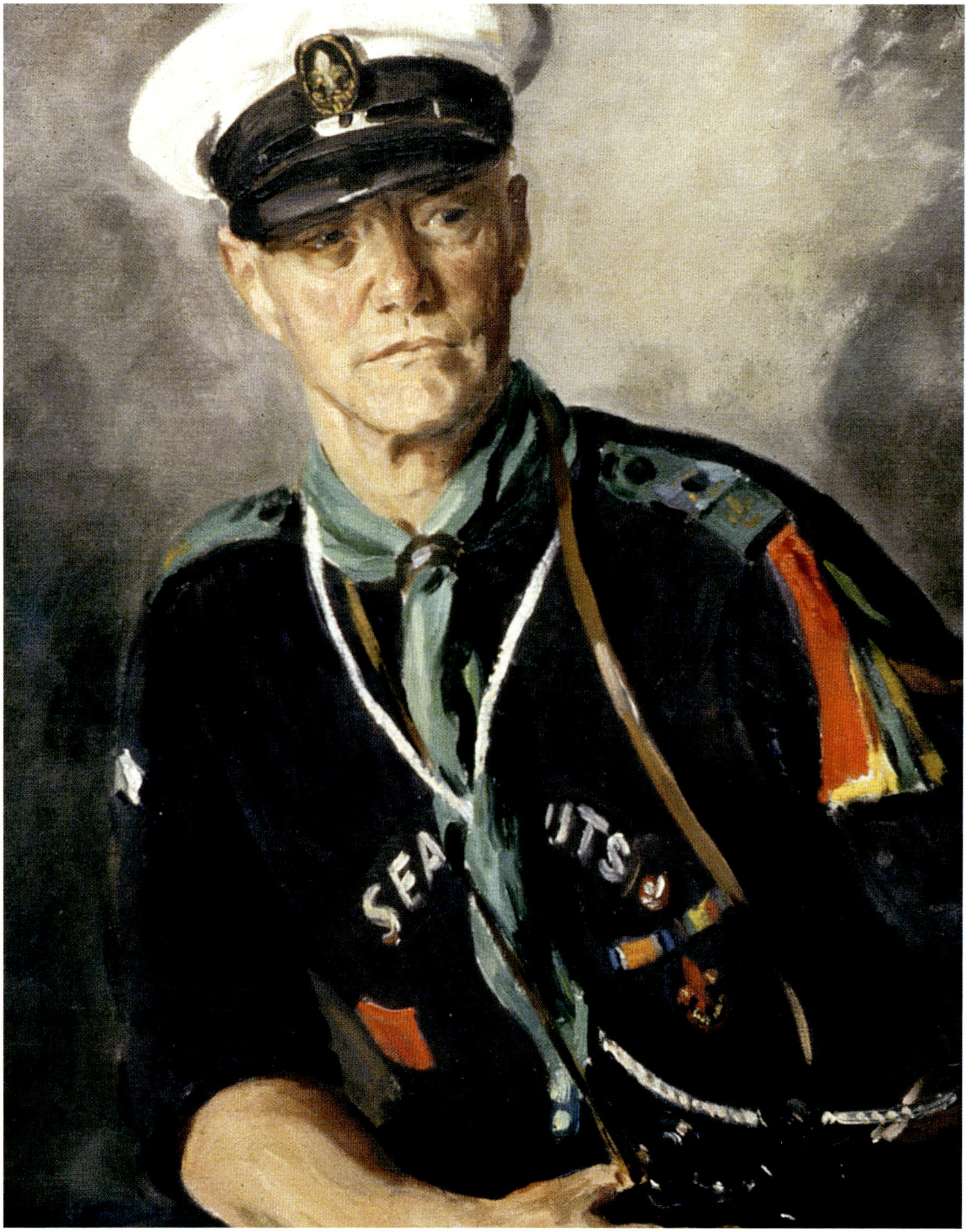
SEA
UTS

through holes in the canvas and were various signals at sea and the Sea Scouts had to read, identify and learn the meaning of the signals. I don't know what happened to that painting."

Opposite: *Portrait of Borlase Smart in his Sea Scout uniform painted by Leonard Fuller.*

Eddy Bassett

"We learnt seamanship, sailing, signalling and had lectures on First Aid. For some, it was the first experience of sailing. It was a good thing. It was lovely. Many of those Sea Scouts joined the Navy but I joined the Air Force. When I returned to St Ives I went fishing. Steven was the Skipper, and then he had a pleasure boat afterwards."

Matthew Care

"We had an ex naval whaler and a cutter. We did a lot of sailing and rowing in the harbour. I remember I spent a week aboard *The Discovery* which was moored alongside the Embankment, in London. There were three of us. Edward Murt and Richard Tanner were with me. I can't remember why we went, but it was very special."

The usefulness and interest shown by the St Ives boys in becoming Sea Scouts paid off when 47 of those lads joined the Navy and others joined the Merchant Navy. Smart's ability to engage the boys in learning various skills was recognised and praised. He resigned his post as District Commissioner because of ill health.

Below left: *Sea Power, with signalling lights behind the canvas.*

Below right: *Commander H V Coates, Chairman of the Executive Officers Deep Sea Scouts and members of the 3rd St Ives Sea Scouts.*

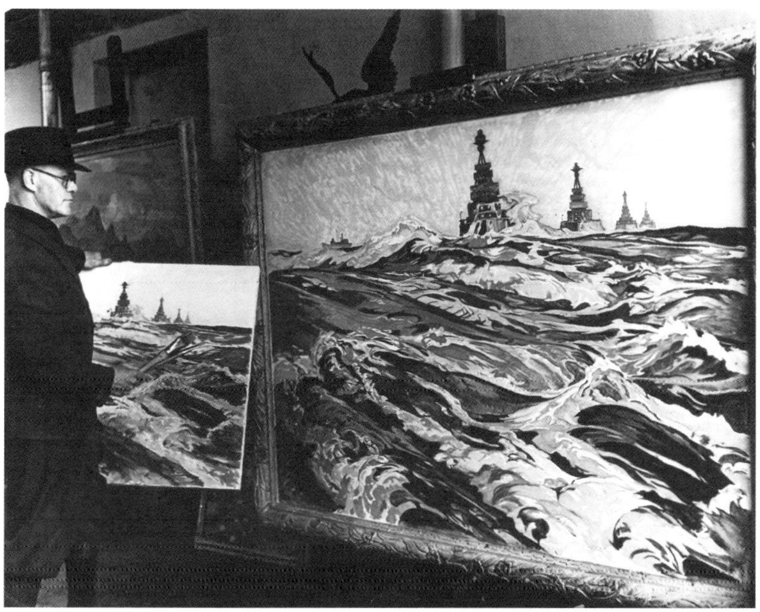

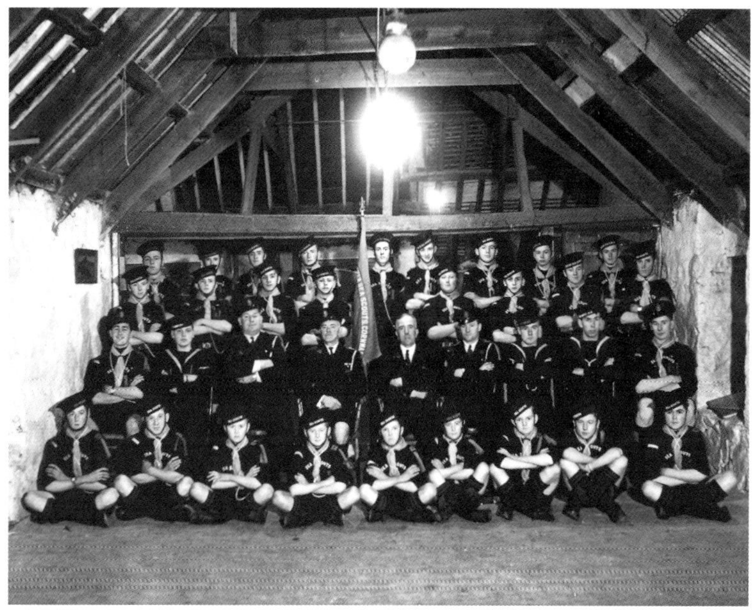

Willie James

"Lads who were fourteen could join one of the cadet forces, but as I was only thirteen I had to be content with a Sea Scout uniform, not that I have any regrets about that however, for I found the time I spent in that group to be full of fun and enjoyment under the supervision of Scout Master Borlase Smart.

The high spots I suppose were the sailing sessions in the whaler. The Scout House was the single story building at the top of the island, adjacent to the Coastguard lookout... At the seaward end was a glass observation tower set as a dormer in the roof, accessible by a ladder and a trap door. Lads would crowd into this limited space on Sunday afternoons and from this vantage point would keep a close watch through binoculars on the immense amount of shipping moving up and down in convoys."

The Battery Scout House with the observation tower, St Ives.

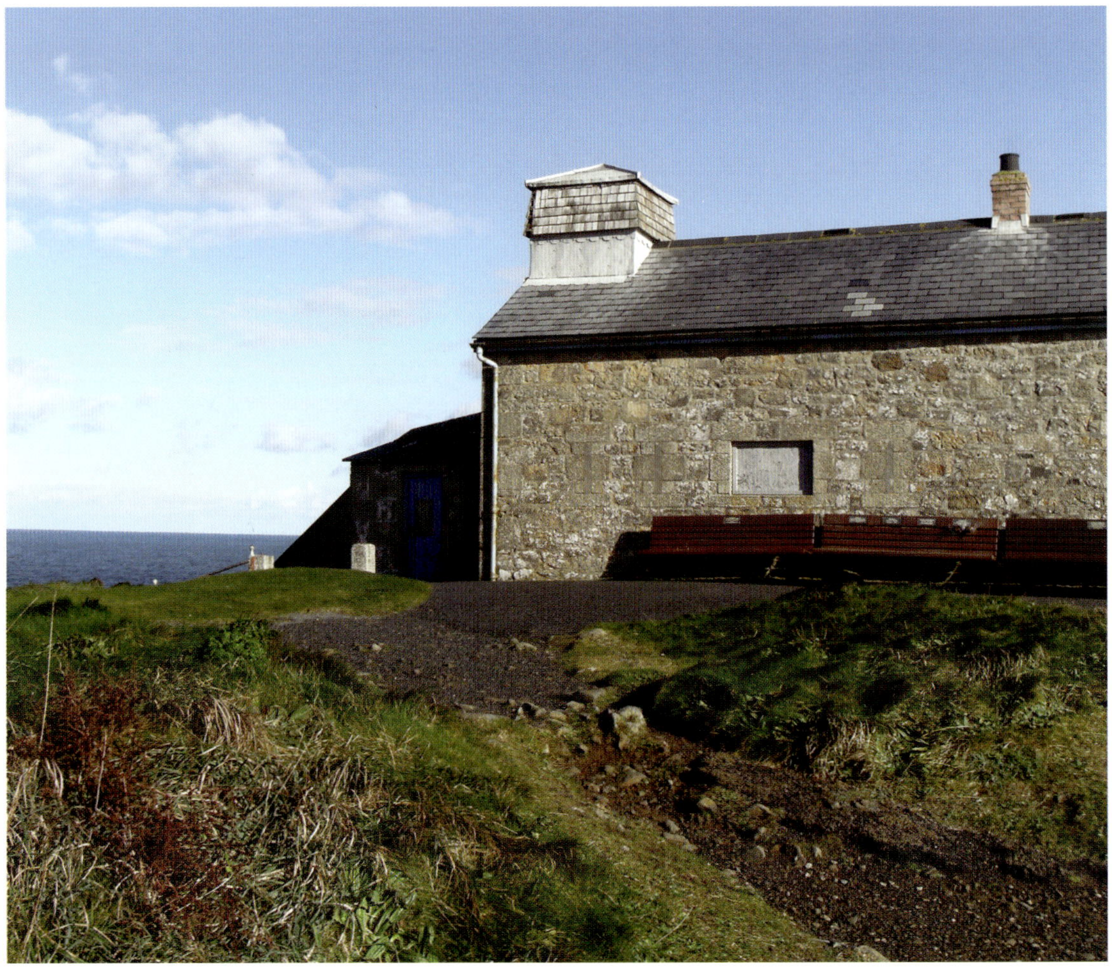

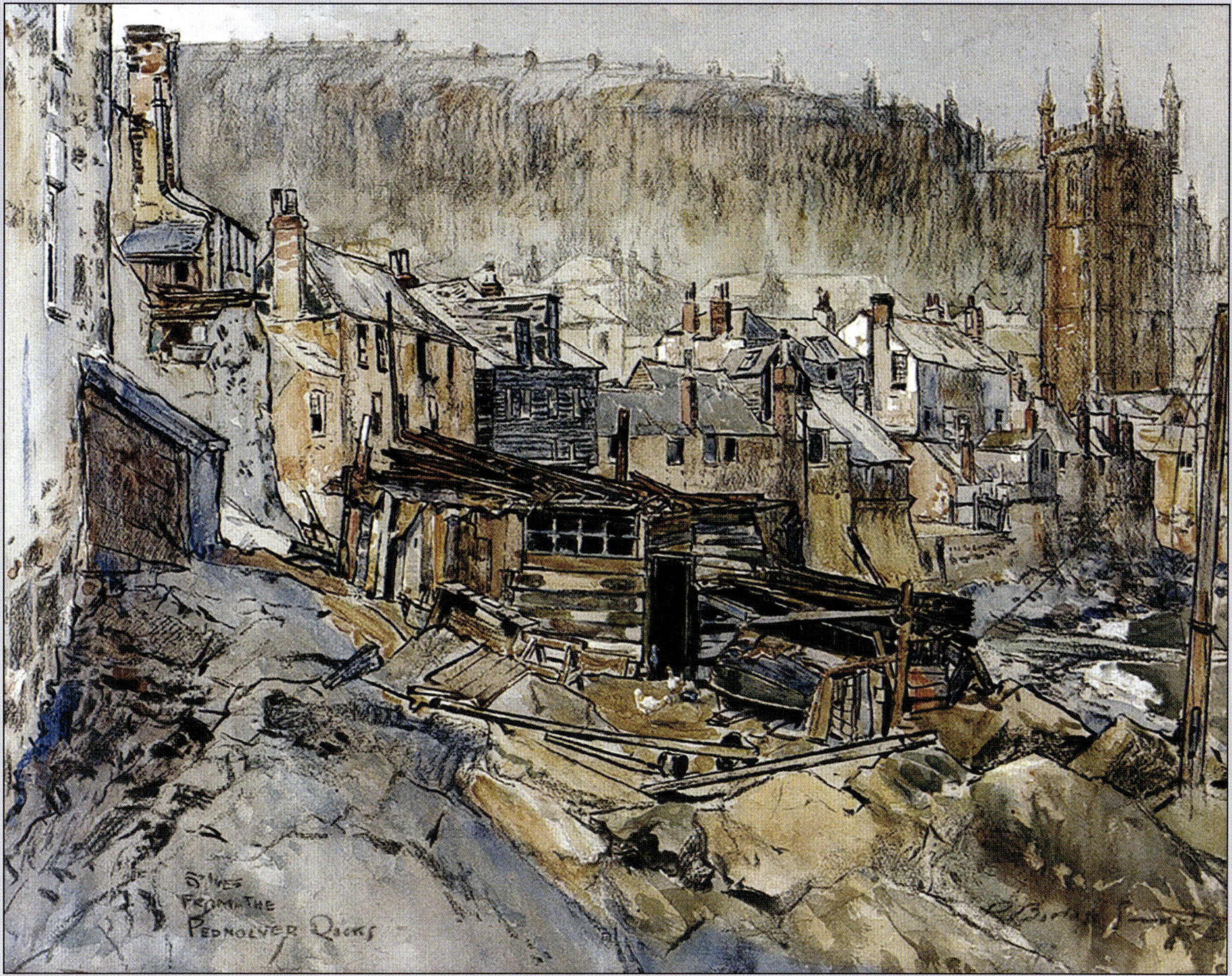

St Ives from Pednolver Rocks.

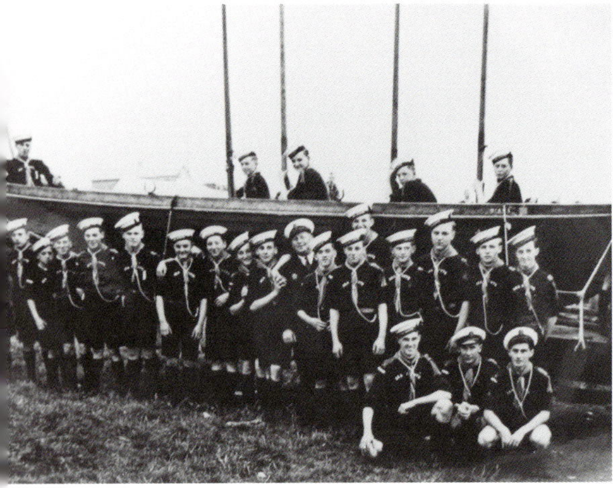

Sea Scouts with the whaler.

The Battery on the Island was built by the War Department in 1860. The capitals of Europe at that time were seen as a possible threat and coastal defences were necessary. A chain of batteries were built around the coast. The St Ives Battery had three gun emplacements, with tracks on which the guns could be directed against an enemy approaching from the sea. The guns were for the use of the (St Ives) Duke of Cornwall Artillery Volunteers. They were never fired and were dismantled in 1895.

Of course Borlase Smart was also interested in the Scouts and the Girl Guides, whose organisations also provided activities for the youngsters. Borlase Smart gave the Girl Guide Leader, Millie English, a seascape painting for her 25 years of running her troupe.

The Home Guard

At the outbreak of the Second World War, Borlase Smart was over age to serve but his interest in the sea and naval affairs led him to ask Commander Bradshaw, who was serving as an officer in Falmouth working for the protection of merchant ships, to find him a position in Falmouth. Bradshaw found him a post as editor of the Royal Navy Magazine. However, Smart's decline in health led him to resign from this post.

Thereafter, he was appointed intelligence officer in the Home Guard. They met at the Drill Hall in St Ives. Also in the Company were, Leonard Fuller (painter) Captain in charge, Denis Mitchell (sculptor) Corporal, Bernard Leach (potter) and Adrian Stokes (painter) were privates. In Carbis Bay, Ben Nicholson (painter) and Naum Gabo (sculptor) were Air Raid Wardens.

Calling on his expertise and army training for the First World War, Borlase Smart lectured, and demonstrated, to the Army, the Home Guard and various societies, like the Rotary Club, the importance of camouflage in a war situation. He also joined the Admiralty police and was sergeant in charge of the munitions dumps at Ponsanooth, near Falmouth, where mines, torpedoes and shells were stored and where his expertise in camouflage was doubly important.

C/O Mrs Gregor
"Glengariff"
Ponsanooth
Nr Truro

My dear Leonard
Sargent can have the old natural wood easel in my studio free loan. It belongs to AC Bailey who lent it to me to mind for him. It is a wind up screw one, & takes a canvas any height. Ask Miss Thompson

to let him have it. It is rather soiled, but it works well. You will recognize it as it is not polished. Bailey won't mind I am sure. Irene and the boys have had a ripping time & I have had my meals with them. It has been a most happy time for us all being together as much as possible in spite of Bombing! Sunday night Jerry dropped about 9 between their farm & next door farm about ¼ mile. They fell in almost a straight line & ended in a direct hit on the main road which was blown to bits. Monday night they dropped about 8 in the farm next to where I live. I thought we were gone! but no damage thank God!

The AA was wonderfully accurate & they had to get rid of the bombs and fly higher. Altogether miraculous escapes. First bomb went off at 8.15 while I was having breakfast & rocked the bungalow. The other has not gone off yet in the field up the road behind "Glengariff". At the same time I shall be glad when they are in safer St Ives!!! They are all tremendously brave & Irene shows a fine example to the farm people. I shall try & come over to see you all about 14th Sept for a day or two. I am sorry to hear about Nancy's rheumatism. I hope she will soon be free from pain. Glad to hear Miss Procter is efficient. Congratulations on your work with the Home Guard. Give my kindest regards to Sargent.

Love from us all to you both in haste
Borlase

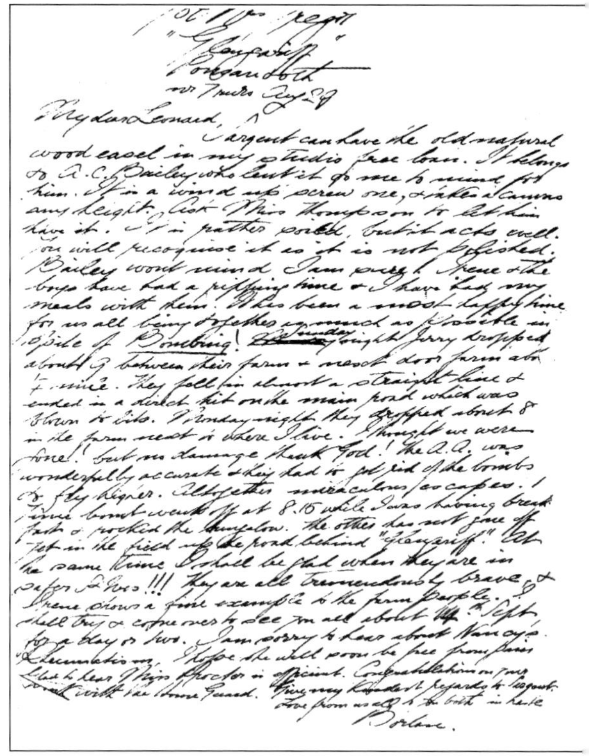
"Glengariff"

My dear Leonard,

Sargent can have the old natural wood easel in my studio free loan. It belongs to A. C. Bailey who lent it to me to mind for him. It is a wind up screw one, & takes canvas any height. Ask Miss Thompson to let him have it. It is rather soiled, but it acts well. You will recognise it as it is not polished. Bailey won't mind I am sure! Irene & the boys have had a ripping time & I have had my meals with them. It has been a most happy time for us all being together as much as possible in spite of Bombing! Sunday night Jerry dropped about 9 between their farm & next door farm about ¼ mile. They fell in almost a straight line & ended in a direct hit on the main road which was blown to bits. Monday night they dropped about 8 in the farm next to where I live. I thought we were gone! but no damage thank God! The A.A. was wonderfully accurate & they had to get rid of the bombs & fly higher. Altogether miraculous escapes. 1st bomb went off at 8.15 while I was having breakfast & rocked the bungalow. The other has not gone off yet in the field up the road behind "Glengariff". At the same time I shall be glad when they are in safer St Ives!!! They are all tremendously brave & Irene shows a fine example to the farm people. I shall try & come over to see you all about 14th Sept for a day or two. I am sorry to hear about Nancy's rheumatism. I hope she will soon be free from pain. Glad to hear Miss Procter is efficient. Congratulations on your work with the Home Guard. Give my kindest regards to Sargent.
Love from us all to you both in haste
Borlase.

Letter from Borlase Smart to Leonard Fuller (undated) probably 1940s.

The Smart family of four was holidaying for a short time on a farm some distance from the dump. There was an air raid one night, with bombs dropping close to the farm. In the morning, after the 'all clear' siren, they walked across the fields to see what damage had been done. They found a line of about ten bomb craters, just short of Borlase's heavily camouflaged ammunition dump. Unfortunately, the onset of Angina forced him to retire from his Naval commitment.

Borlase was very much in demand as a designer of posters with regard to raising money for the war effort. Anxious to do his bit he always gave these services free of charge and drew the town's attention to these money raising activities for the National Savings Campaign, Navy Week and the collection of waste paper for the Red Cross.

The paper was housed in the attractive building which is now Oates Travel, near Market Square, and Irene Smart of the Women's Voluntary Service took over the job from her husband who had left the town on Government work. She said she allowed herself two afternoons for tennis and the rest of the time was spent in the salvage operations. These and other campaigns were all helped by a striking poster.

St Ives folk bought a Spitfire for £5,000 for the RAF and Borlase designed a big arrowed indicator which was mounted on the side of Barclays Bank, in the High Street, to show how much money the town was collecting. A Spitfire was on display in the Palais de Dance on Barnoon Hill. The building was later taken over by Barbara Hepworth for producing and storing her larger sculp-

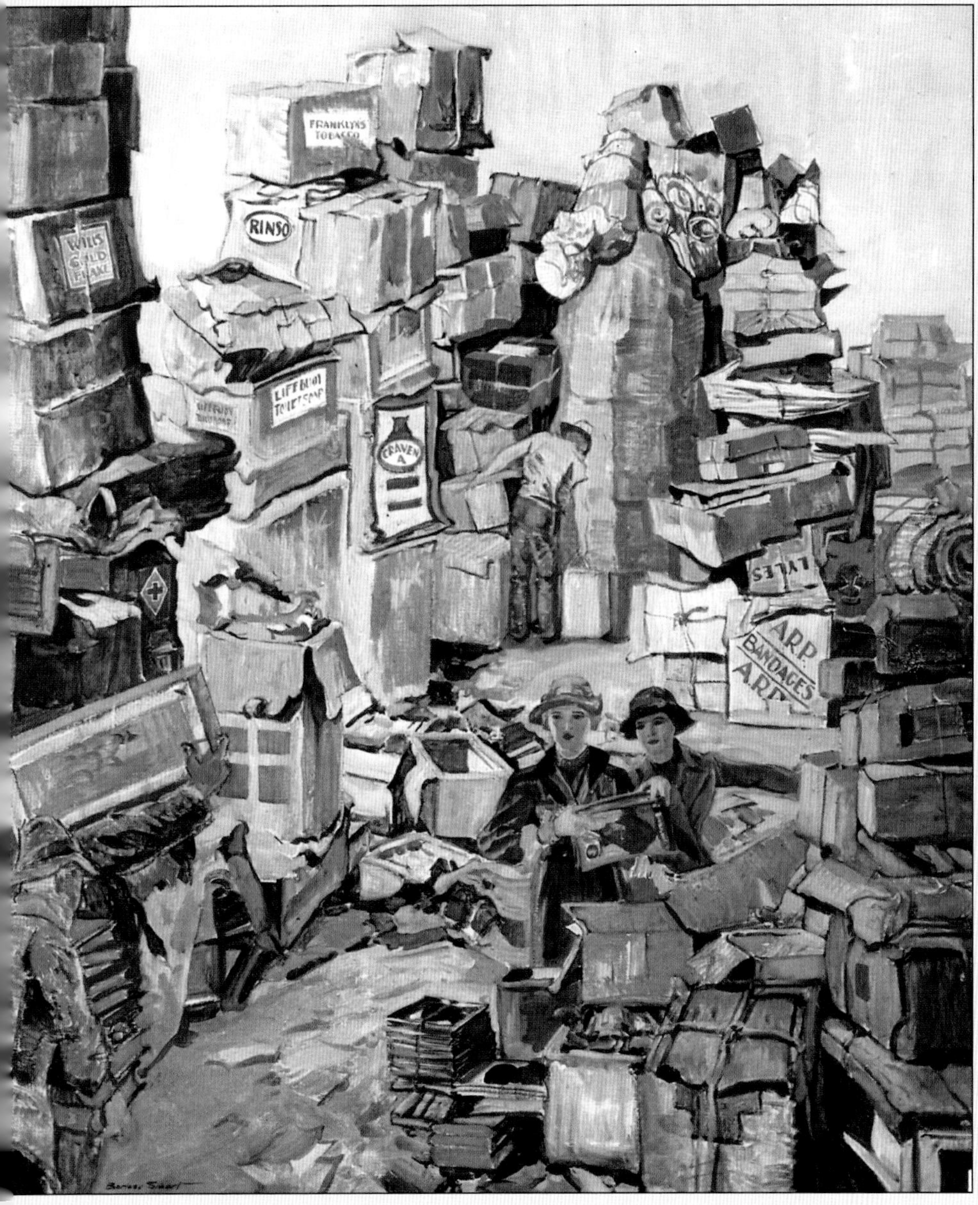

Borlase Smart's painting for the Royal Academy.

Borlase Smart's continued association with the Western Morning News.

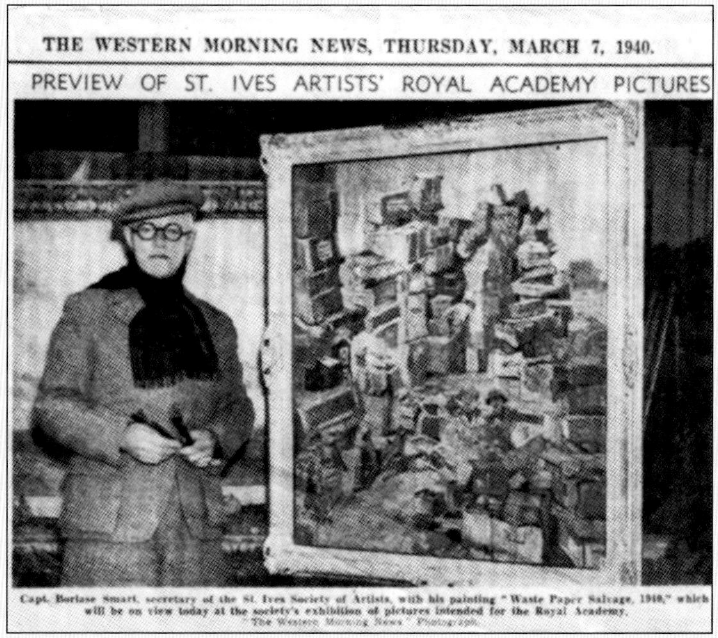

THE WESTERN MORNING NEWS, THURSDAY, MARCH 7, 1940.

PREVIEW OF ST. IVES ARTISTS' ROYAL ACADEMY PICTURES

Capt. Borlase Smart, secretary of the St. Ives Society of Artists, with his painting "Waste Paper Salvage, 1940," which will be on view today at the society's exhibition of pictures intended for the Royal Academy.

"The Western Morning News" Photograph.

tures, one of which was *Winged Figure* commissioned by John Lewis for their Oxford Street store in London.

Both Commander Bradshaw and Captain Smart were asked to design posters for Navy Week, which took place in Portsmouth in the autumn of 1936. The message was two-fold. It demonstrated to other nations that the British Navy was a force to be reckoned with , and it reassured its citizens that Great Britain was a powerful nation and well able to defend itself against an encroaching tide of hostilities developing in Europe.

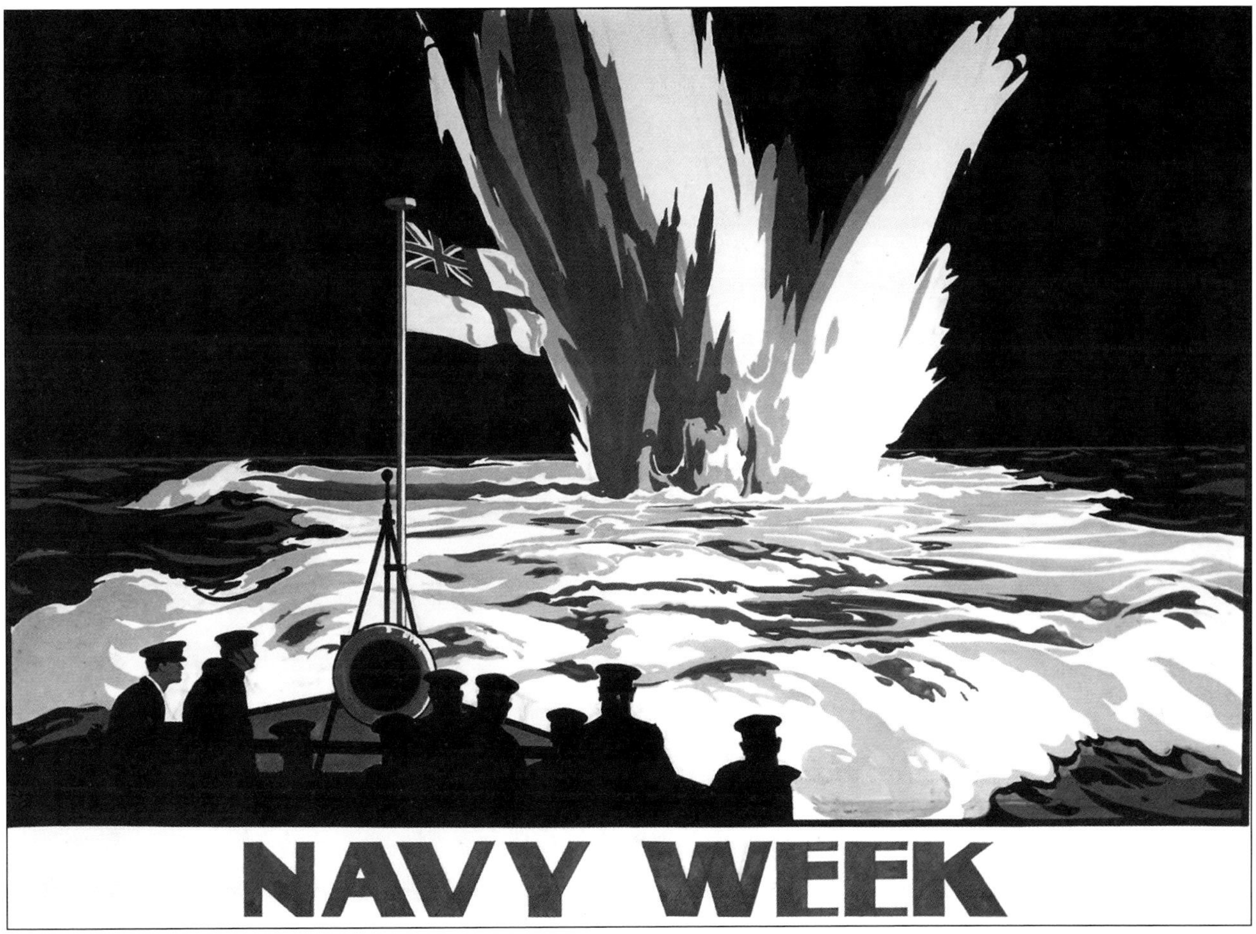

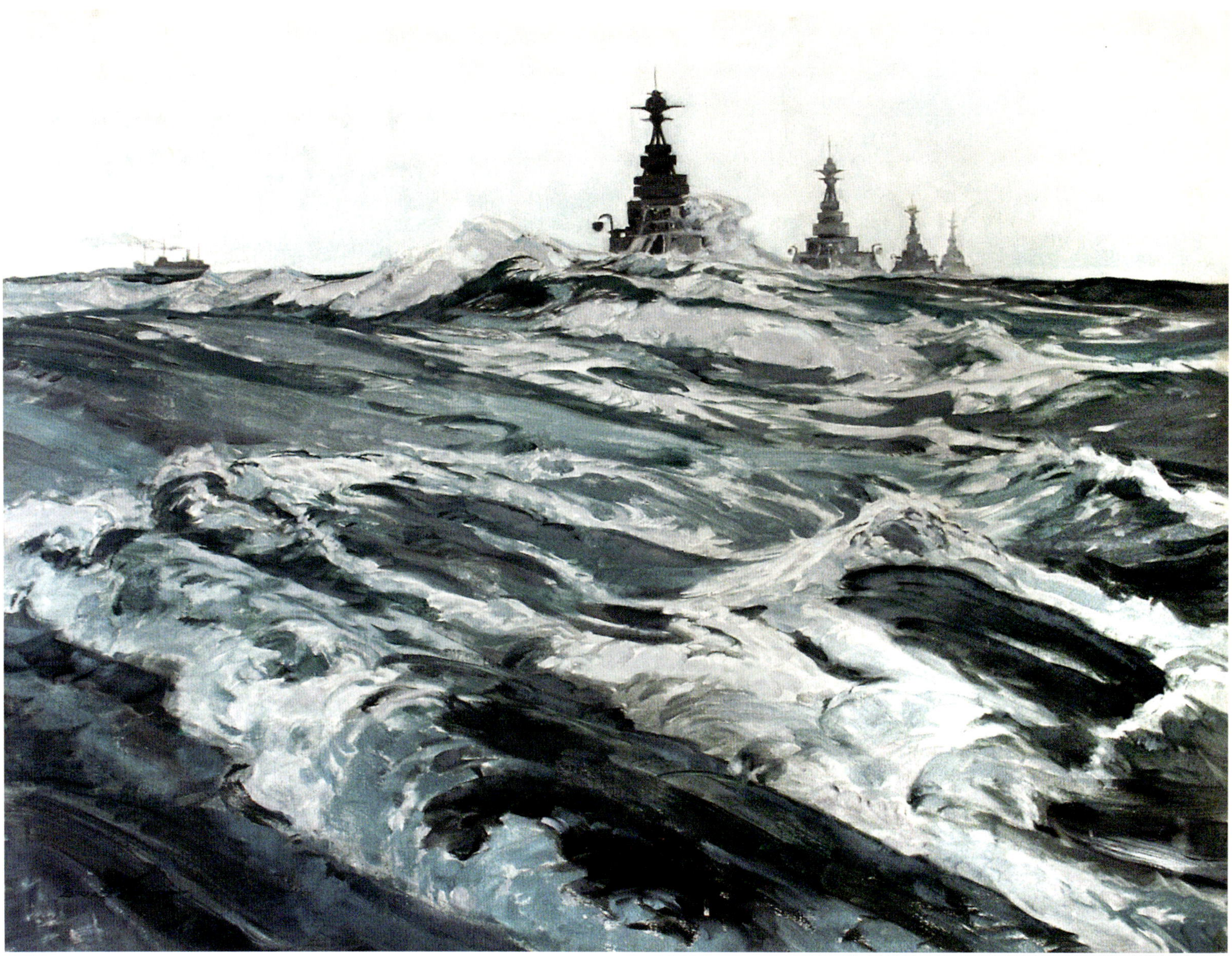

Battleships.

Studios Open Day

Again, there was a revival of the Studios Open Day for those wishing to show their paintings intended for the Royal Academy Summer Exhibition. Borlase Smart in his Ocean Wave studio, with balcony overlooking the harbour and St Ives bay, welcomed school children.

He said, *'I had scores of young children in my studio, unaccompanied by any grown up, and I found their behaviour all that could be desired. They showed an intelligent interest in what they saw. I always make it a practice to endeavour to interest the children in the various pictures, and anything I feel may appeal to them, I give them a little talk on it. I have invariably found them very attentive listeners, and that they appreciate such consideration is shown by their general behaviour.'* [23]

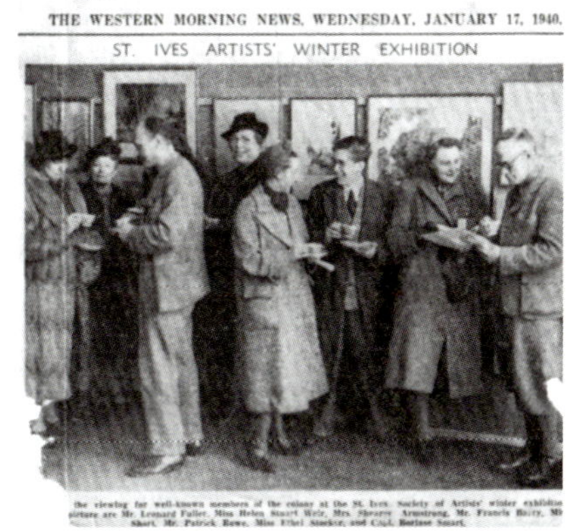

The hanging committee at Newlyn, 1940, Borlase Smart far right.

This comment was made in reply to a complaint a visitor had made about the bad behaviour of children, spoiling the enjoyment of their visit to the studios. It was typical of Borlase to respond and defend those under attack, or accused unjustifiably.

A letter from the headmaster of a local school, Charles Bray, wrote, *'I would express my sincere thanks to the artists of St Ives who invited our children to visit the studios on the morning of Show Day… the courtesy shown to us by the artists is greatly appreciated.'* [24]

The headmaster extended an invitation for the artists to visit his school. These visits were very much favoured by Borlase Smart, who taught art at the Grammar school in Hayle and encouraged his fellow artists to demonstrate their interest in teaching the young.

Amateur Art Exhibitions

Smart organized amateur art exhibitions which included the work of children; as a teacher himself, he encouraged all their endeavours, even advertising in the local paper, *'I shall be glad to receive postcards from intending exhibitors and schools desiring to participate, so that I can make the necessary arrangements.'* [25]

The advert produced some surprising results. The youngest artist was Nina-Serafina Gabo, aged four-and-a-half years, daughter of the artists, Naum Gabo and his wife Miriam, living in Carbis Bay. There were also paintings by Telfer Stokes, aged five, son of artists Adrian Stokes and his wife Margaret Mellis, living at Little Parc Owles. One wonders if they were wryly making fun of Borlase Smart's super enthusiasm. It is how Willie Barns-Graham described her friend Borlase to Ben Nicholson, *'He's an enthusiast,'* she said, knowing Ben, who was also an enthusiast, would be intrigued.

The amateur exhibitions were held in the Guildhall and had previously attracted 850 entries. No professional work was admitted.

A local woman, Catherine Bowtell, told me of her memories of Borlase Smart. *"He used to come to the schools and choose pictures for Show Day. I had mine hung in Moffat Lindner's studio. We were very pleased if we were chosen. That's why I have always been interested in art and enjoy painting."* [26]

An exhibition of the work of the Czech soldiers stationed in St Ives took place in the St Ives Society Gallery, organized by Smart and opened by Leonard Fuller; one of the soldiers taking part was Joza Belahorsky, who was said to be producing some good work.

Captain Smart was eager to promote an interest in art for the local community and said he was hoping to open a free public art class in the Crypt of the Mariners Church. He expressed the view that the professional artists would willingly co-operate in giving free lectures and advice on painting.

Some of Borlase's sketches are on view at the St Ives Museum, at Wheal Dream, which was established in 1921 and houses the working history of the town and its environs.

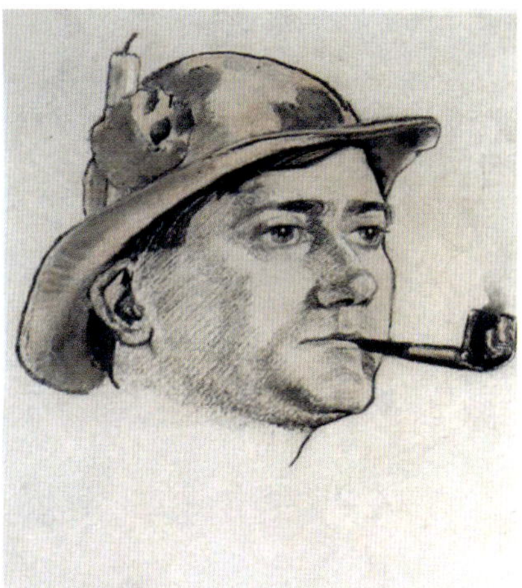

Above: *A Miner.*

Right: *Two studies of Daniel.*

Far right: *A study.*

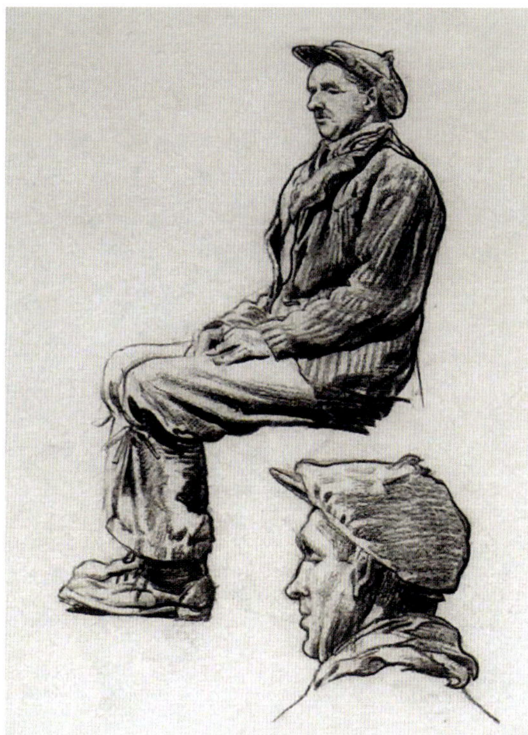

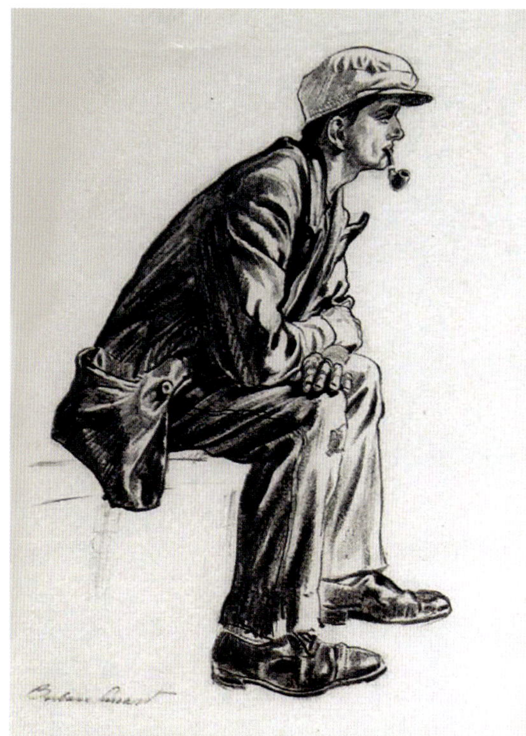

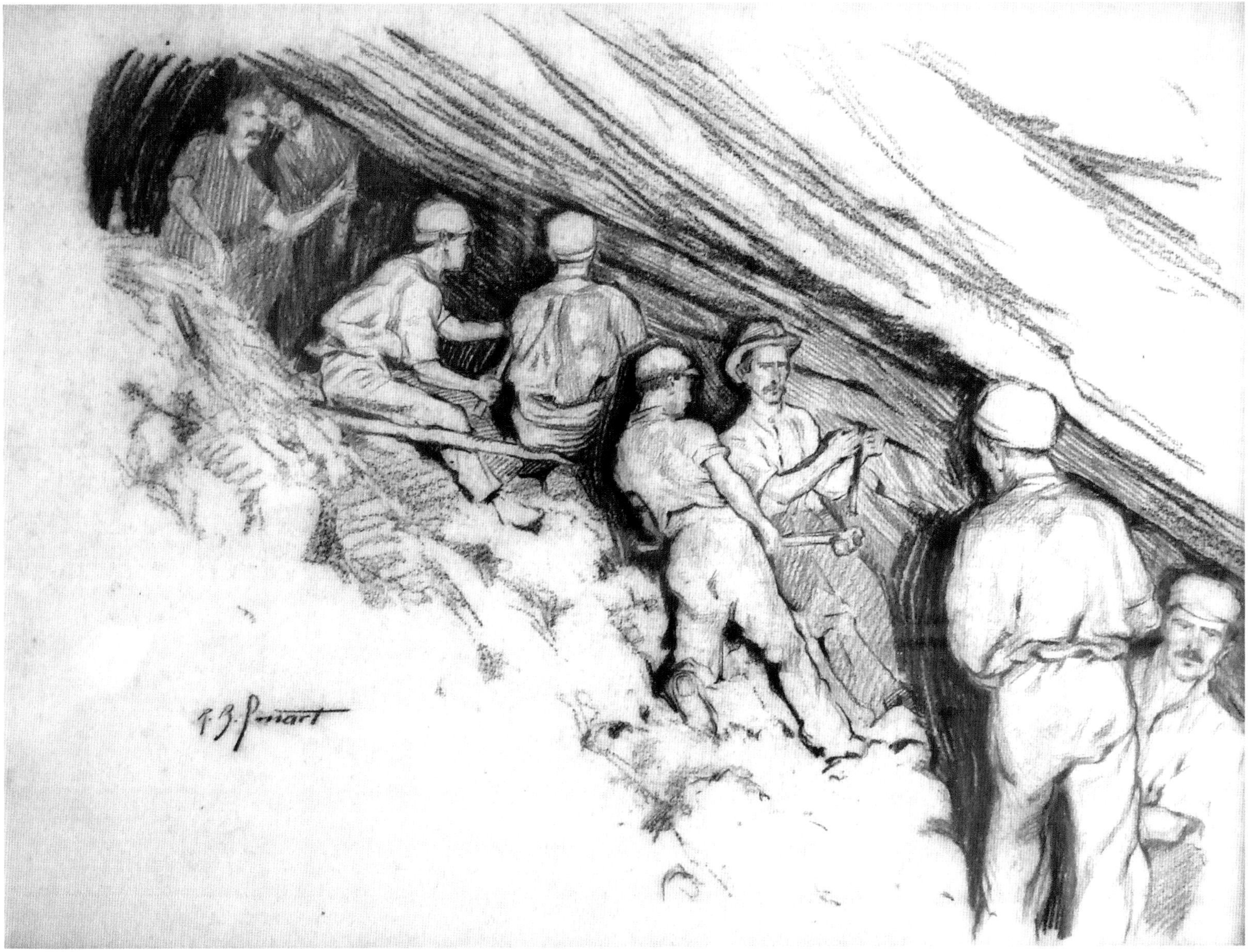

Tin Miners at Geevor.

Treloyhan Manor

In 1944 the newly elected Mayor of St Ives, Councillor Mr W J Sullivan, stressed the need for a museum and art gallery to house the paintings owned by the Council. The proposed venue was Treloyhan Manor. He felt this would be a fitting war memorial and was located on the edge of town. Smart supported the Mayor's suggestion and saw great possibilities of this happening. It was previously the home of Sir Edward Hain and family, who owned the Hain shipping line. Many sons of the town went to sea with their local fleet before it was sold to the P and O line.

Smart agreed that the town should capitalize on the artists' influence on the holiday trade on which the town was more and more dependent. The artists were a permanent feature and one of the town's industries, living, working, contributing to the economy of the town and promoting St Ives with their paintings. Borlase Smart reminded the Town Council, '*The art colony has advertised this town for the last fifty years throughout the world and by comparison with which the propaganda of the Publicity Committee of the Council and the Chamber of Commerce is a mere pin-prick, and such a half-century of endeavour has not cost the town one penny.*' [27]

Treloyhan Manor.

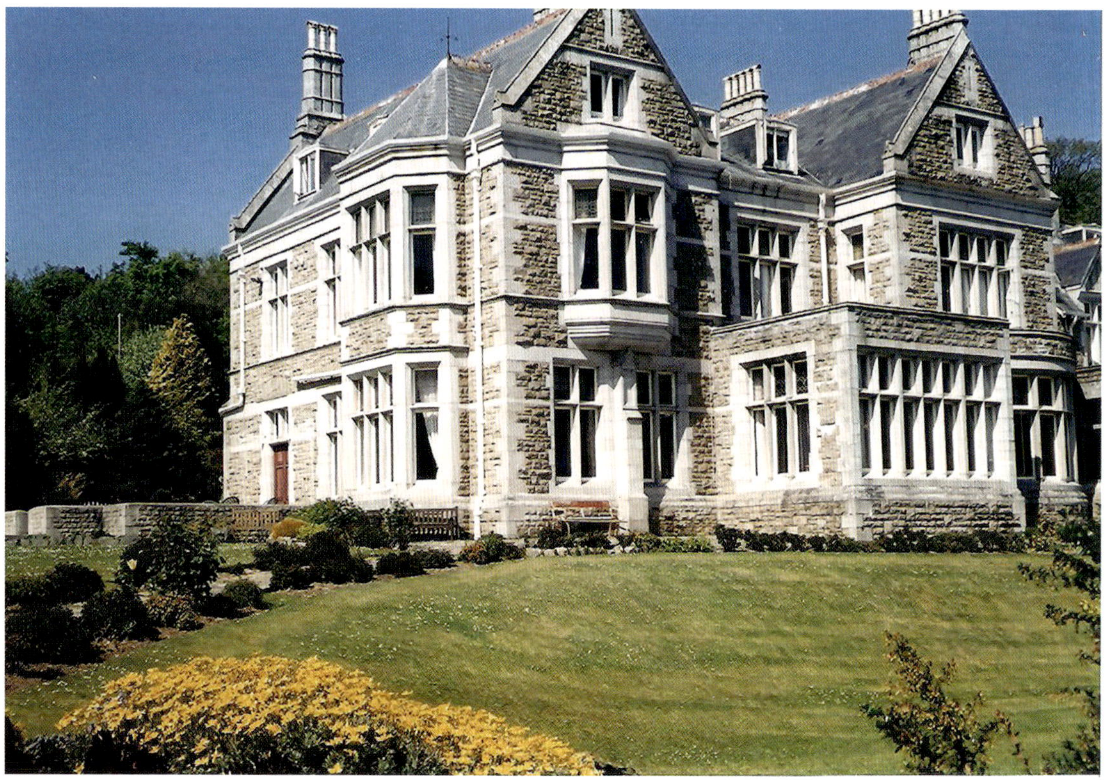

A quarter of a century after his first attempts to secure an art gallery, Smart was trying once again and hoping, this time, to succeed in his ambition to provide a permanent home for the accumulated work of St Ives artists. Treloyhan Manor, a large house with extensive gardens was the ideal venue and up for sale. Smart suggested that the building be bought by public subscription and urged the Council to call a meeting to invite the townsfolk to support this idea. He made an impassioned plea. *'The extensive grounds would provide the long-felt want of a public park... the museum could house treasures of local or Cornish origin such as pottery, coinage, geological and prehistoric specimens, and even a collection of old Cornish dresses, many of which are still treasured in St Ives. The art gallery might exhibit the work of distinguished artists of the colony showing the history of painting in St Ives for the past 60 years...even a recreation room may be set aside for St Ives ex-Service men... The grounds are large enough to include tennis courts, bowling and putting green. Borlase Smart, Hon. Sec. St Ives Society of Artists.'*[28]

In spite of the backing of the Mayor, the proposal was lost by 14 votes to 9. Smart then decided to call a public meeting himself, but was prevented by the news that the building was under offer. This lost opportunity cost St Ives a large building and substantial grounds. Having adequate housing for works of art would undoubtedly have saved a great number of paintings being sold off throughout the years because there was no public building to display the history of the town and for a lack of hanging space in Council offices. Fortunately, some of the art works were later transferred to St Ives Library in Gabriel Street, including a seascape painting by Borlase Smart.

Mariners Church, St Ives Society of Artists Gallery.

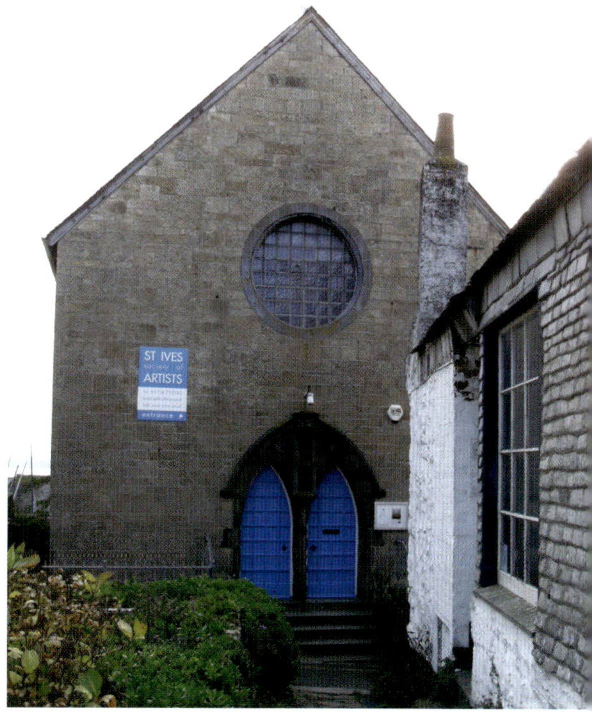

However, coming to the rescue for the town were Marion and George Pearce, both former mayors of St Ives, and two other partners, who bought Treloyhan Manor to save it falling into the hands of developers. They spent considerable sums of money repairing the building after its occupation by the Downs School who were evacuated there during the war. They then sold it to the Methodist Society, who was prepared to preserve the character of the estate. It is still in the hands of the Methodist movement.

The Mariners Church

In Norway Lane, opposite Norway square, a disused church built in 1902, was on the market. It was supposedly built for the sea farers of St Ives, however, those mariners and fishermen had their own Methodist chapels; buildings which were modest and sat comfortably among the cottages and were part of the architecture of Downalong. This new church dominated its surroundings and imposed its size upon the inhabitants. It was largely ignored and neglected by local people and fell into disuse.

Borlase Smart, always with an eye to the future, had some years before secured a promise from the church authorities that if the building were to come up for sale it should be offered to the St

Ives Society. Now that opportunity presented itself and as secretary of the Society he negotiated the transfer of the building. In 1945 they were firmly established in their new home with a large exhibition area. Smart persuaded the 'Moderns' to exhibit in their New Gallery.

'In 1944 Ben Nicholson had sent work to the St Ives Society of Artists spring and summer shows, as well as to the one-day show mounted in Borlase Smart's studio, where his 'group of geometrical designs for which he is famous' contrasted sharply with the normal local product.' [29]

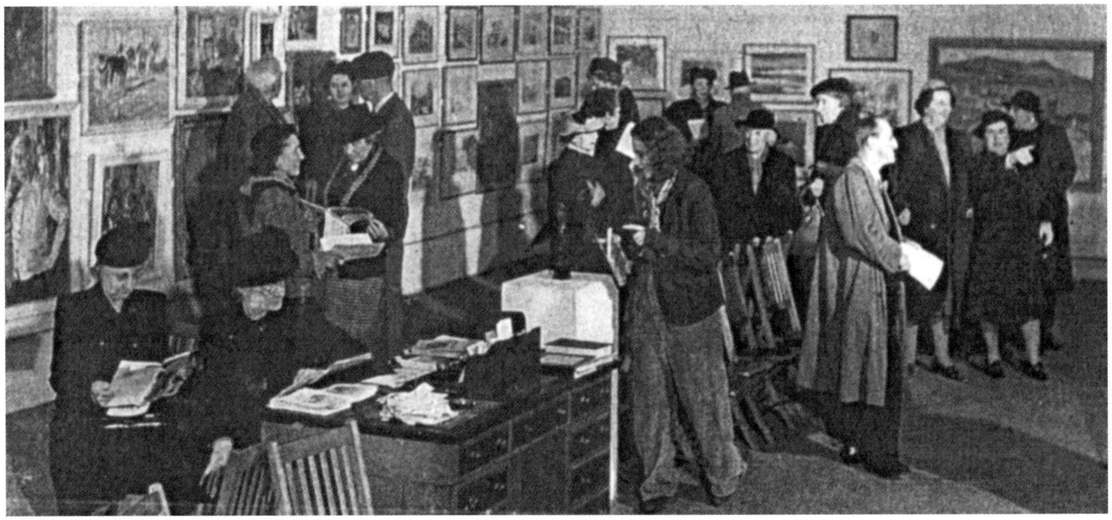

Exhibition of 1947 at the St Ives Society of Artists, Mariners Church. Willie Barns-Graham, standing left, talking to Dorothy Everard. Left, Fred Bottomley and Leonard Richmond. Marion Grace Hocken, centre, wearing trousers. Behind her are Dorothea Sharp in wide-brimmed hat and Pauline Hewitt in beret.

Regular visitors to St Ives to view the work in the St Ives Society of Artists expected to see the familiar landscapes, still lifes, flower studies and portraits. It proved a shock to visitors and the residents to see abstract works that they couldn't identify with or understand. It also angered the local painters, who were staunch supporters and members of a Society steeped in history and the painting of subjects true to their likeness and known and loved for generations.

'The 1945 exhibition included paintings by Ben Nicholson and, at last new sculptures by Hepworth. Thanks to Borlase Smart's efforts, the Society now had more extensive premises in the Mariners Church, between Porthmeor Studios and the harbour.' [30]

Those artists given space were Barbara Hepworth, Miriam Gabo, Margaret Mellis, Ben Nicholson, John Wells, Sven Berlin, Barns-Graham and his young friend, Peter Lanyon. Their allocated space was at the far end of the building known as, 'around the font' up three steps to where the altar had once stood. The large main body of the building exhibited the work of the traditionalists.

'I and a few of the others like Nicholson, Barns-Graham, Stokes, had already joined at the invitation of that ebullient and honest person, Borlase Smart. We were gathered round the font and were called the Font Group. Peter Lanyon, being a local, had been in this for much longer: he was taught by Borlase Smart and Leonard Fuller, later by Ben and Gabo.' [31]

Not only had Borlase to deal with the dissent from his colleagues by introducing the new young artists with their fresh ideas into the St Ives Society, but also to counter any problems in hanging the work and conflict within the two groups. Disagreements were rife but in spite of objections and criticism Smart was unrelenting in wishing to encourage and promote the work of the modern artists, as well as remaining loyal to those traditional painters, whose work was closest to his own.

'...under the broad-minded and intelligent plans of Borlase Smart the St Ives Society of Artists was beginning to show modern works alongside the more traditional. A policy not without its problems.' [32]

Denis Mitchell thought Smart an interesting character who 'backed the modern lot.' He remembered that Borlase went up to London to see a Klee exhibition. He turned to his son Brian and said, 'Well I think they are amazing.' He came back very excited and inspired by the experience. He also attended an exhibition with Brian who remembers his father being very impressed with the work of Picasso and Matisse. With this new experience of modern art he was fully prepared to understand and accept the different forms of art that were happening in St Ives, although he didn't emulate them. However, given a few more years and his open mind, he may have developed a more radical style of painting, whilst maintaining his traditional and skilful drawing techniques and masterful sea paintings.

Other Exhibitions

Just a year before he died Borlase Smart, in an explosion of activity, embarked on a series of touring shows; in spite of his ill health. One of his greatest achievements was in co-coordinating an exhibition of the work of the established names in the world of art, with the support of the Arts Council, in his own number five Porthmeor Studios in 1946. The works exhibited were by, Thomas Gainsborough, Anthony Van Dyck, JMW Turner, John Everett Millais, Henry Raeburn, Richard Wilson, Joshua Reynolds, Walter Sickert, Wilson Steer, Peter Lely, George Stubbs, John Sell Cotman and others of that class.

This same year Smart organised a touring exhibition which took in Sunderland, Gateshead, Darlington and Swindon. With the Sunderland show Smart stayed in the town for a week, acted as guide, and gave an illustrated talk, '100 Years of Cornish Painting'. In the 90 works of art exhibited there must have been several from the newly accommodated young 'Moderns.'

He arranged a touring exhibition to South Africa in 1947, coinciding with the Royal Tour of the King and Queen and the hope that they would visit Cape Town when the 150 paintings from the St Ives Society of Artists were on exhibition at the Maskew Millar Gallery. The proprietors had extended invitations to a few British artists to visit and paint the scenery. They included Dame Laura Knight, Stanley Spencer and Borlase Smart, who again acted as guide/lecturer during his six months stay. This must have been an exhausting effort for a man in such ill health. The exhibition continued its journey to Johannesburg and various other towns where they possessed 'very fine galleries worthy of such a great colony.'

'In a further talk with Mr Smart, he the [proprietor] *remarked that there was much scope in the future development of exhibitions abroad … and he* [Smart] *hoped on his return to see if it were possible to have a similar exhibition in New York, having in mind the important fact that USA troops were stationed in St Ives during the war.'* [33]

An exhibition in the United States would surely have happened, given Borlase's determined efforts in every field in which he tried to promote St Ives artists and the art colony, but now he was in very precarious health and there was a shortness of time in which preparations would need to be made.

The Crypt Group

Borlase Smart felt very strongly that the St Ives Society, to be truly representative should reflect modern and abstract art as well as the traditional, and to this end he managed to carry through an arrangement for a special corner of the New Gallery to be given over to the modernists.

However, under pressure from increasing tensions in the society, eventually the more progressive artists were given space by Borlase Smart in the Crypt below the Mariner's church to exhibit their work separately. This became known as, The Crypt Group. The space was unused for exhibitions and before any shows could be mounted the crypt had to be cleaned and painted to make it presentable. Two of the founder members were Peter Lanyon and Sven Berlin, returning to normal life from the Services and anxious to re-establish themselves as artists. John Wells, Bryan Wynter, Willie Barns-Graham, Patrick Heron, David Haughton, Kit Barker and Adrian Ryan were also part of this group. They even had their own designer/printer for the catalogue, Guido Morris. They continued exhibiting for three years in their own private space.

The art critic Charles Marriott said he had a notion that even in their abstractions, the later recruits to the colony, such as Ben Nicholson, got nearer to representing the 'peculiar magic of West Cornwall' than did the painters of his day.

The indomitable, peace maker and go-between, Borlase Smart opened their first show, much to the disapproval and anger of many of the members. In response to criticism he said:

'In this exhibition young artists have on view works of exceptional Merit, four have become members of the Society. They have just returned from the services and brought back new ideas which they are endeavouring to carry out in their artistic works.' [34]

He wrote to his friend Willie Barns-Graham, who was at that time away in her country house in Scotland, that his name was 'mud' in certain circles.

The Clash

Weighing in with wrathful criticism was Harry Rountree in the letters page of *The Western Echo* in 1946, which set off an avalanche of replies from both artists and the general public. Rountree declared, 'Surely those who are encouraging our young 'Moderns' are doing a great disservice both to the artists and art… I see nothing original in these alleged modern ideas. I have seen them all – most of them in the work of children aged six to ten years.'

Bryan Wynter replied that Mr Rountree had not visited the exhibition which he so strenuously condemned and hoped he would remedy 'this initial error.'

John Wells remarked that his vulgar attack was, '…evidence of an unfortunate constriction of his field of vision…'

And Sven Berlin wrote that Rountree's letter was an, '… uncultured and bigoted attack on the integrity of the artists themselves.'

Even that traditional craftsman potter Bernard Leach was provoked to remark, 'St Ives ought to be glad to have fresh young blood in its art-world.'

In answering his critics Borlase Smart said, *'the intolerance to any kind of individuality is one of the unpleasant features of post-war clashes between the old and the new order.'* He further stated, *'I have been accused of running with the horse and hunting with the hounds. That is precisely my outlook, as I definitely intend to like the best in both traditional and advance art.'* [35]

Smart announced that the correspondence between the artists and Rountree about the first Crypt exhibition was framed and on display in the gallery and had increased visitor numbers. Rountree was very much a commercial illustrator and designer and worked on a series of posters and advertisements. A plaque on Smeaton's Pier confirms that the fishermen approved his caricatures of the locals on display at the Sloop.

The last word in the correspondence was given to Rountree who declared, 'It was a grand fight while it lasted … let's hope there are left behind no personal wounds. As sportsmen we gave it: as sportsmen we can take it.' However, this jovial note denies the vitriolic attack which began this controversy.

Also exhibiting at the Crypt was Hyman Segal, newly arrived with a kit-bag of drawings from his army duty in Africa. Segal said, '*Borlase Smart came in, had a quick look and went out again. I thought, well that's it, but he returned with the press and a photographer. Very few people in St Ives had seen coloured faces in those days so they created quite a sensation.*' [36] Smart also obtained for him John Park's studio number 10 Porthmeor, below the painting school, which Segal occupied until his death in 2004, aged ninety

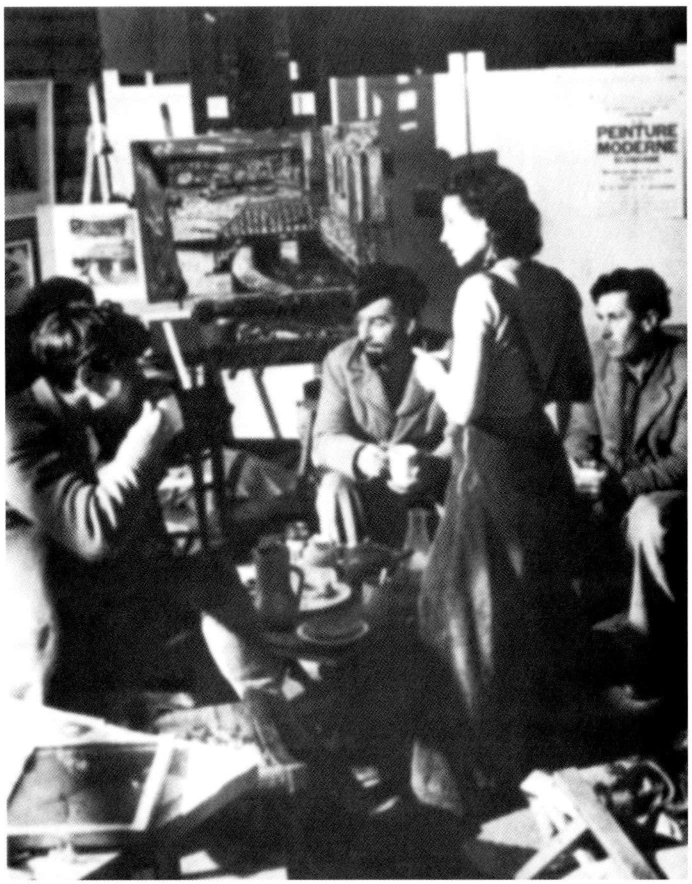

Below left: *Crypt Group 1947. Peter Lanyon, Bryan Wynter (behind), Sven Berlin, Wilhelmina Barns-Graham, John Wells, Guido Morris.*

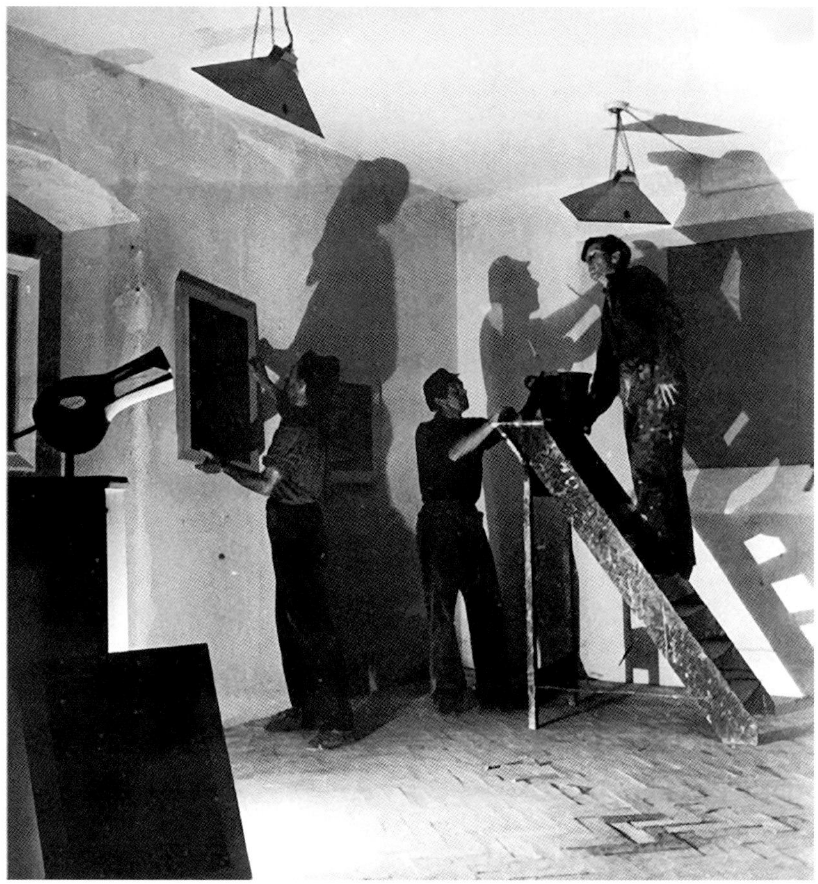

Below right: *Sven Berlin, John Wells, Peter Lanyon.*

Artists had been prevented from painting or drawing from any vantage point by the sea or coast during the war for fear of unwittingly informing the enemy of geographical areas which might prove useful to them if their drawings fell accidentally into the wrong hands. It was goodbye to paintings of the fishing fleet setting out to ply their trade and to pilgrimages to Land's End and St Michael's Mount, and other interesting areas. Landscape painting within five miles of a military site or objective was prohibited. Any breach of these restrictions could have meant imprisonment. One year after the war the artists were anxious to be freed from these constraints. At the opening of the Spring exhibition at the St Ives Society, Smart addressed the audience, saying, *'We have had the utmost difficulty in getting artists' materials, some are unobtainable. If we tackle the Leader of the Opposition to raise the point with the House or the Ministry of Supply, we might get something done, so I would ask the members and visitors to sign the petition and I will send it to Mr Churchill.'* [37]

President and Secretary

Early in 1947, Borlase Smart achieved the status of both President and Secretary of the Society, succeeding the artist Dod Procter's term of office as President. He was largely responsible for organising an exhibition at the National Museum of Wales in Cardiff in October. It can be said that Smart realised his dream-come-true with well over a hundred selected items displayed, featuring both the traditionalists and the modernists side by side. It was the direction in which Smart was steering the St Ives Society of Artists.

However, the two parties, modern and representational did not sit comfortably together and Denis Mitchell managed to persuade his brother Endell, landlord of the Castle Inn in Fore Street, to allow his friends, the moderns, to exhibit their work. They were also exhibiting in George Downing's bookshop in Fore Street but a desire to establish their own premises was growing.

Tragically, Borlase Smart died in November 1947 and his ambitions for the Society to become all-embracing of every faction of art were not fully realised. Disagreements within the group led to the fragmentation of the Society and a long running dispute between the old and the new was shortly to be resolved by a major split.

In 1948 it was learned that Sir Alfred Munnings, famed painter of race horses and the hunt and at one time living in Lamorna, and friend of Laura Knight, accepted the role of President of the St Ives Society of Artists – the very antithesis to Borlase Smart's ideology. Munnings was knighted in 1944 and elected President of the Royal Academy in the same year. This new appointment in St Ives would have pleased the traditional painters, who probably applauded the notorious retiring speech he addressed to the Royal Academy banquet in 1949 condemning the 'modernists' such as Picasso, Matisse and 'foreign' artists in general, working in a progressive style, as corrupters of art. This BBC radio broadcast was heard throughout the country and it was feared that words from such an authoritative voice would be taken as truth and acted upon to the detriment of the young 'Moderns' in St Ives who were striving for recognition of their status and value in the art world.

Death of Borlase Smart

Captain Robert Borlase Smart died of a heart attack on the 3 November 1947. It was whilst he was helping with the opening of the Society exhibition at Fowey in October that he was taken ill. Many friends and members of the societies to which Borlase was associated were at St Ives Parish Church to commemorate his life. He had been a regular member of the church and had carried out his duties as a sidesman. Leonard Fuller in paying tribute said, '*As a life-long friend, may I be allowed to pay my tribute to his wonderful spirit and goodness. He will never be forgotten. His tremendous energy, his absolute integrity in artistic matters have won for him a place that can never adequately be filled.*' [38]

It seems that Borlase Smart had previously shown a deterioration in his health. Sylvia Sirrett remembers her mother's connection with the Smarts. "*The Smarts lived in the Cabin and during a great storm they were washed out. Borlase Smart had had a heart attack some time previously. He was brought over to our house in a blanket. Mother went and tackled the after effects of the water and he gave mother a painting in appreciation of her help.*" [39]

Usually, Mrs Smart would close the wooden shutters of the Cabin at night, but one balmy night she left them open, only to wake to find several windows had been smashed by the force of the sea at high tide, which flooded the building and unfortunately, washed through and saturated the interior.

It is probable that Borlase Smart could have lived a few more years with the condition of angina, if he had slowed down and taken more care of his health, but he was as ambitious as ever in his plans to promote the artists and secure their welfare, ignoring his own well-being. His first daughter-in-law, Martha, remarked that his energy, rather than focusing inwards upon his own development, always flowed vigorously outwards towards life.

Leonard Fuller recognised his friend's self-sacrifice, for which he paid the price in an untimely death. Irene Smart provided a bench to be placed in Norway Square, adjacent to the St Ives Society of Artists Gallery, in memory of her husband. Her friend the painter, Eileen Cross, was responsible for transforming the bleak space into a garden, with seedlings provided by Irene and other contributors of plants. Another bench recognizes 'Eileen Cross 1900-1991 who reclaimed this square and inspired Downalong in bloom.' The Council gardeners finally took over its upkeep. The garden was now a valuable green space for the townfolk to enjoy, and hopefully will remain so in the years to come.

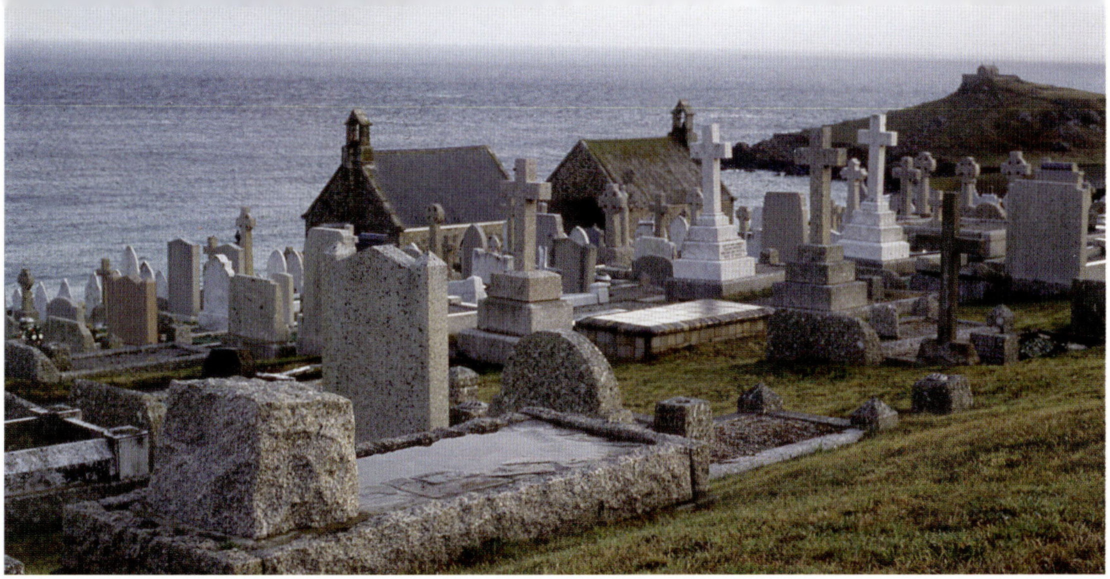

The rough hewn stone is the grave of Borlase Smart in Barnoon Cemetery. Nearby is the tiled grave designed by Bernard Leach for fisherman and painter, Alfred Wallis.

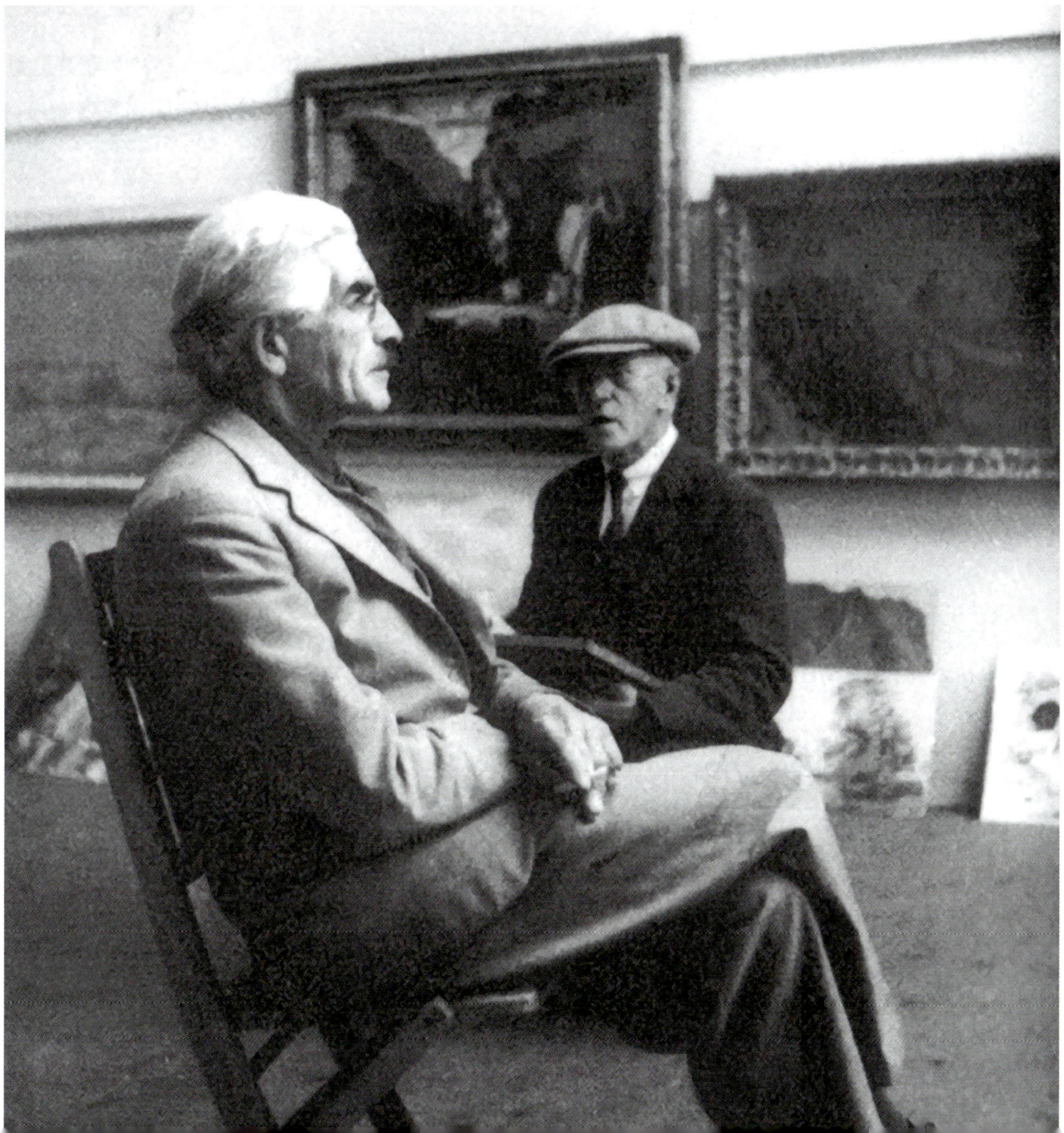

Borlase sketching photographer Gilbert Adams.

The final portrait of Borlase was painted in the year of his death by Allan Gairdner Wyon, sculptor. He was ordained Deacon in 1933 and served as Vicar of St Peter's Church, Newlyn until 1955. He produced 40 sculptures and memorials for Cornish churches, including Truro Cathedral.

Last portrait of Borlase Smart, by W. G. Wyon, 1947.

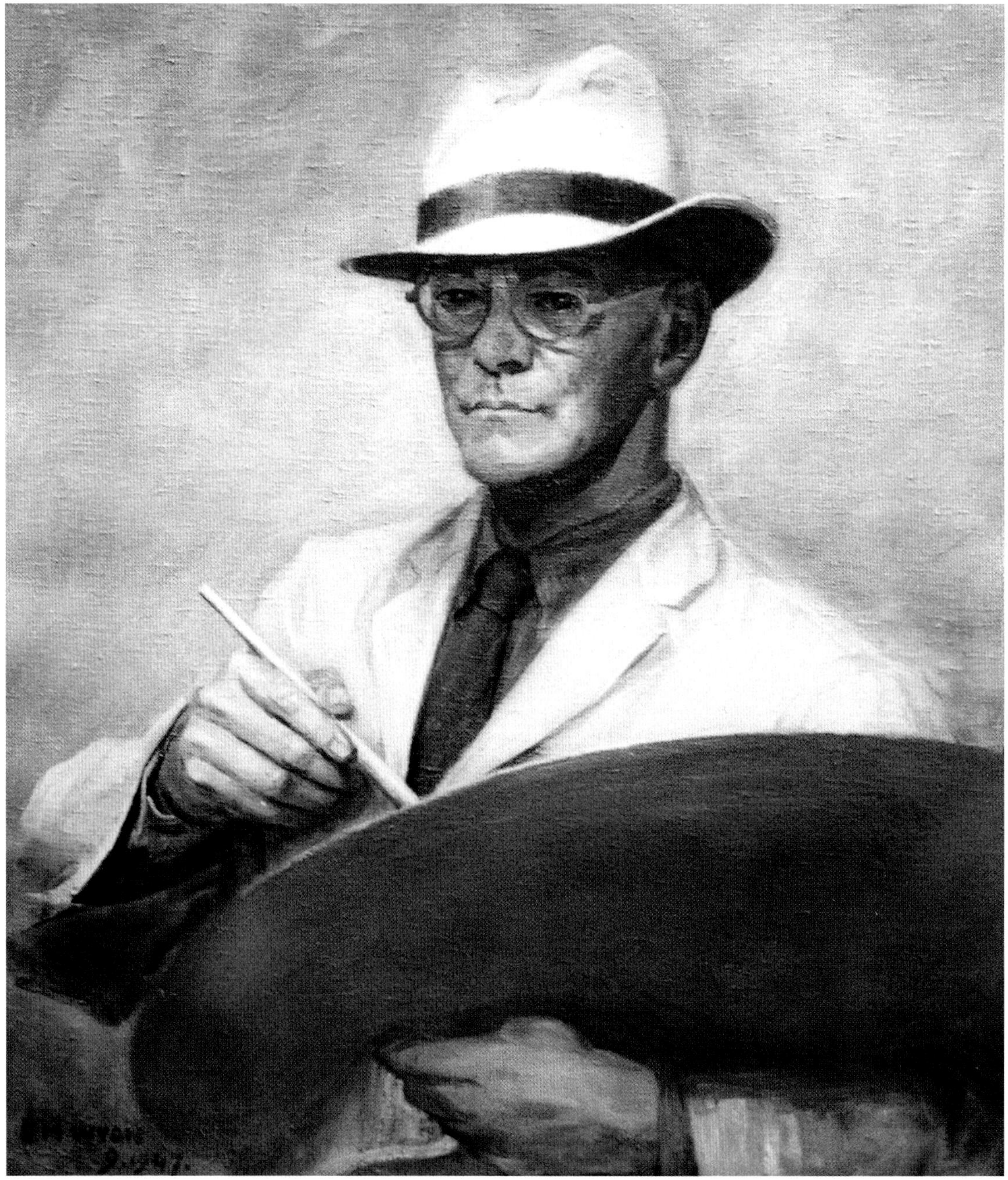

The Penwith Society of Arts in Cornwall

Not even Borlase Smart could have intervened, with his tact, diplomacy and understanding, in the huge row that developed among the membership of the St Ives Society of Artists when a breakaway group of nineteen formed The Penwith Society of Arts in Cornwall, in 1949. To smooth its new forward thinking it was decided to dedicate the founding as a tribute to Borlase Smart. This would seem like a tug of love between the two societies, except that the newly elected Chairman for the modernist society was Borlase Smart's loyal friend, Leonard Fuller. The President was Herbert Read, distinguished art critic. The Committee were Barbara Hepworth, Peter Lanyon, Bernard Leach, Denis Mitchell, Ben Nicholson and Misome Peile. There was no counter argument from the traditionalists; that Borlase Smart was held in high esteem by both parties is obvious.

The Public Hall, in Fore Street was the Penwith Society's first showroom. It was suitable for social functions, as well as exhibitions, with its modern gas heating system, its fire and club room atmosphere.

The first exhibition in 1949 was an eclectic mix of styles and techniques. One hundred items included paintings, embroidery, pottery, sculpture and furniture were shown. Lanyon's painting was described as 'curvilinear' and Nicholson's as 'geometric.' Among the wide range of works exhibited were Bryan Wynter, Alfred Wallis, Bernard Leach, Borlase Smart, Dod Procter and Leonard Fuller.

Patrick Heron wrote, '*The strange partnership on these walls, not only of abstract with representational and non-figurative with impressionist and even ante impressionist paintings and sculpture, is not without its advantages. It cannot fail to stimulate critical activity in the spectators.*' [40]

Unfortunately, this welcoming of all-comers was not to last and it became a society devoted only to more abstract works of art in spite of the Society's claim that it was 'entirely opposed to exclusiveness and antagonism'.

In his honour, and to show their respect and commitment to his progressive ideas and his name, the newly found society held an exhibition of Borlase Smart's work at their new premises in the Public Hall. On show were 66 paintings, drawings and etchings. Among them were aquatints of the Oxford and Cambridge Colleges, which had been commissioned by the colleges. The etching press given by Mrs Irene Smart had been set up for members' use. There were drawings and paintings of St Ives and West Penwith with Cornish cliffs and various seascapes, Devonshire valleys, the Scottish landscape, Venice and miscellaneous subjects. The foreword to the catalogue was written by Leonard Fuller. In 1950 Smart's Memorial Exhibition was shown at the City Art Gallery, Plymouth.

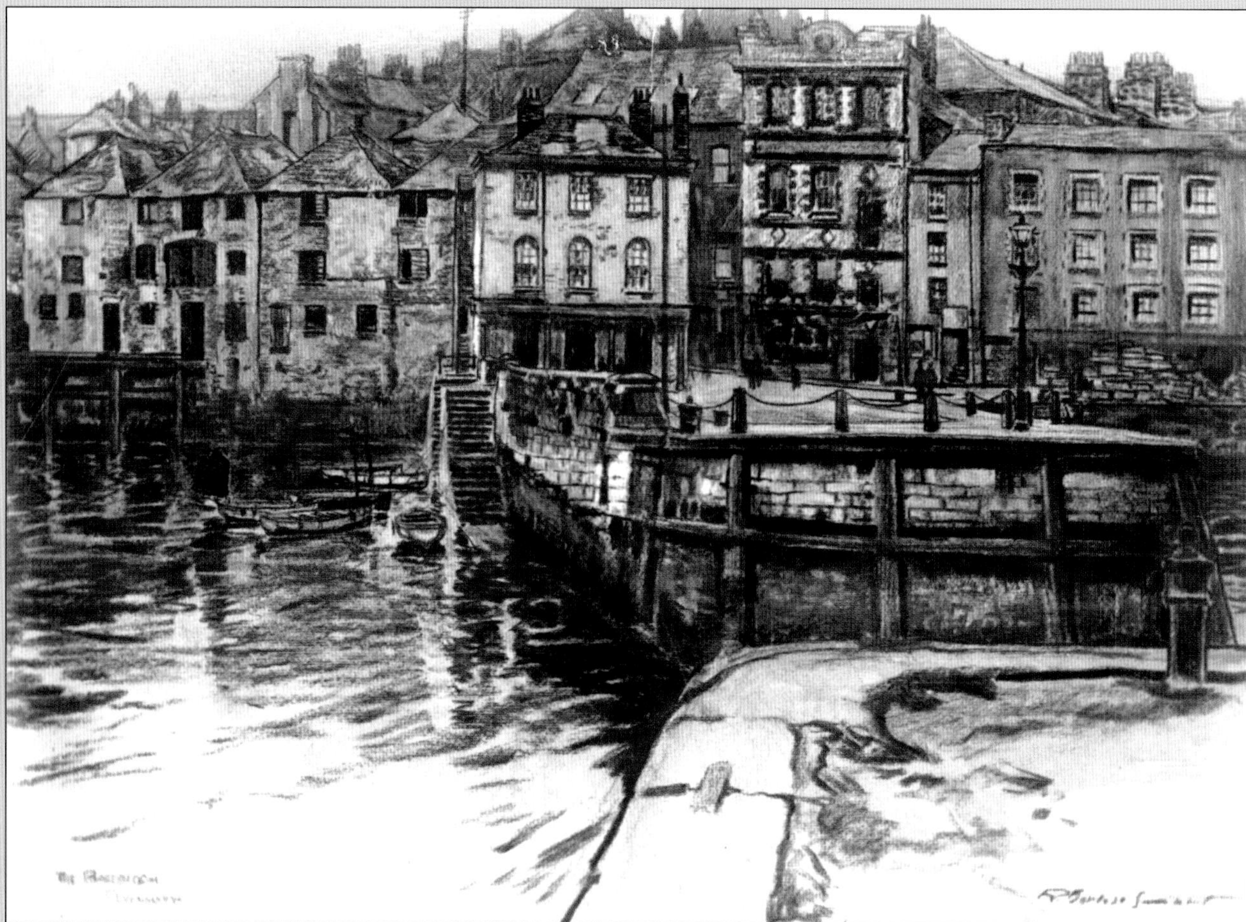

The Barbican, Plymouth.

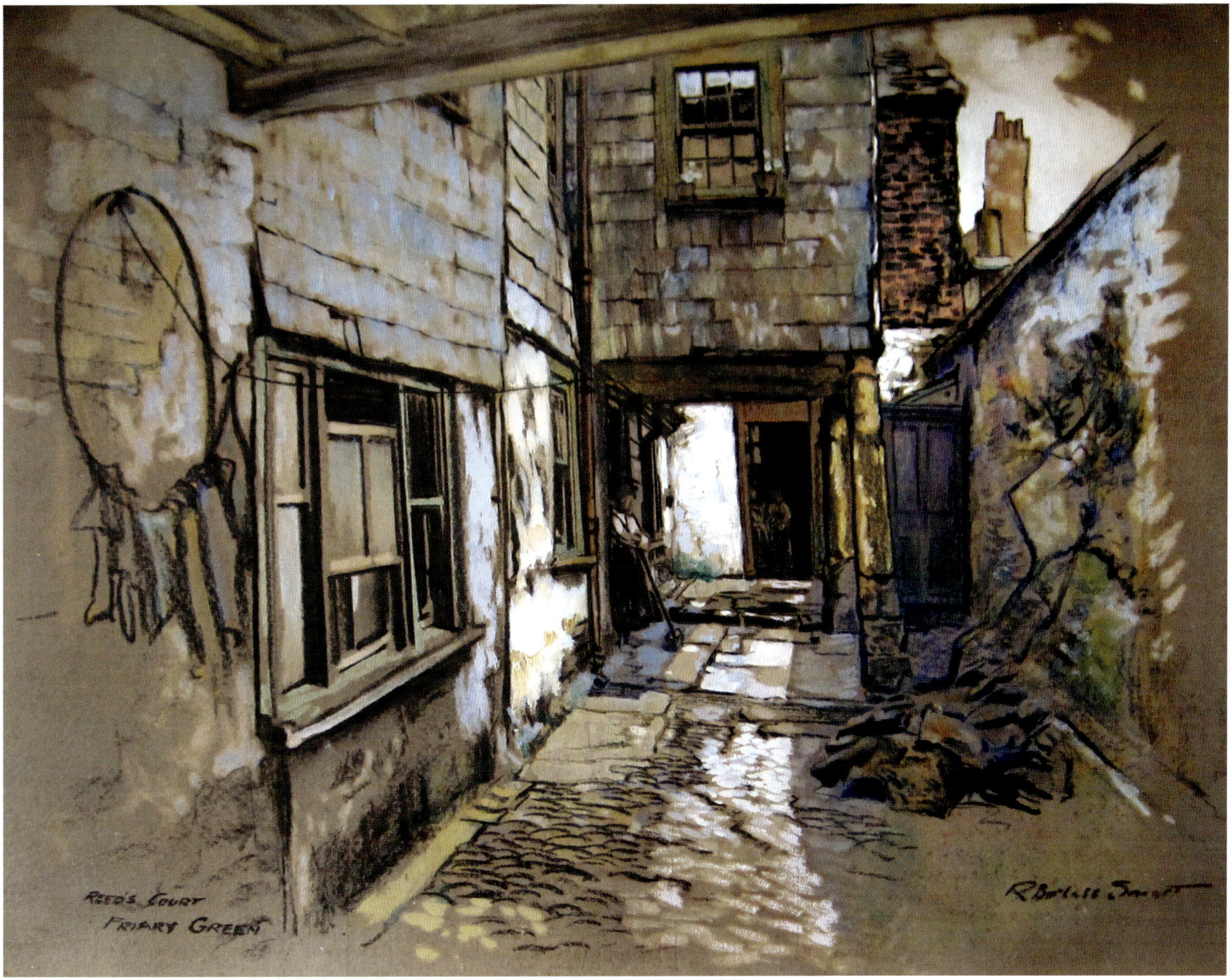

Reeds Court, Friary Green, Plymouth.

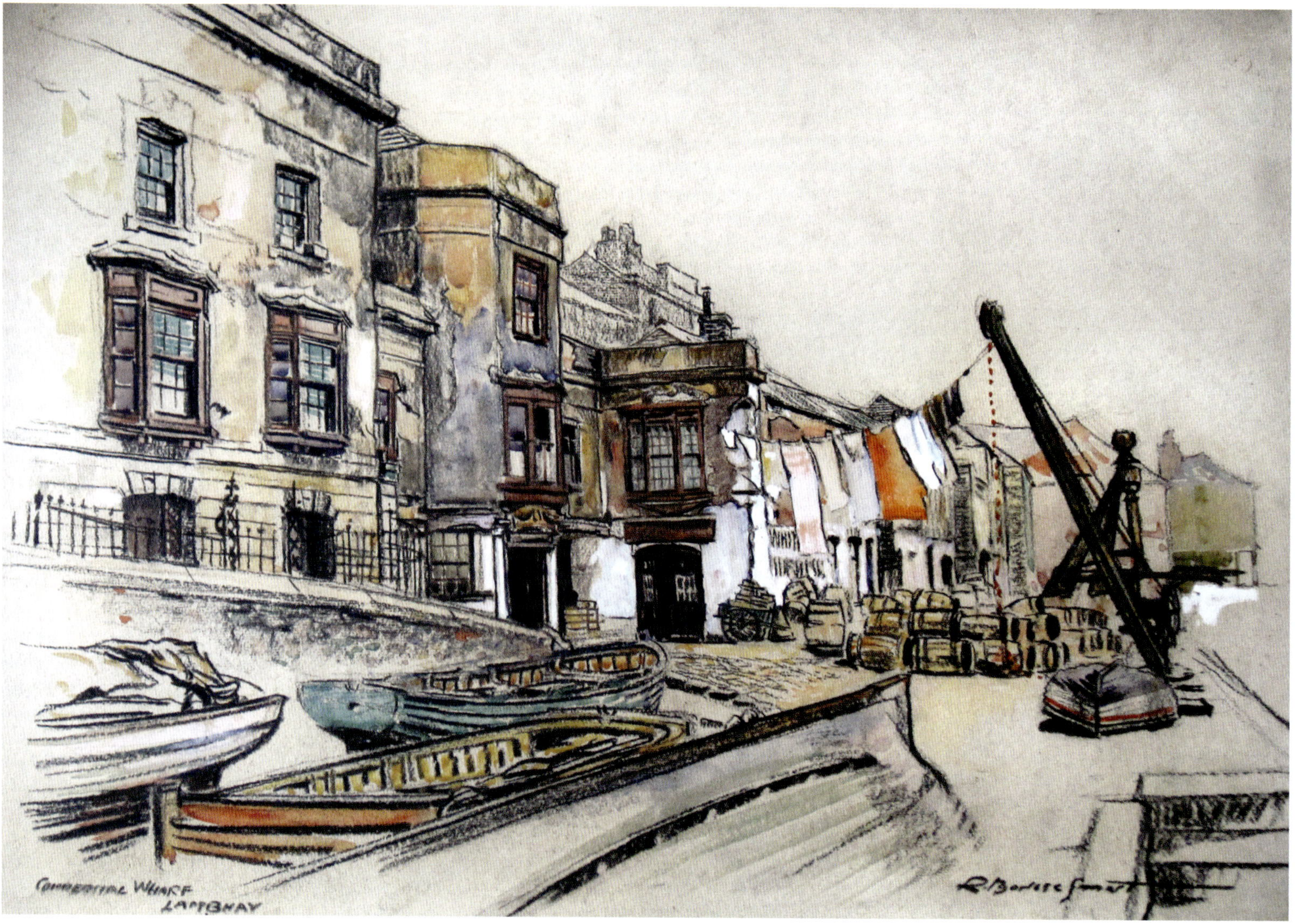

Commercial Wharf, Lambhay, Plymouth.

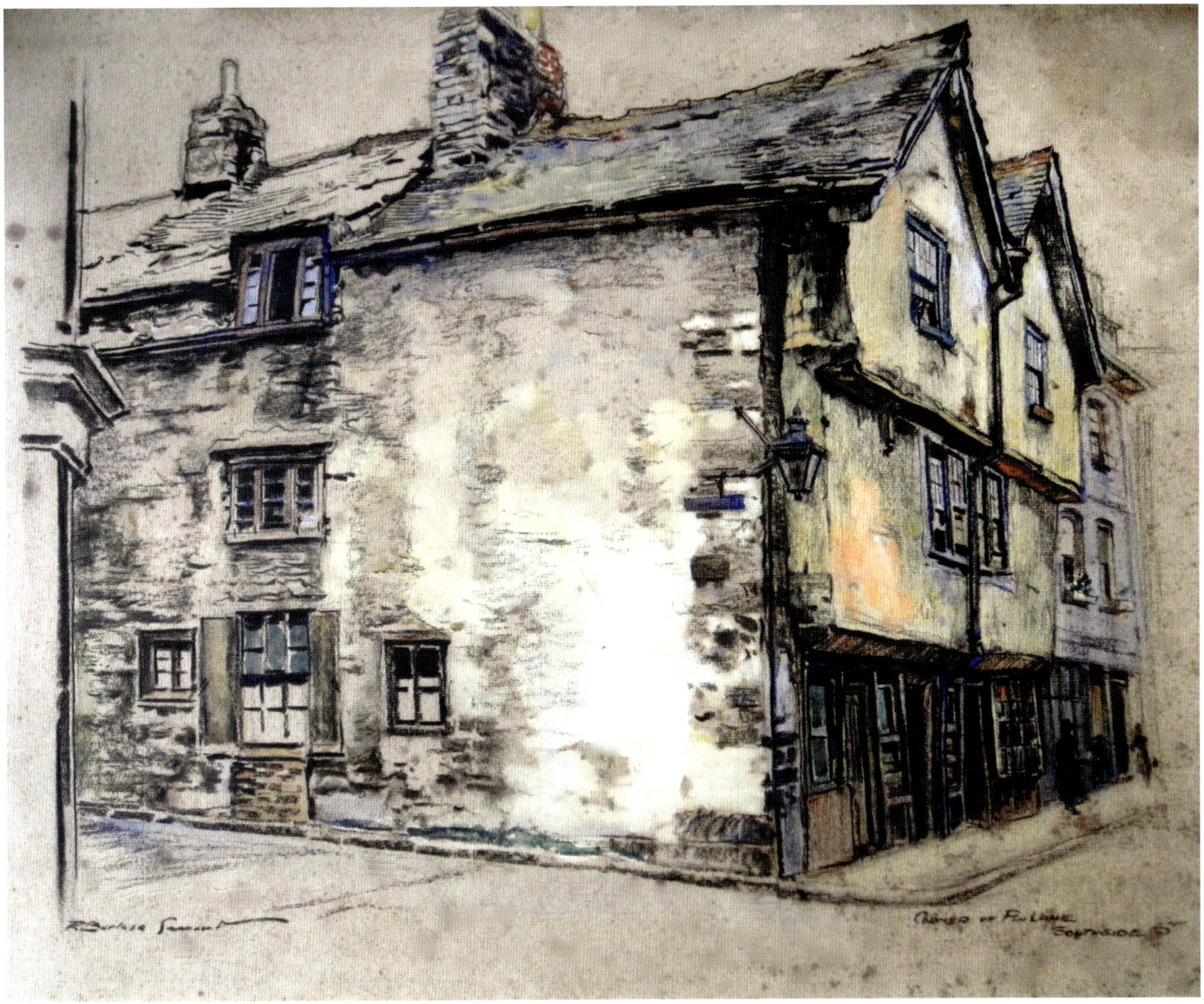

Corner of Pin Lane, Plymouth.

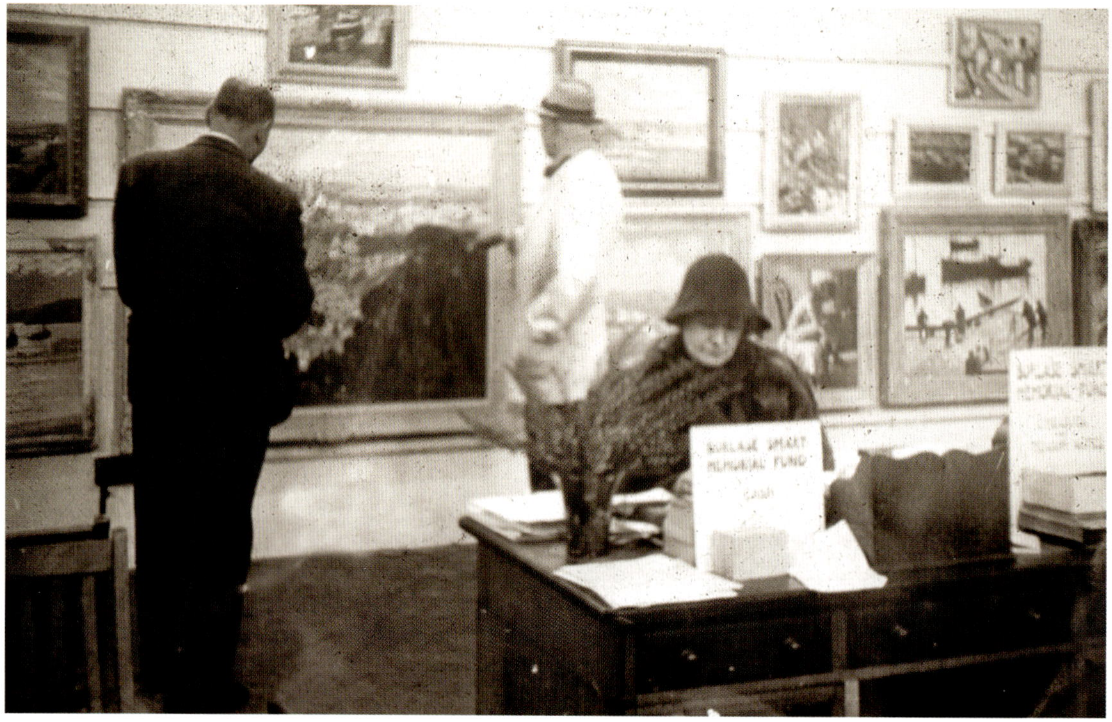

St Ives Society, Mariners Gallery.

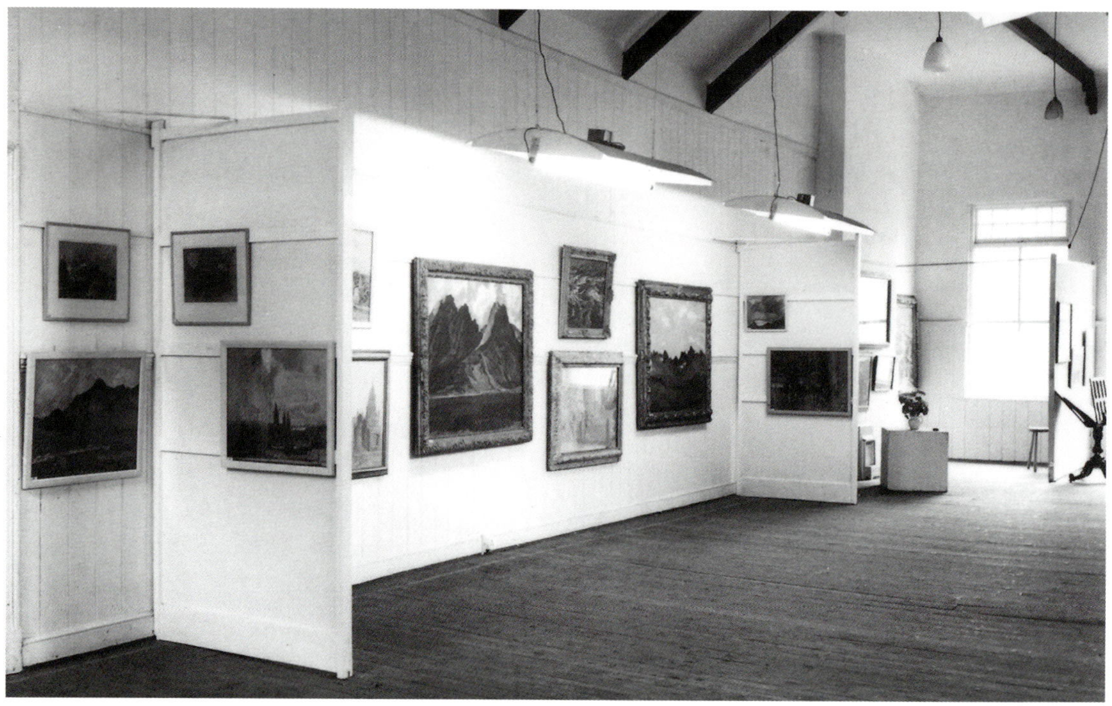

Public Hall, Fore Street, showing Borlase Smart's Work 1949.

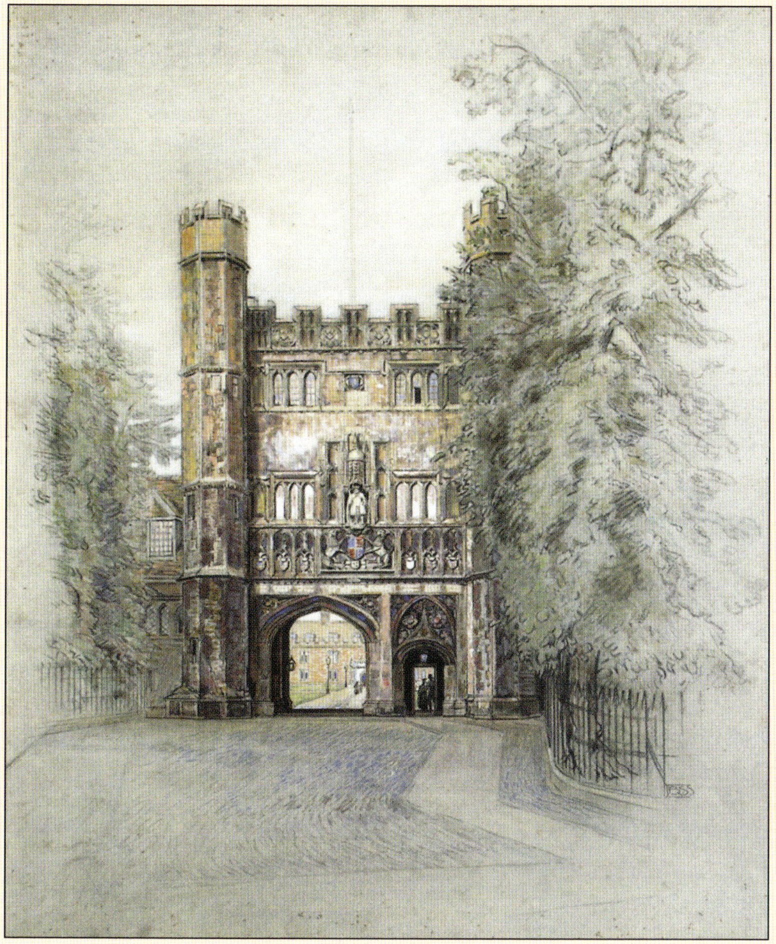

Trinity College, Cambridge.

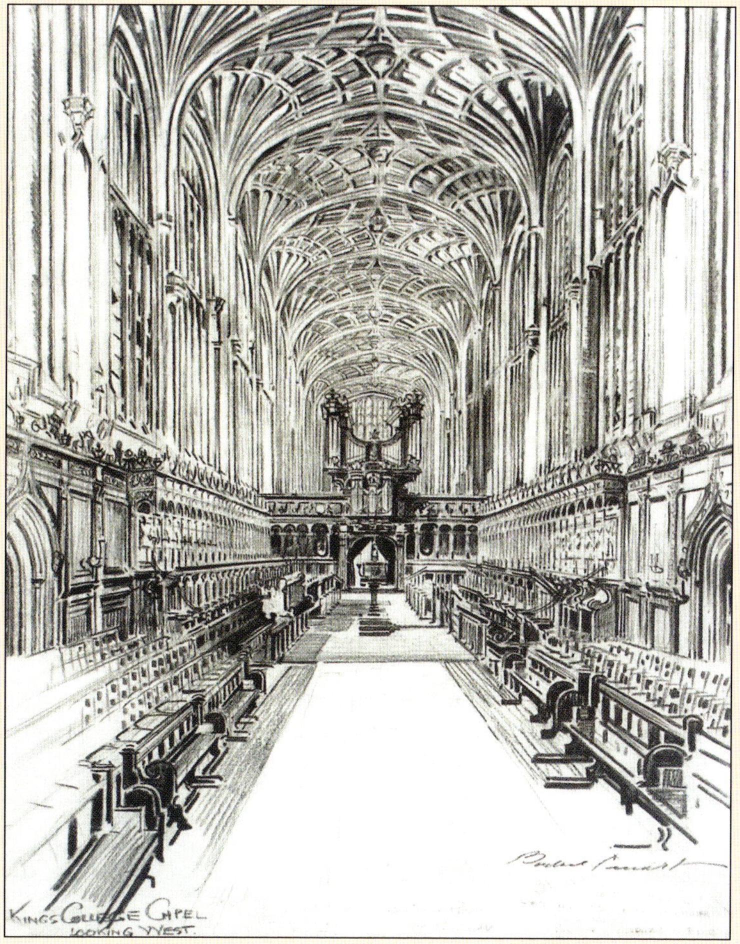

King's College chapel.

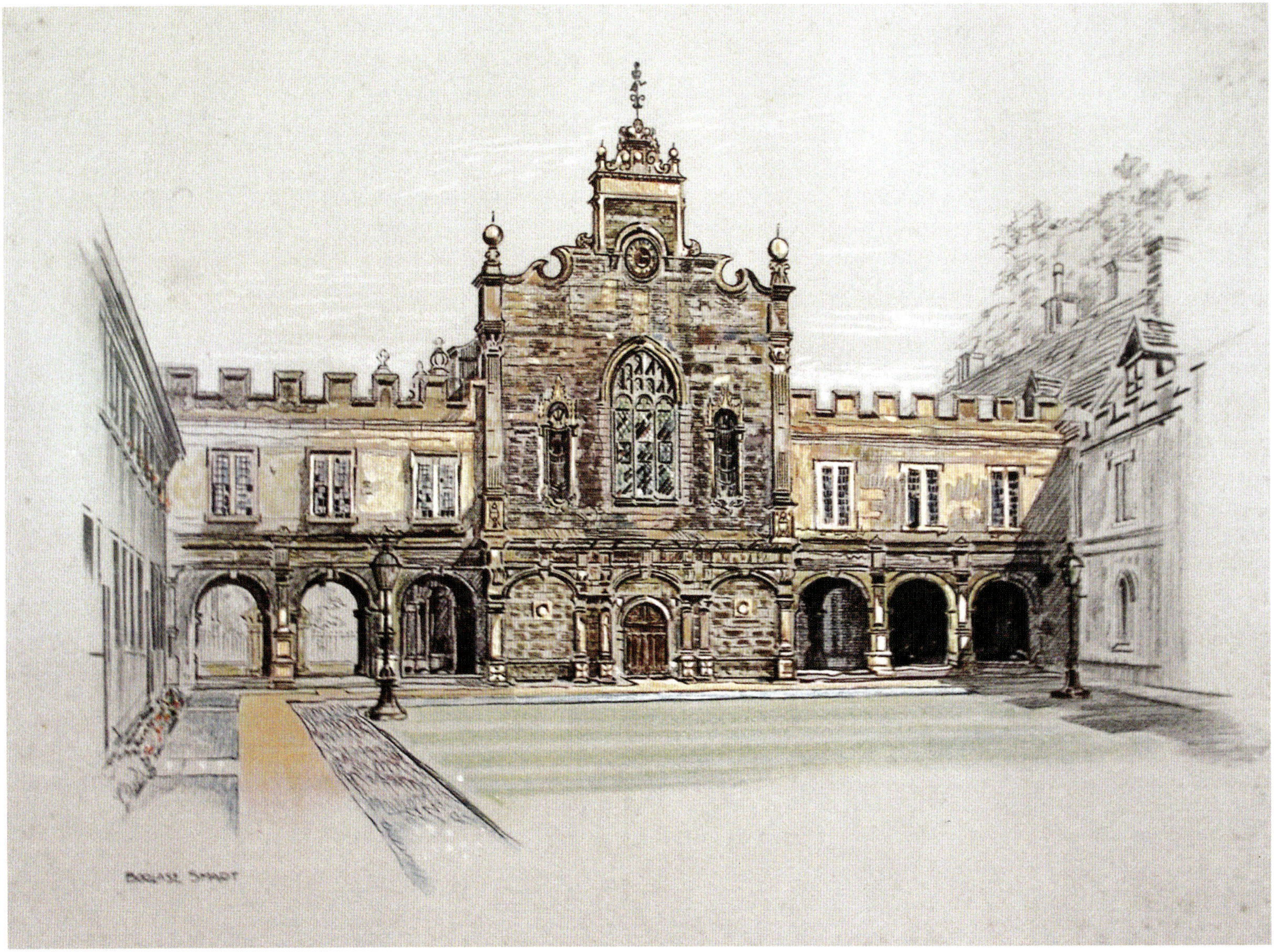

Peterhouse, Cambridge.

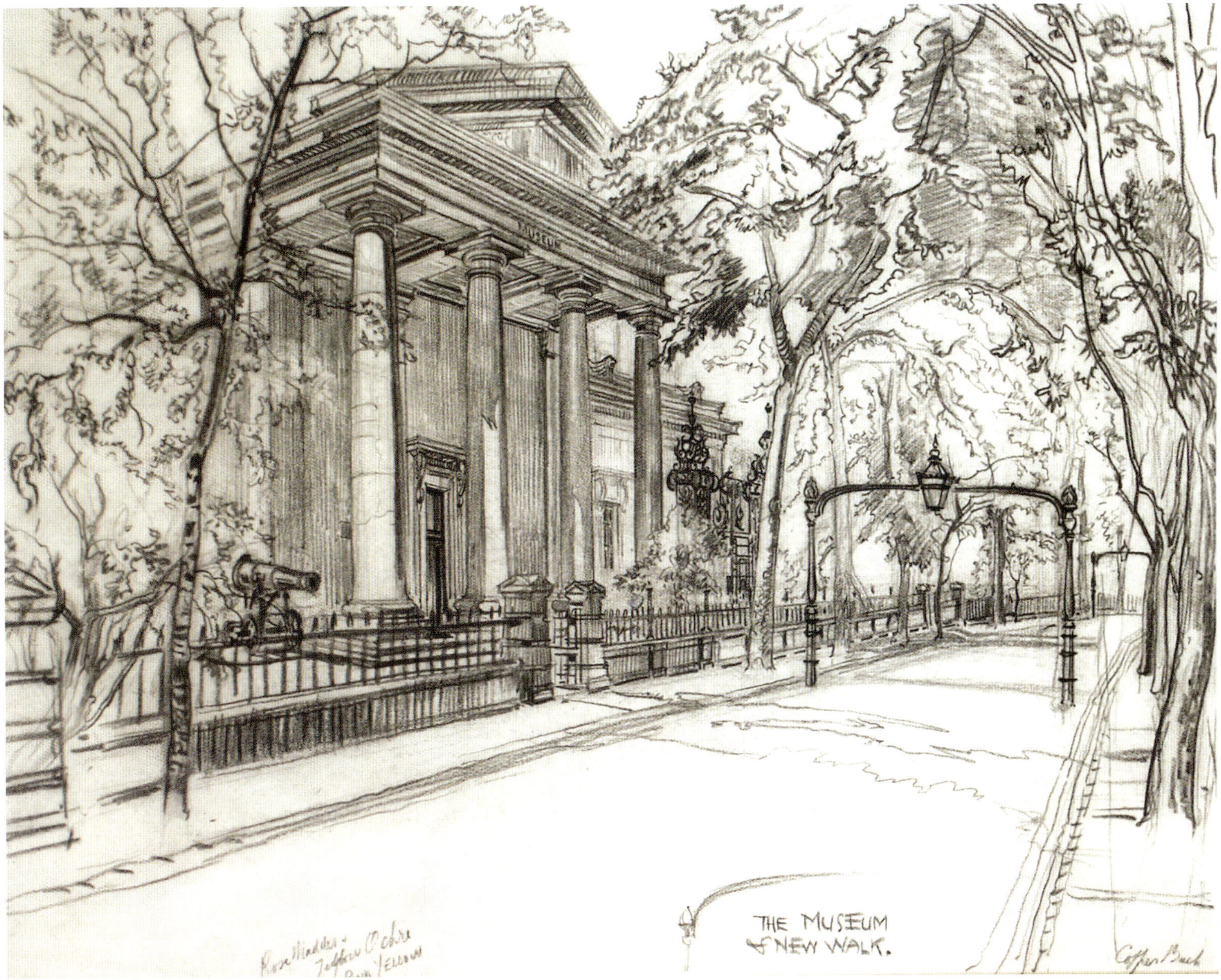

Museum and New Walk, Leicester.

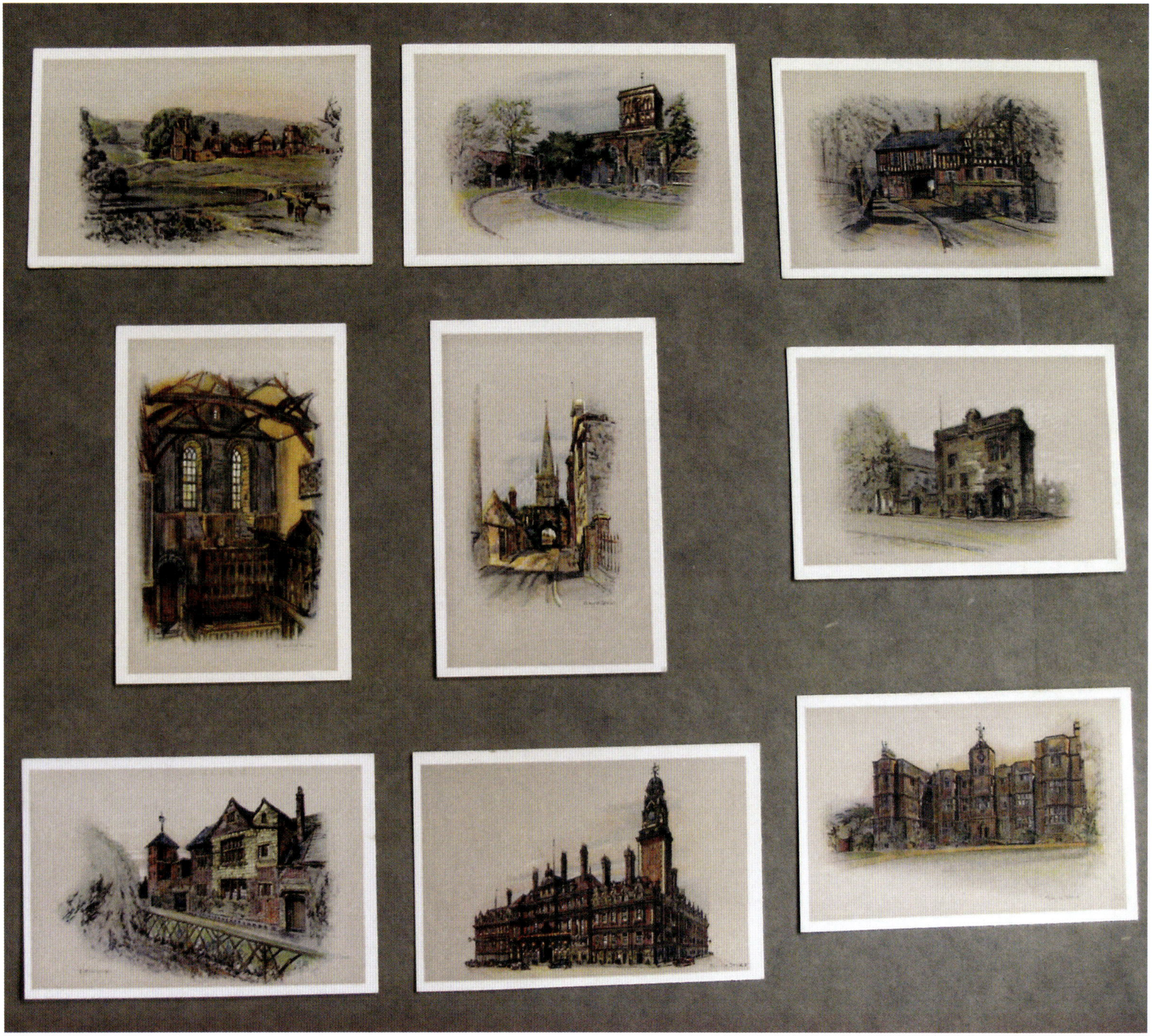

Sketches of Oxford and Cambridge Colleges in Borlase's album.

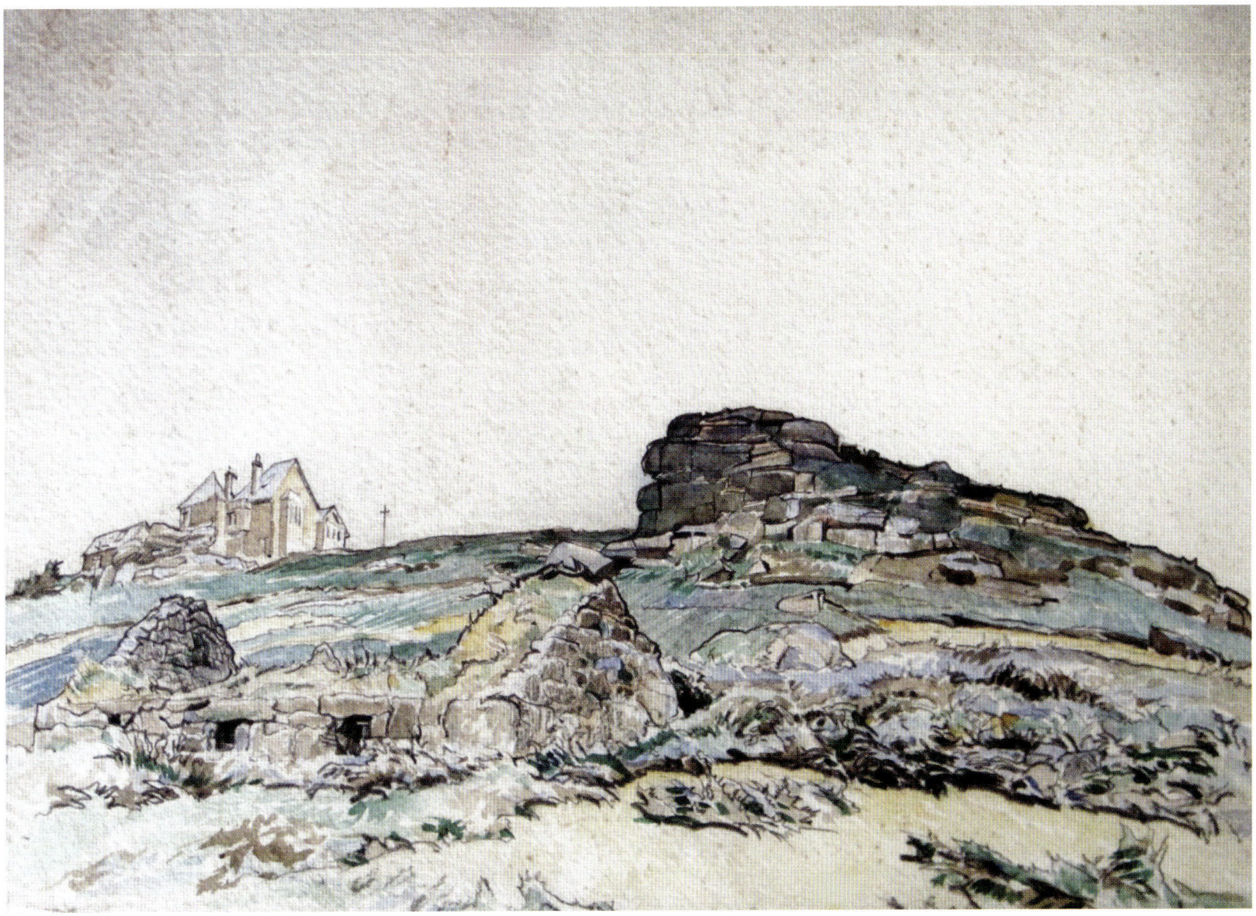

Eagle's Nest, Zennor.

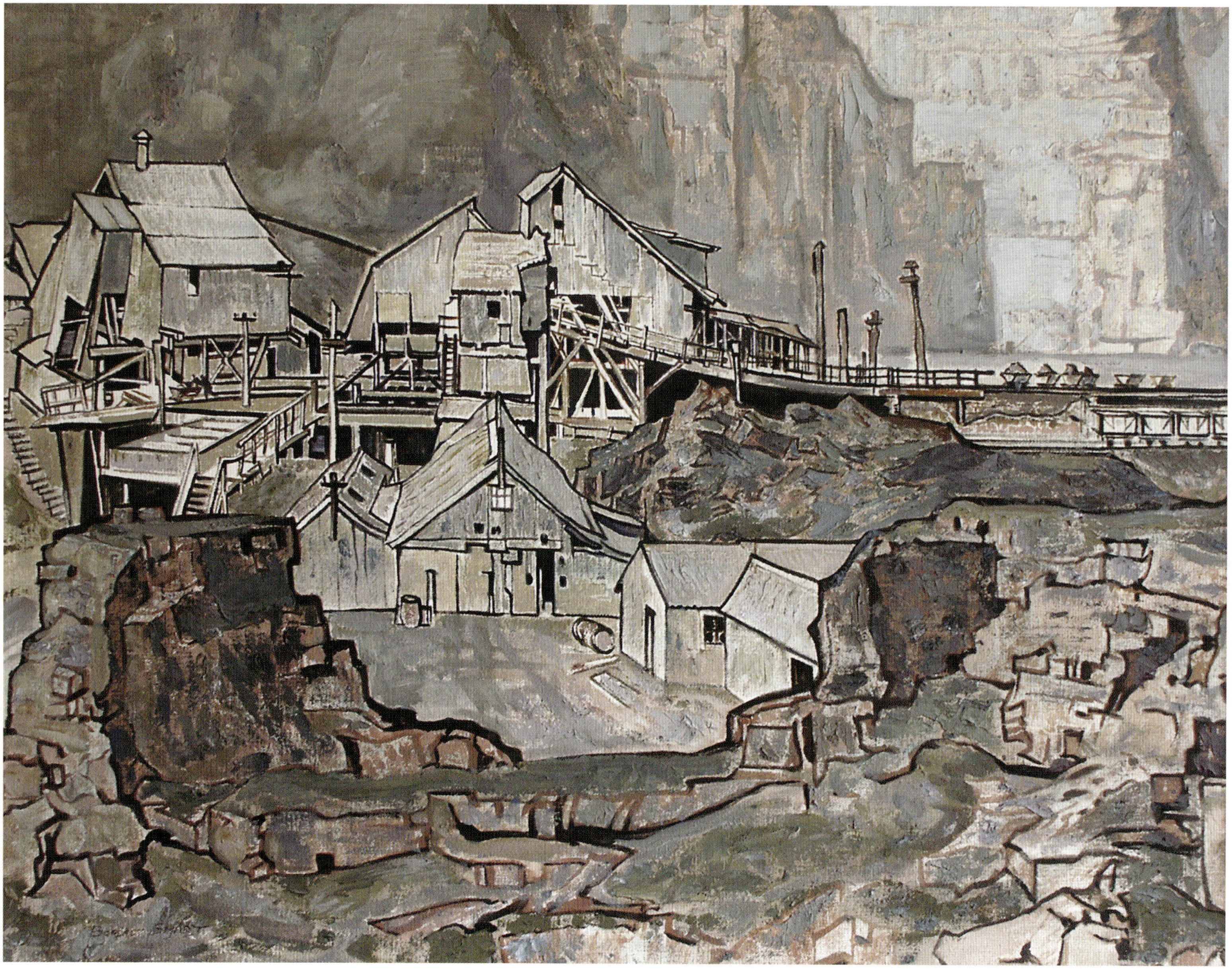

St Austell Claypits.

The wrangling which took place between the two societies (both claimed him as their own) and indeed within the societies themselves, took many years to resolve. Borlase Smart's name was mentioned as one who would support the various warring factions but Mrs Smart knew that her husband would not have sided with either party and reprimanded them, *'Having split the Society on this question of principle, it is amazing to have Mr Ninnes now use my husband's name as he did at the Annual General Meeting on March 31st*. [saying the new Society represented the ideals of Borlase Smart] *Borlase Smart stood for kindliness and tolerance and would never have associated with a policy based on vindictiveness and intrigue as displayed at the Extraordinary General Meeting.'* [41]

There were those who were dissatisfied with the rules of the newly formed group and resigned, Peter Lanyon among them. He was brought up in St Ives with traditional artists and shared their respect for such art. He refused to accept that 'modern art is apart from traditional art,' and such forms 'can live together.'

Acquisition of Porthmeor Studios

Moffat Lindner, nearing the end of his active life as a painter, chairman and president of societies, desired to relinquish his ownership and responsibility for the Porthmeor studios complex, of which there were thirteen, occupied by St Ives artists. These also included the St Ives School of Painting. Lindner stipulated that the sale would only take place on the understanding that the buyers would safeguard the studios as affordable work places for artists. It had long been Smart's wish to procure these studios as permanent buildings for the use of the artists, fearing the art colony's decline on an already greatly reduced number of studios available in the town.

The St Ives Society of Artists launched the Borlase Smart Memorial Trust Fund and gave an assurance that Lindner's legacy to the artists would be honoured and Borlase Smart's dream become a reality. Over the years Lindner had drawn modest rents and even given free access to those artists who could not afford a studio, such as New Zealand painter, Frances Hodgkins, during the First World War.

The sum of £6,000 was the sale price. The Arts Council offered an interest free loan of £4,500 and the sum of £2,036 was raised by the new Trust Fund. This would have cheered the heart of Borlase Smart who had occupied many of the studios and where the first exhibitions of the St Ives Society of Artists were held. At the time of his death he was renting number five. It had previously been held by Julius Olsson. After Borlase Smart, David Cox occupied it for a year when he became secretary of the Society and involved in setting up and fund raising for the newly formed Borlase Smart Trust. Number five then passed to Ben Nicholson who was one of the first to apply to the Trust for a studio. Nicholson worked there until 1958, when it was taken over by Patrick Heron who occupied it until his death in 1999.

The Penwith Gallery

The Penwith Society of Arts in Cornwall eventually established itself in the Penwith Gallery in Back Road West. An article in the *St Ives Times & Echo* dated January 1961, reported, '*St Ives status as a world art centre has been recognised by the Calouste Gulbenkian Foundation… The Penwith Society, founded in 1949 as a nursery of the Avant-garde in painting and sculpture, has produced more artists of standing and more impact on the art world than any other society in the country…*' [42]

The premises were former fish cellars and fish packing areas with granite columns, which would be preserved. The building was large with upper and lower storeys. The lower contained two spacious rooms with facilities for paintings; the floor area was ideal for the display of sculpture and pottery, with other smaller rooms for display and storage, and a courtyard for sculpture.

The area was formerly known as Maid Betsy's Yard where a great number of men and women were employed in salting and packing pilchards for export to Italy and the continent. But this major industry was now defunct and St Ives would have slipped into a depression but for the influx of artists, who lived and worked in the town.

Leonard Fuller, Principal of the St Ives School of Painting, member of the Society of Artists and the Penwith Society said, '*Without it* [the Penwith Gallery] *there would be no place at which the more advanced elements in St Ives could show their work.*' [43]

Eight months after the conversion of the cellars to a modern art gallery, designed by Henry C. Gilbert (Gillie) the Penwith Society mounted their first members' show of 174 exhibits of paintings, pottery and sculpture.

Barbara Hepworth, who had been instrumental in gaining the Gulbenkian grant, declared the new gallery was wonderful news for the Society and for the town. The number of modern artists who had arrived in St Ives ensured an adequate membership and the Penwith Gallery and Society began to flourish, eventually becoming the more dominant in its development of new ideas. Indeed, many of its members were to take their place in the world of modern art, overshadowing French art, which had for many years been centre stage and was now in decline, and challenging the dominance of the New York Abstract Expressionists. St Ives took its place in the prominence of art colonies which occur from time to time when artists of like minds come to the fore and spearhead their way forward to new developments in the field of the arts.

To back the objective of a permanent collection of the work of the 'Moderns', artists donated paintings, pottery and sculpture, which fulfilled Borlase Smart's prediction that artists would freely give their work. They believed in the idea that their art would attract attention from art lovers and visitors to St Ives to see creations that had emanated from Cornwall to influence the flow of modernists ideas and make an impact globally. The collection was housed in a large gallery adjacent to the Penwith Gallery which was acquired by the Penwith Society in 1976.

An American View of Art at St Ives, noted in the *St Ives Times and Echo* states,

'By far the largest colony outside London, competing with London as one of the centres of art in Europe, is the tiny community of St Ives, a picturesque fishing village which juts out at Land's End on the Western Coast of Cornwall. One finds there a community of painters that is almost too typical of an artists' colony to be believable.' [44]

After its first successful fanfare, by 1980 at a special meeting, the members of the Penwith Society were told of a decision by the Arts Council to withdraw its funding for housing the permanent collection. The Society faced bankruptcy. In this moment of crisis a hasty decision was taken by the committee to dispose of the permanent collection in order to ensure the Society's survival. It freed up hanging space for the current members, with possibilities of extra sales, which would keep the roof over their heads. Borlase would have been turning over in his grave in Barnoon cemetery at such a decision; before a rescue plan could be formulated and put into action.

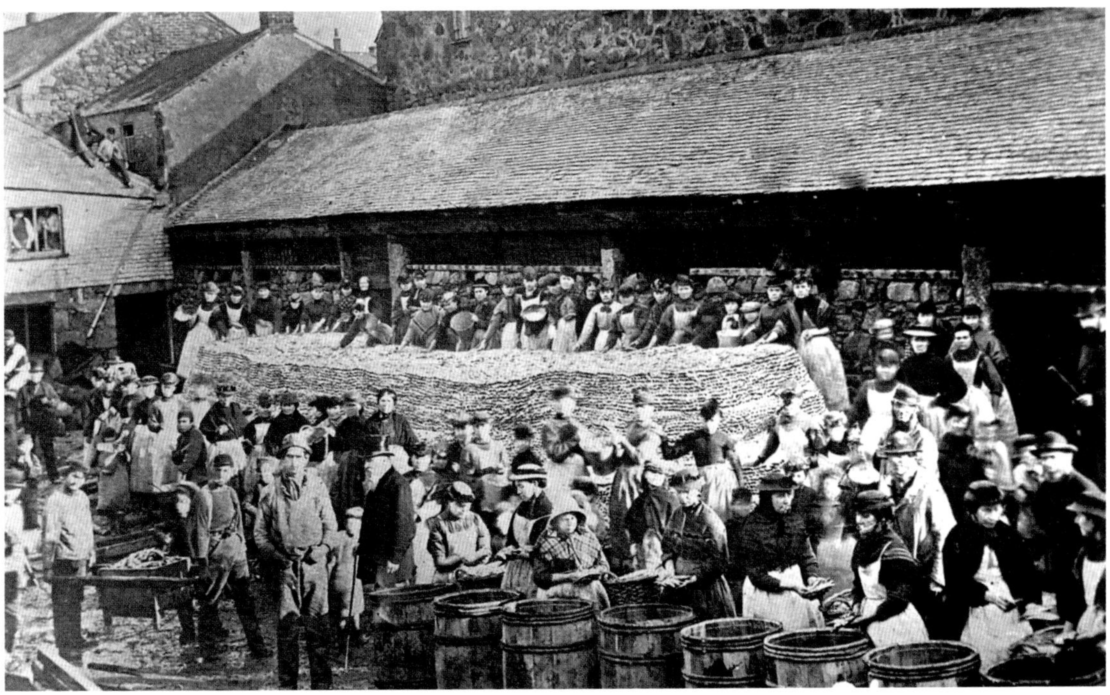

Maid Betsy's Yard, 1871.

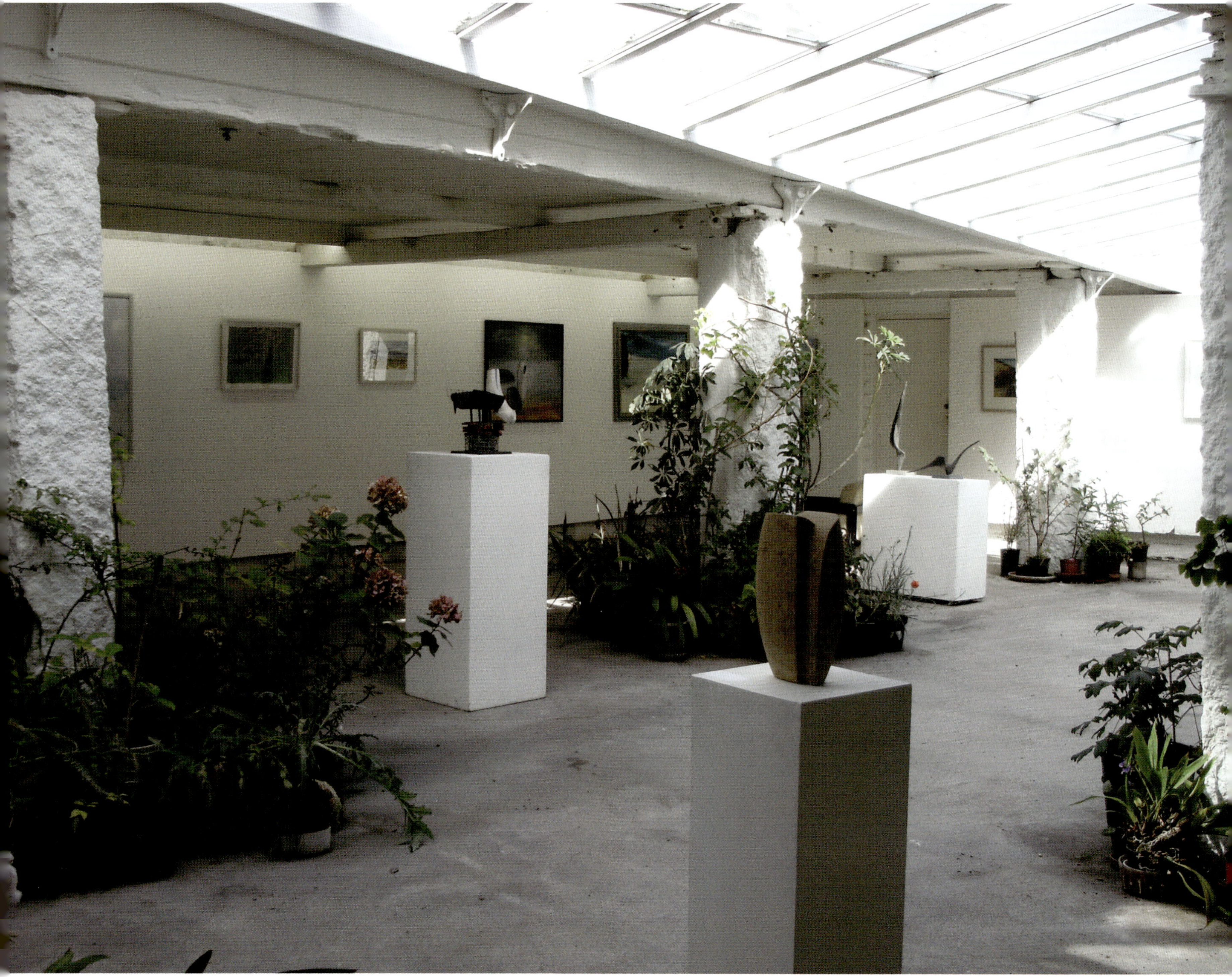

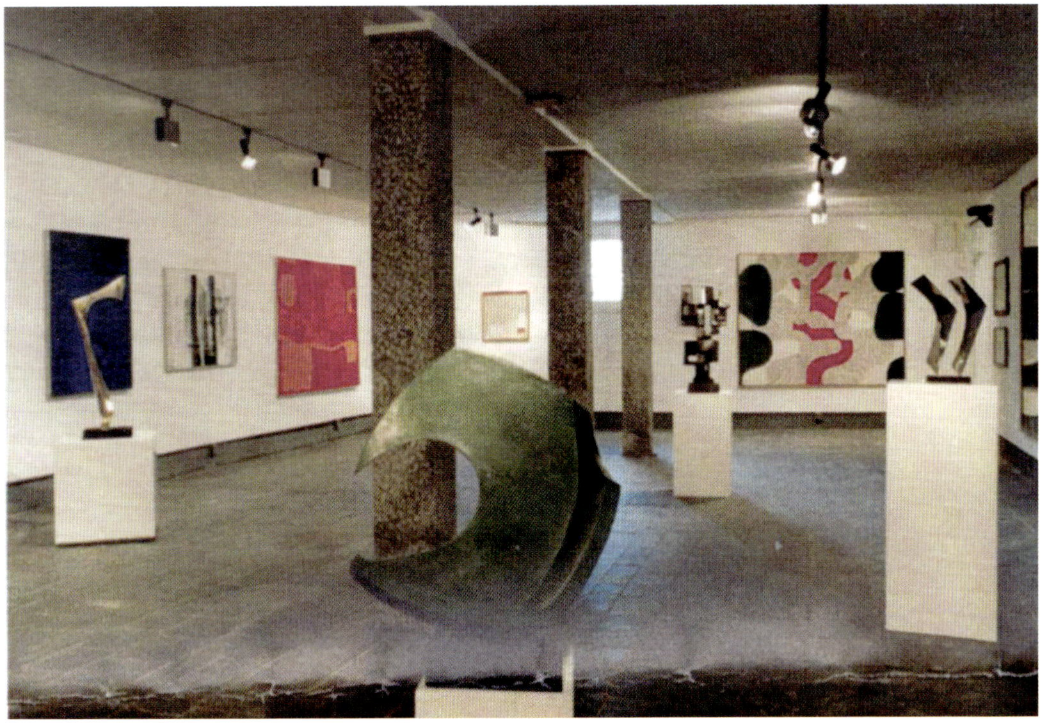

Penwith permanent collection is disbanded in the 1980s.

Opposite: *The Penwith Gallery.*

Retrospective Exhibition

To fulfil the prediction that Borlase Smart would never be forgotten, the Penwith Gallery mounted a retrospective exhibition in the St Ives September Festival of 1981 entitled 'The Man and his Work'. Accompanying the show was a booklet written by Martha Smart, his daughter-in-law, first wife of younger son, Brian. It was sponsored by the then young auctioneer, David Lay.

Martha wrote, *'In his art as in his life, Borlase was poised between tradition and modernity.'* She describes his painting *Atlantic Reefs '...painted with a restricted use of colour, showing his prevailing interest in structure, the ability to abstract, and a preoccupation with form that overrides the incidental romance of the subject matter ... and looks towards Cubism.'* [45]

Atlantic Reefs and Sea Cliff, the paintings seen overleaf, show this treatment of the subject.

In answer to a letter from Brian Smart in the *St Ives Times and Echo*, appealing for the whereabouts of paintings, drawings and etchings, many paintings were discovered, owned by townsfolk and private collectors and others loaned by art galleries from their collections.

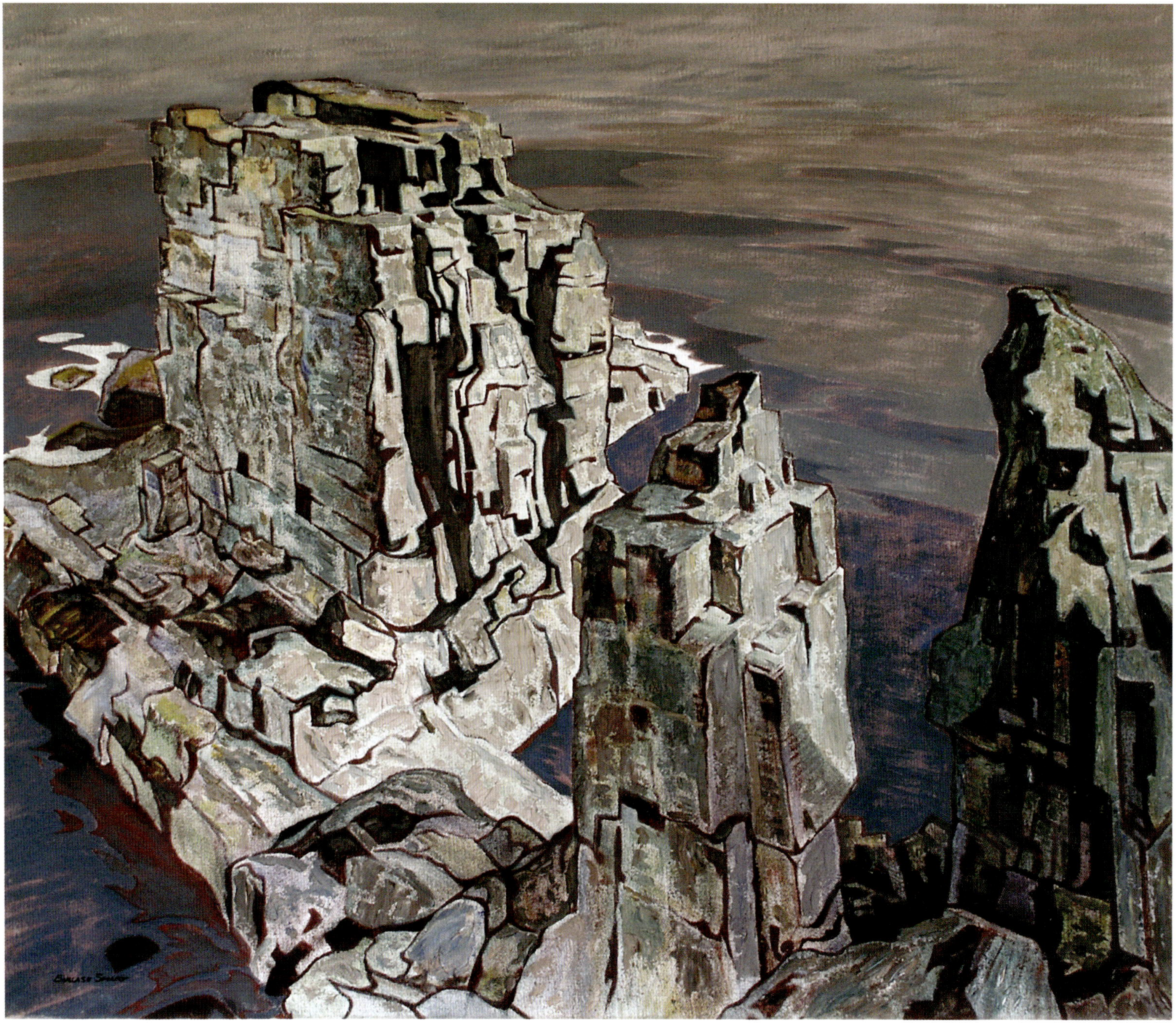

Atlantic Reefs.

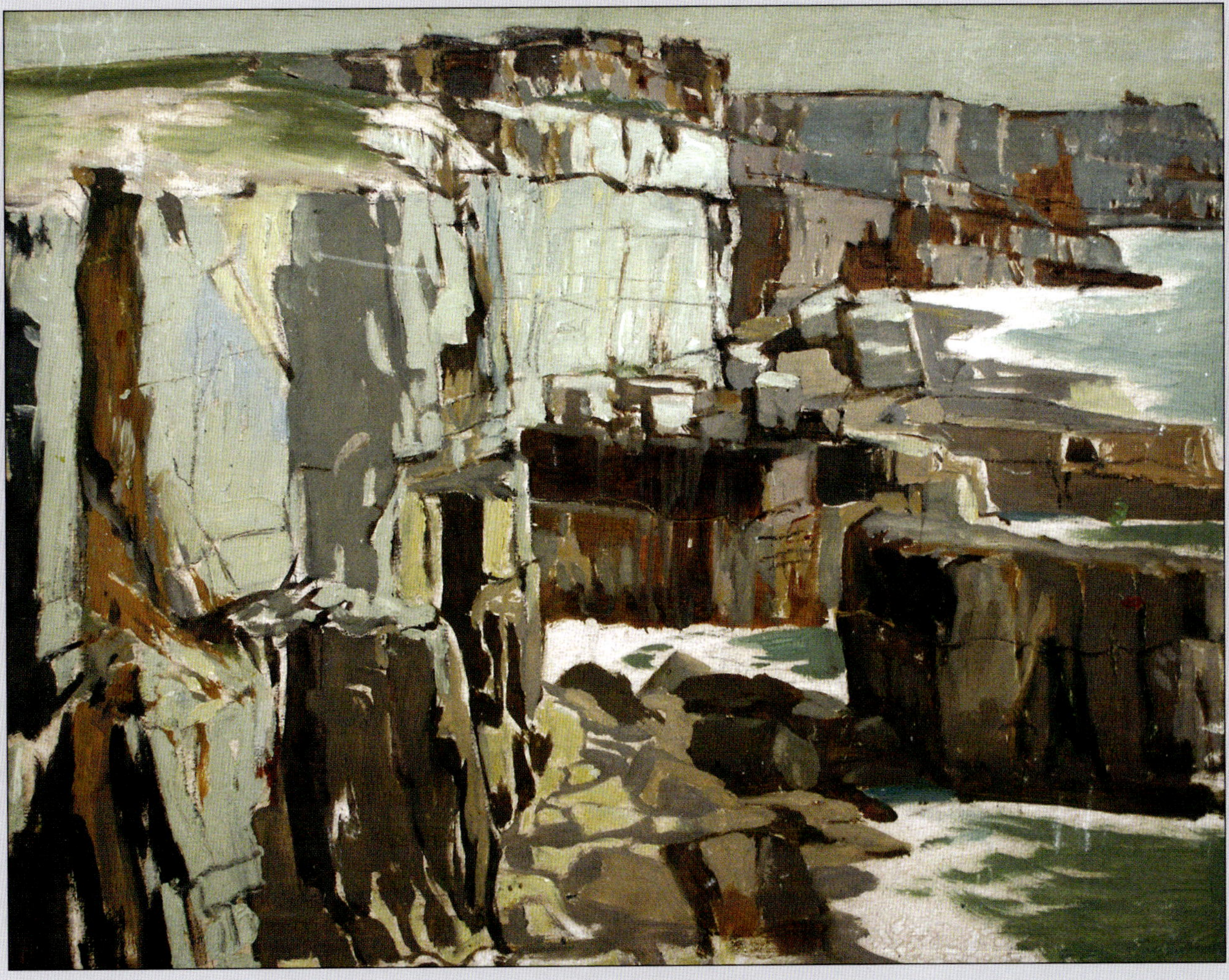

Sea Cliff.

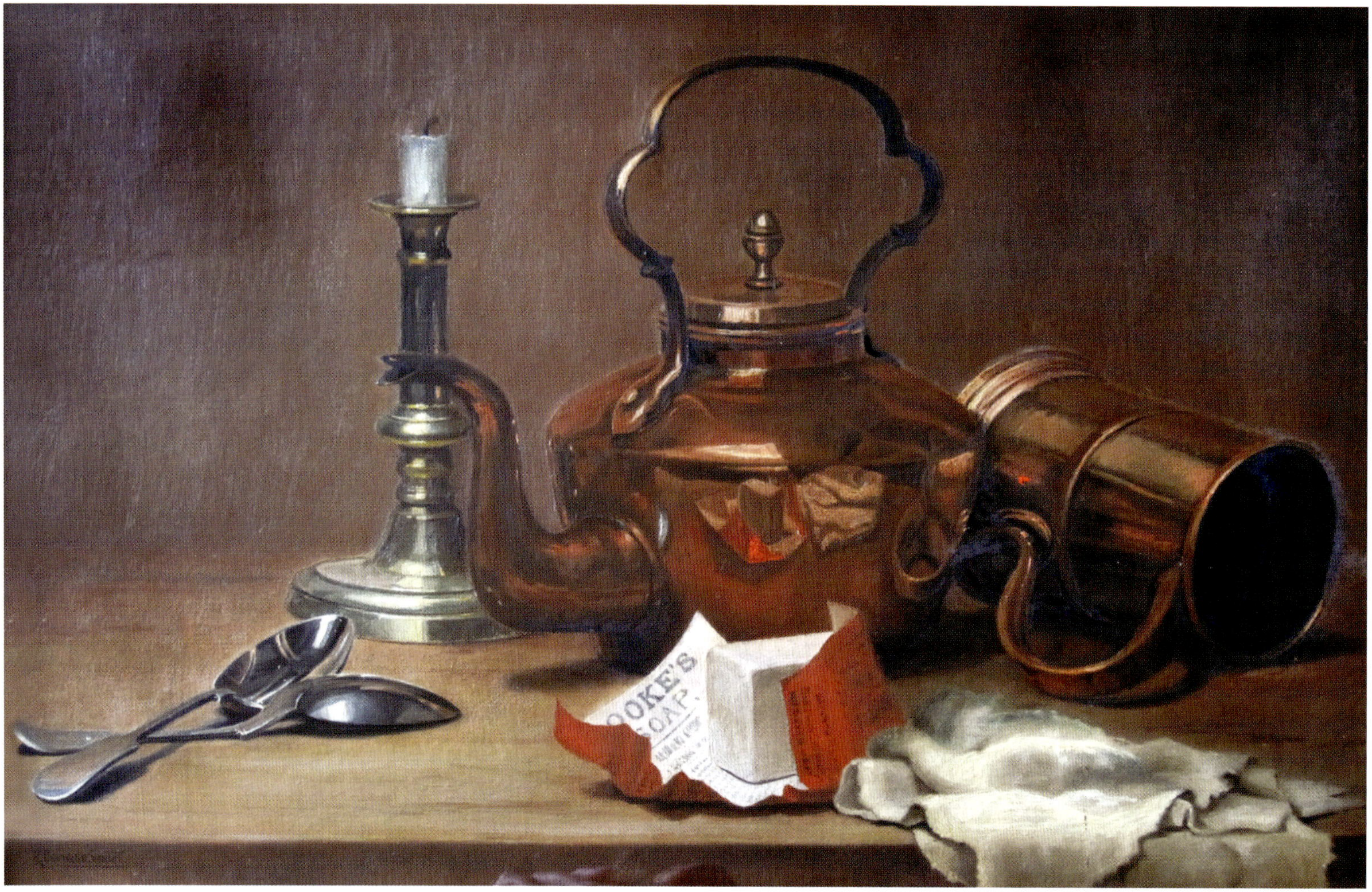

Still Life with Kettle, painted when Borlase was seventeen.

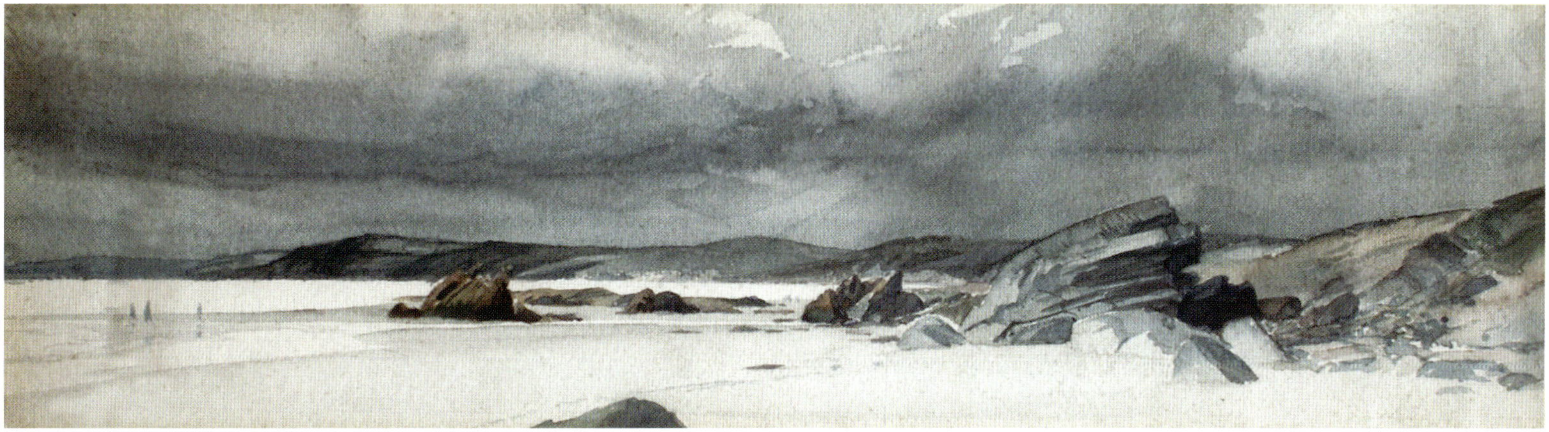

Rocky Shore.

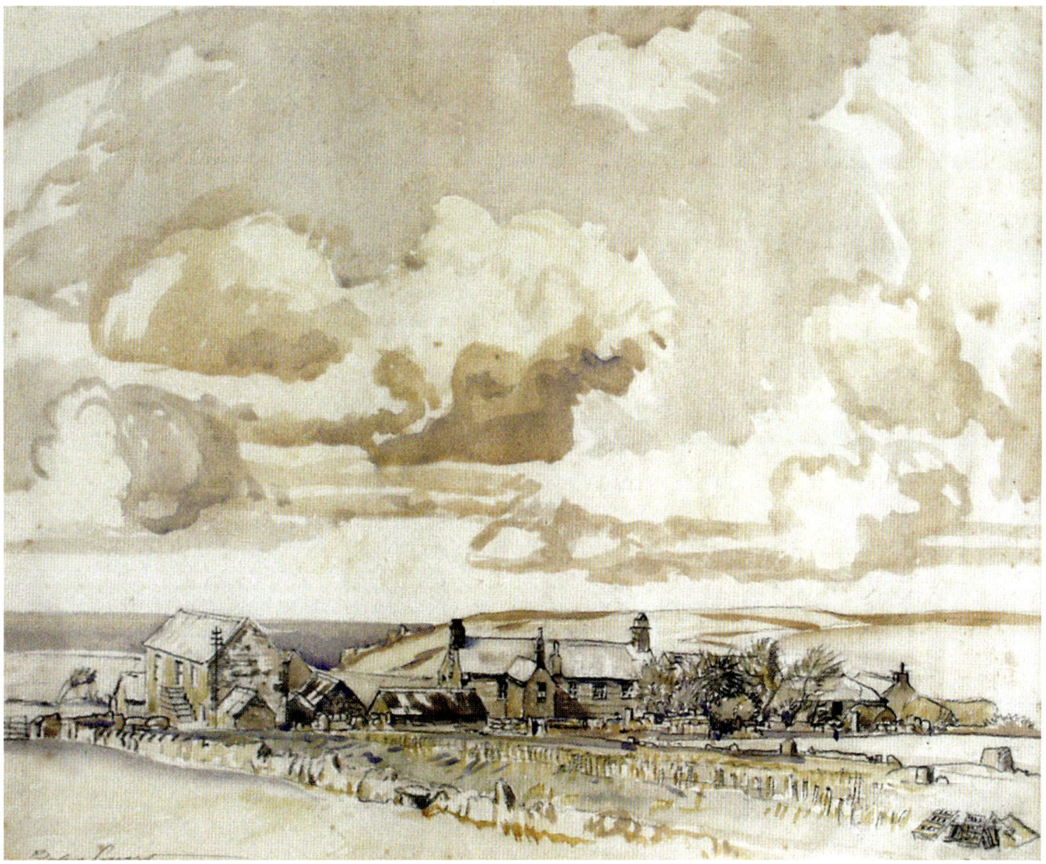

Farm cottages near Zennor.

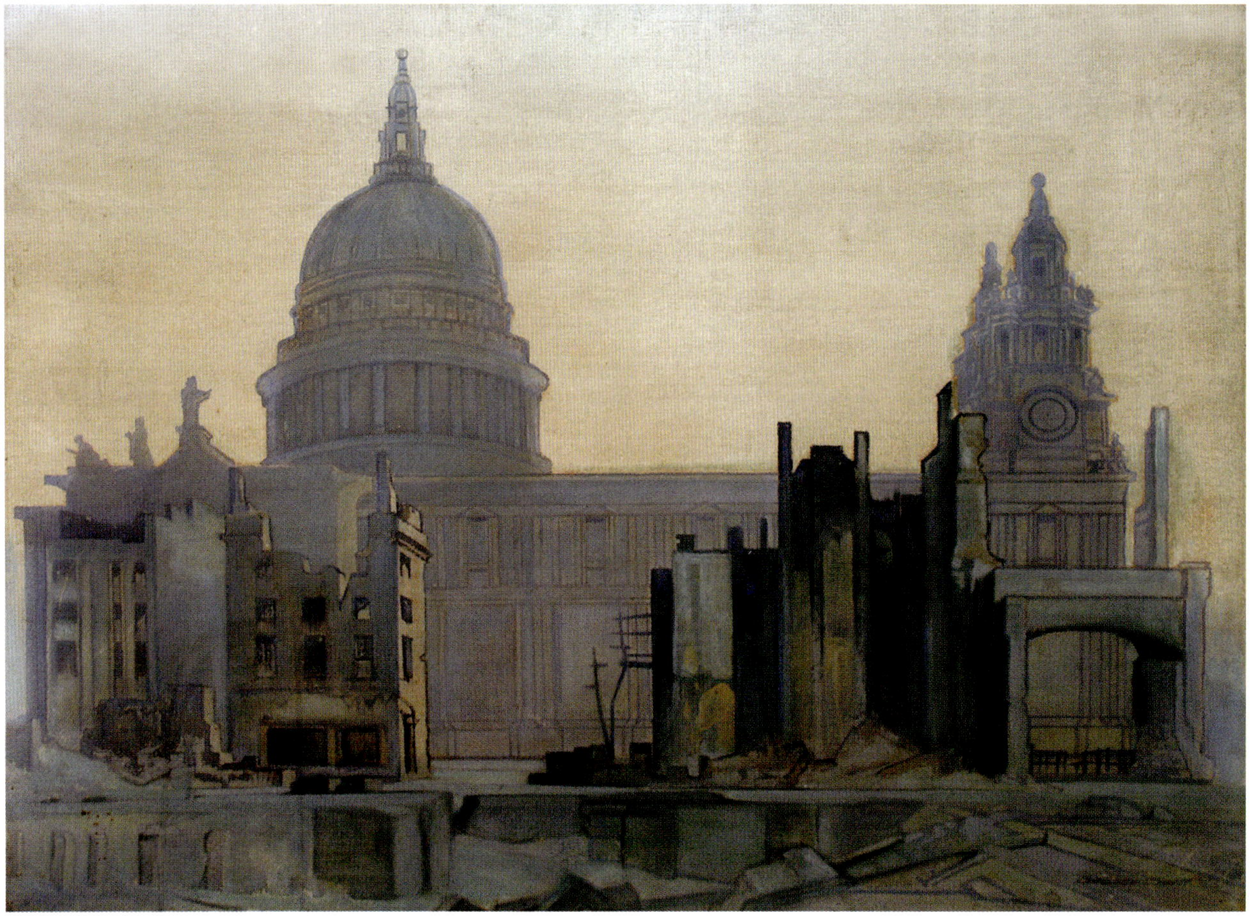

St Paul's Cathedral in the Blitz.

Shearer Armstrong, who responded to this appeal wrote that she had known Brian's parents, and had served with Borlase on hanging committees on many occasions, 'Borlase was very kind to me. I still have the Porthmeor studio [No.9] near his.' She offered a small oil painting on loan for the exhibition, '…the building of a dam, but I don't know where.'

From the response of many people who had known him Brian Smart had confirmation that his father 'was obviously well-loved and remembered in the town.' Alongside this show Bob Devereux and Roy Ray presented a show of slides, prose and poetry in the form of a Borlase Smart biography.

A request for details of Borlase's work at the Plymouth newspaper, for inclusion in the centenary exhibition of 1981, brought the response from the assistant editor, K W Doble: 'I regret that I have not been able to establish the details of your late father's connection with the *Western Morning News* as all our old records have been destroyed.' They almost certainly lost in the devastating bombing of the City of Plymouth during the Second World War. However, his design for their poster 1860 -1910 surely shows his working relationship with the paper, although he left their employment shortly after this.

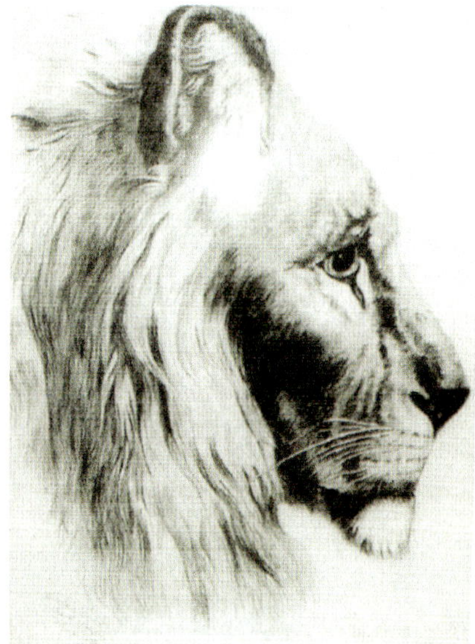

Drawing of lion by Borlase age 12.

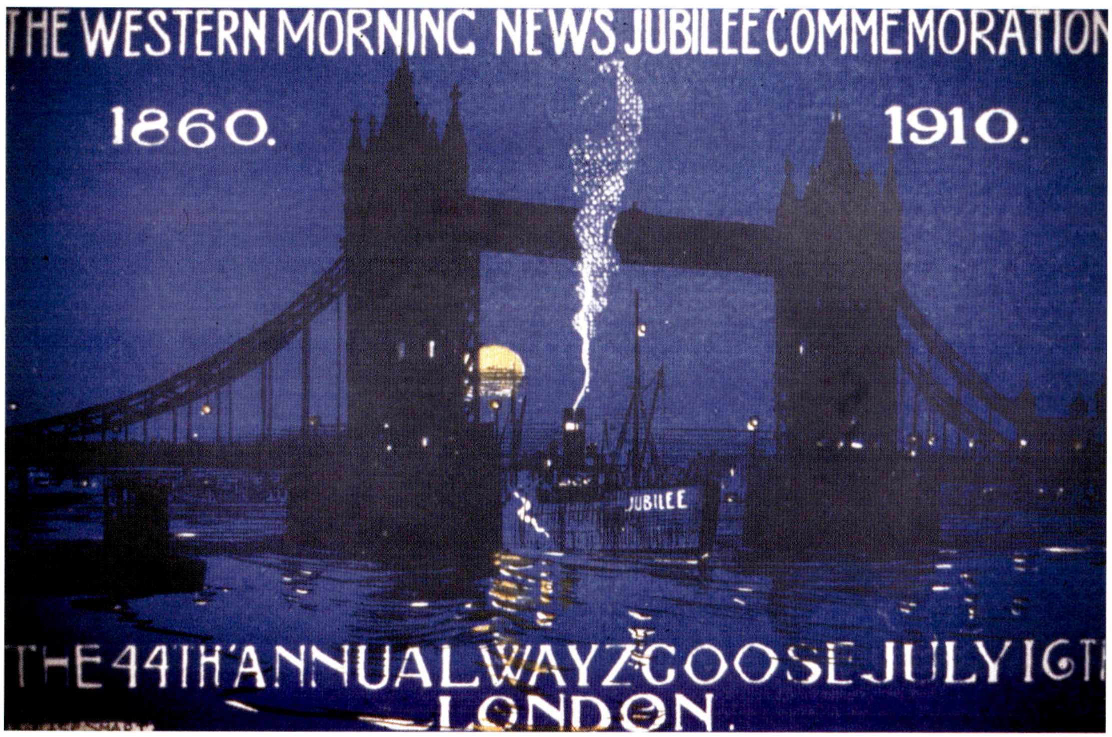

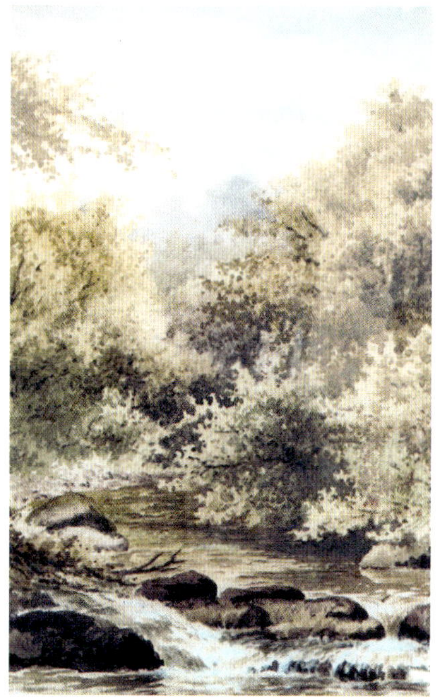

Forest stream.

Poster designed by Borlase Smart.

Brian Smart also commissioned a piece of music composed by the musician Christopher Brown with libretto written by Bob Devereux and performed by soprano Wendy Eathorne and baritone John Barrow, backed by a choir and brass ensemble. The piece was performed at the St Ives Guildhall and aptly named 'Seascape,' a fitting tribute to Borlase Smart, whose very first love was the intimate study and creation of paintings of the sea. However, his commitment to the town is shown in his portraits of fishermen, miners and in the USA Marine Commandos training on the cliffs at Bosigran, and fine line drawings of the architectural features of Downalong.

Left: *St Andrew's Street, St Ives.*

Right: *A Quaint Corner, St Ives.*

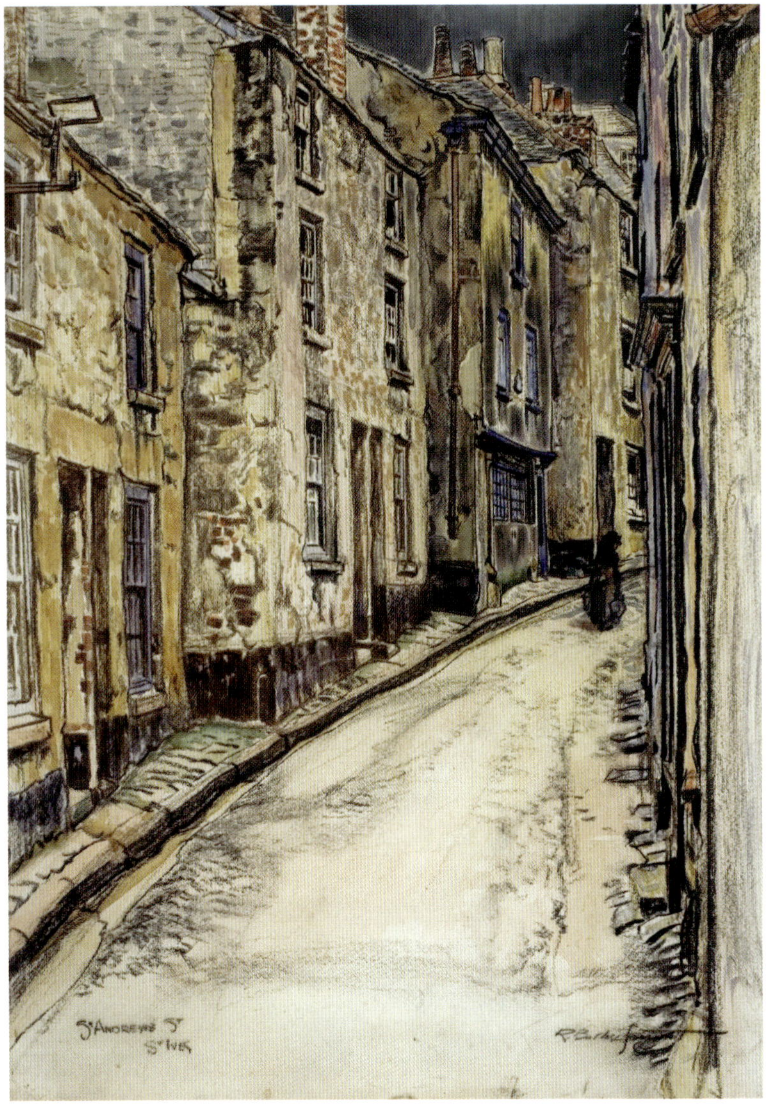

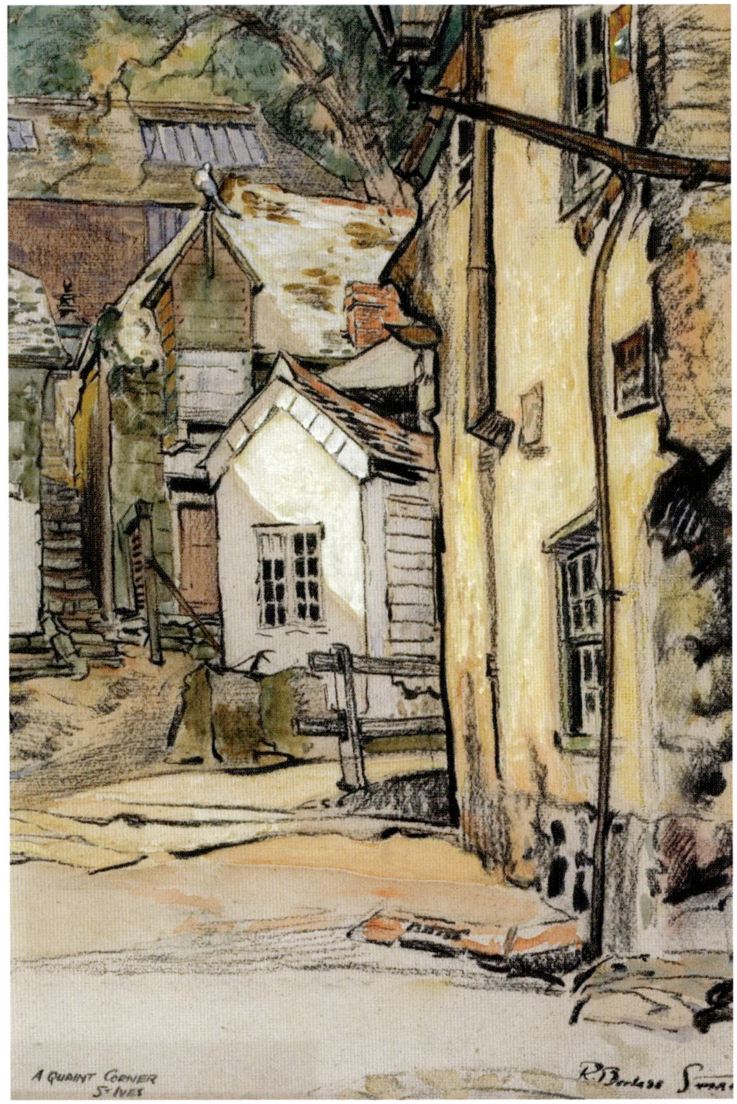

Development of Piazza and Porthmeor Beach

In 1957 Ben Nicholson stated that St Ives could become a world art centre, but there was a danger that it would lose this distinction if its art colony was prevented from expanding and artists were prevented from living and working there. A year later, Mr Percy Williams, the builder, declared he was prepared to build twenty three residential studios to accommodate artists on the Barnaloft site. These were completed in 1963.

The Piazza cottages, net lofts and studios, adjacent to the Barnaloft site were replaced by luxury flats for holiday accommodation in 1967. Both blocks overlooked Porthmeor Beach. It was formerly the site of large pilchard cellars, where fish were salted and prepared for export to Italy. Above the ground floor were net lofts, where nets were made and supplied to the local fishing industry. The Piazza studios were made almost entirely of wood, supported by granite pillars and wooden beams. They had been something of an eye sore for years and the Borough Council and private enterprise, in the form of builders Percy Williams & Sons of Redruth, were anxious to develop the Porthmeor beach area.

'The block of flats now in course of erection at Back Road West and overlooking Porthmeor beach are Piazza flats.' [46]

The widow of Borlase Smart wrote to the *St Ives Times & Echo* in December 1966 deploring the excessive height of the five storey building of the new Piazza. They over shadowed the Barnaloft flats and paved the way for any other developers to exceed this height. Harding Laity, then on the Town Council, had also complained of this breach of building regulations.

Borlase Smart/John Wells Trust

It certainly would have cheered the heart of Borlase Smart to know that the Porthmeor Studios, which for many years suffered neglect and dilapidation, were taking on a new lease of life in the safe hands of sympathetic architects, M. J. Long and Kentish, who were able to draw up plans for the studios' survival, and trust them to the local builders, Symons Construction and other Cornish based craftsmen.

John Wells, one of the abstract painters, a member of the Newlyn Society and the Penwith Society of Arts in St Ives, entrusted his studio complex to the Smart Trust, thus enlarging this organization to the Borlase Smart/John Wells Trust. Wells and Denis Mitchell, the sculptor, had worked together in an old school building in Newlyn and, like Borlase Smart and Moffat Lindner, Wells wanted

Trewarveneth Studios safeguarded for the use of artists. His friend Denis had died in 1993 and Wells was the sole occupant until his death in 2000.

The Secretary of State for Culture, Media and Sport upgraded the listing of the buildings to Grade 11* following research into their historic significance *'which is now seen to be considerable.'*

The Trust Manager, Chris Hibbert was appointed. He sought funds from Cornwall County Council, European Union, Regional Development Agency, Heritage Lottery Fund, The Arts Council, English Heritage and National and International agencies and numerous others. A campaign from the local community was launched to raise funds under the name of Smart Regeneration.

Fund raising within the artists' and fishing communities was put into action in June 2006, largely by the efforts of Jane Val Baker, daughter of the writer, Dennis Val Baker, who told a large audience in Studio number three, *'Smart Regeneration is all about raising awareness of these buildings. This is a unique complex of studios and cellars and we want to save them.'* [47]

Below: *Porthmeor Studios from the beach.*

Bottom: *Elevation of proposed alterations to Porthmeor Studios.*

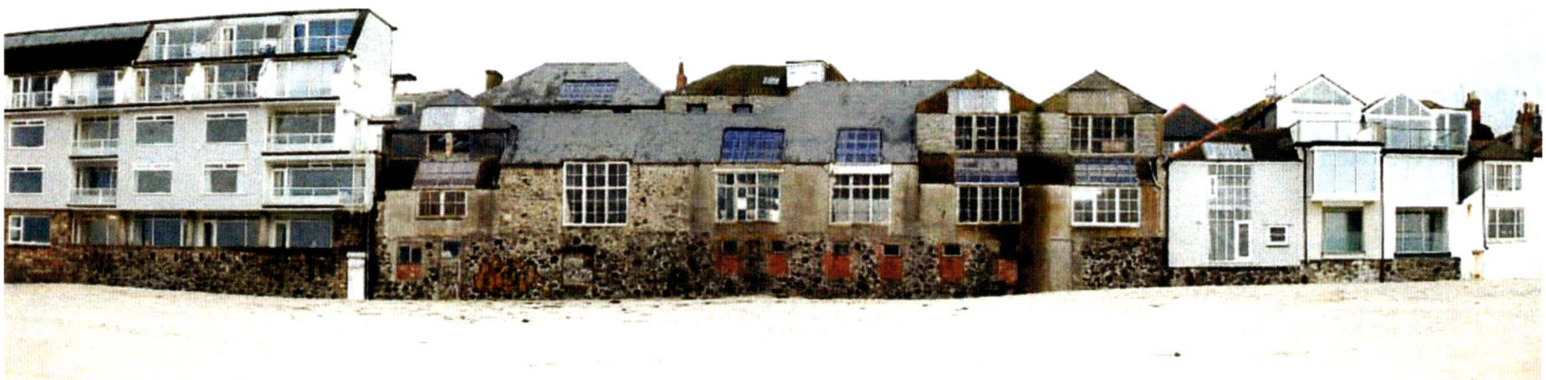

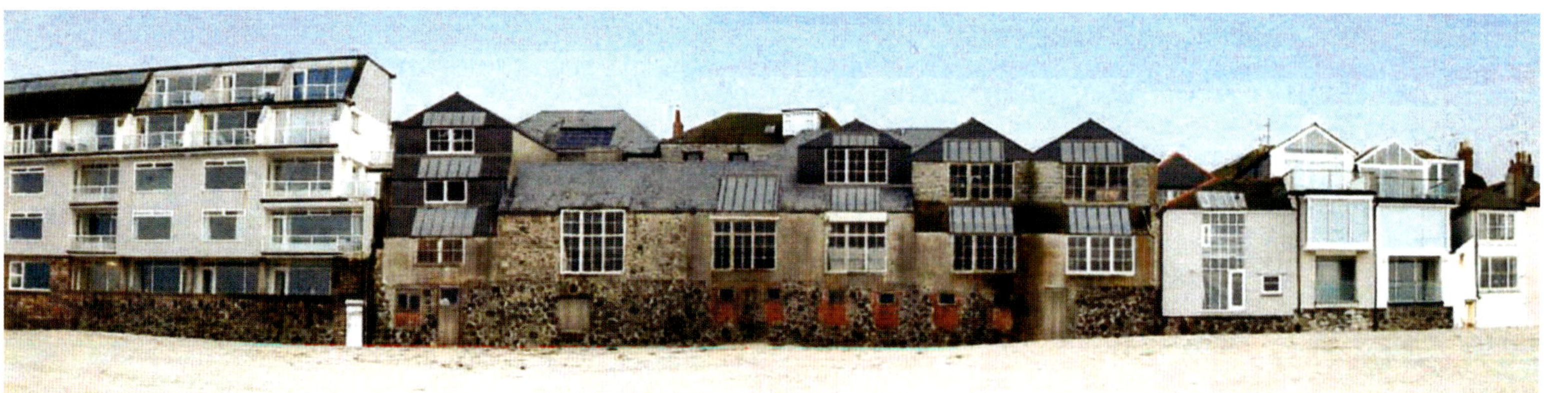

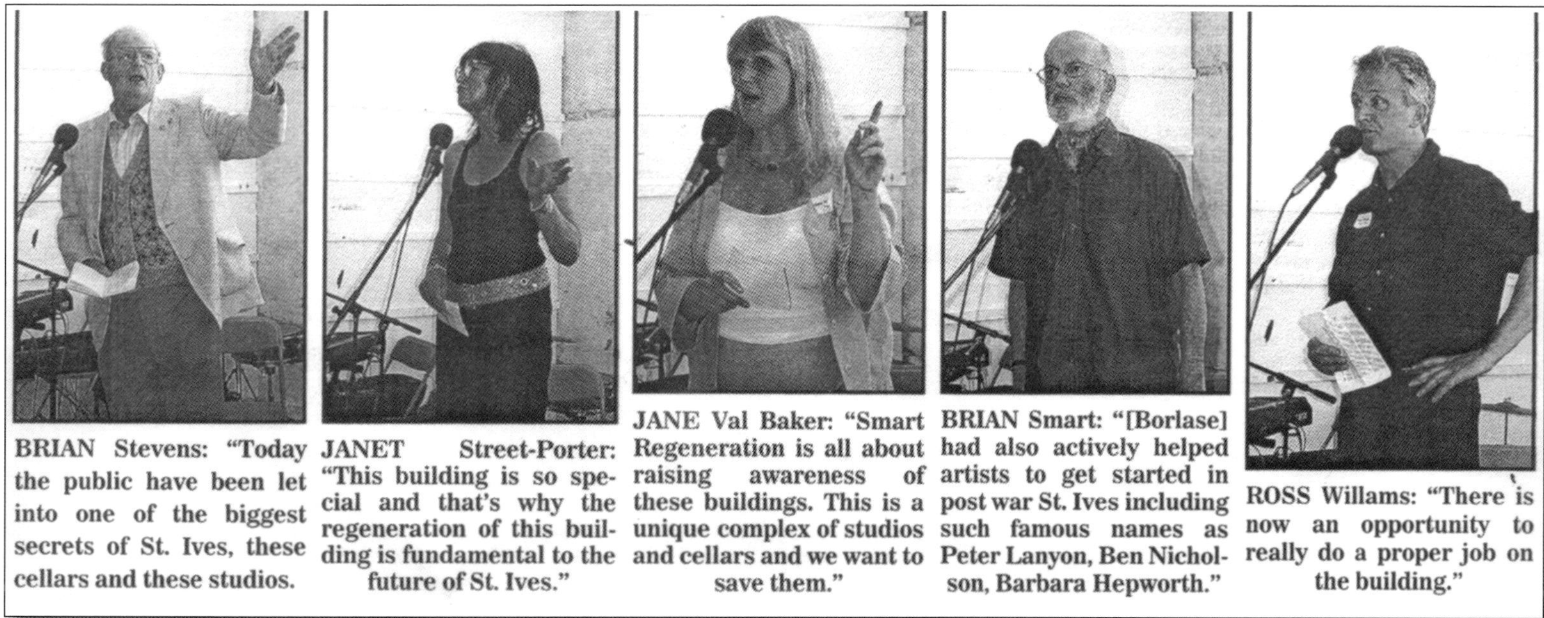

BRIAN Stevens: "Today the public have been let into one of the biggest secrets of St. Ives, these cellars and these studios.

JANET Street-Porter: "This building is so special and that's why the regeneration of this building is fundamental to the future of St. Ives."

JANE Val Baker: "Smart Regeneration is all about raising awareness of these buildings. This is a unique complex of studios and cellars and we want to save them."

BRIAN Smart: "[Borlase] had also actively helped artists to get started in post war St. Ives including such famous names as Peter Lanyon, Ben Nicholson, Barbara Hepworth."

ROSS Willams: "There is now an opportunity to really do a proper job on the building."

Among the supporters on that day, who each gave an impassioned speech, was Janet Street Porter, who had studied architecture with Patrick Heron's daughter, Katharine and spent time with the family at Eagles Nest.

Brian Stevens, local historian and curator of St Ives Museum, revealed the history of the pilchard industry and the fishermen's quarters, unseen by many until now. And Brian, son of Borlase Smart, who had been appointed to the Trust, reminded folk of his father's input into helping to secure the studios, culminating in the setting up of the Borlase Smart Trust. Ross Williams, another Trustee, celebrated the idea of at last being able to progress the building plans.

At the start of the project The Trust Chairman, Sir Nicholas Serota, Director of the Tate Gallery, London, assured the tenants of the studios and fish cellars that new leases and contracts would be issued and they would be able to move back into the new premises. Never have artists and fishermen enjoyed a closer relationship, now more than ever; each relies on the other for a continued existence.

Some years ago, Peter Lanyon, a St Ives Cornishman stated, 'St Ives is primarily a fishing and an artists' town.'

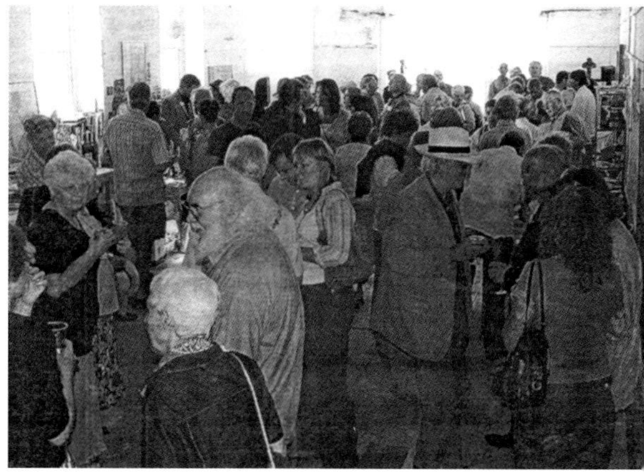

Launch of Borlase Smart/John Wells Trust.

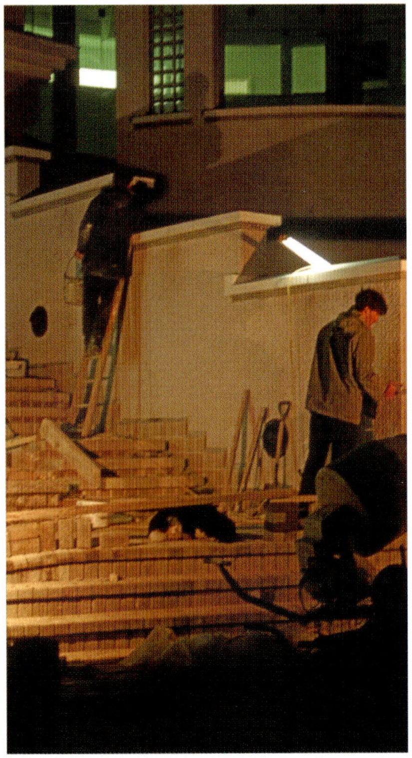

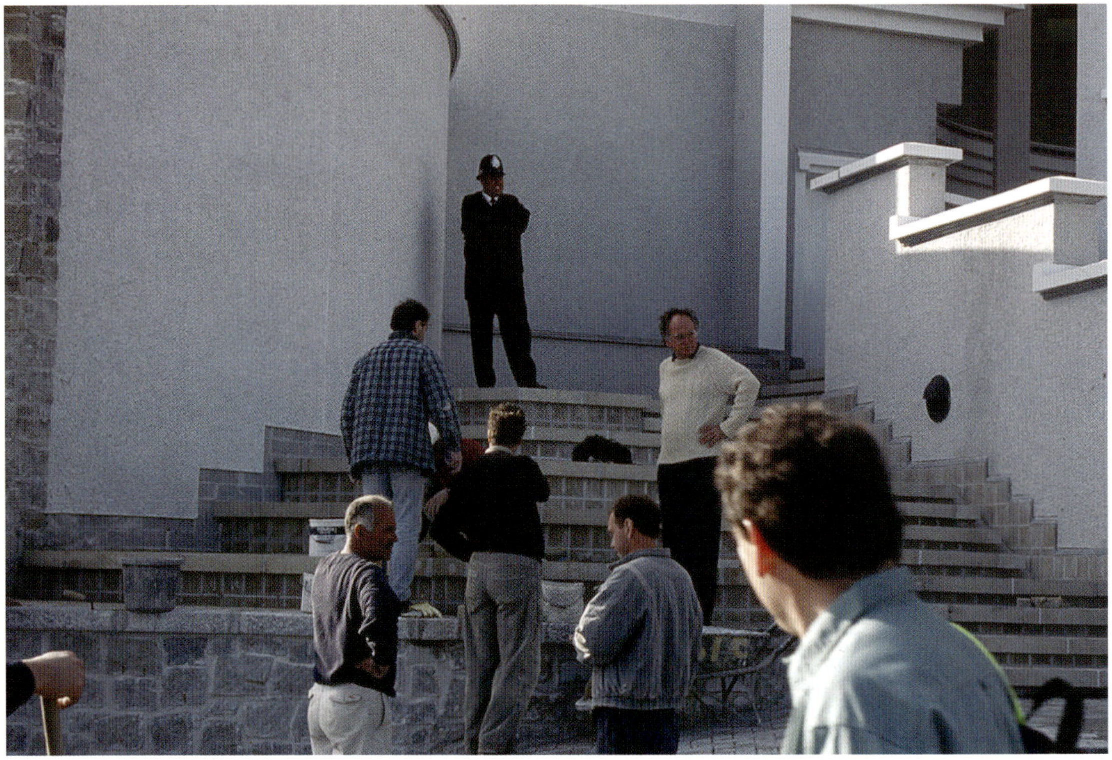

Above left: *Tate Steps with builders still at work, and dog.*

Above right: *Policeman, dog, architect in white jumper, and tired builders.*

Opening of Tate Gallery St Ives

On a beautiful summer morning on 23rd June 1993 St Ives town awaited the arrival of the Prince of Wales to open the new Tate Gallery, St Ives, overlooking Porthmeor Beach. Builders had worked all night to complete the final touches. At 4 o'clock in the morning when the sun was showing as a red glow in the sky, promising a warm and lovely day, I walked round to the gallery. Men were still finishing the steps up which Royalty and the Dignitaries would in a few hours ascend. A worried architect arrived a little later. The workmen and a builder's dog, which had stayed all night, were at last removed by a security policeman and crowds gathered outside to witness the opening ceremony.

In 1993 the *St Ives Times and Echo* produced a colour supplement whose editorial, by Toni Carver, with a sigh of satisfaction after prolonged support for STAG, (St Ives Tate Action Group) commented, 'The dreaming is over; the building has risen and Borlase would be pleased; for the detail of Tate Gallery St Ives is beyond all visualization but that of [architects] Eldred Evans and David Shalev.'

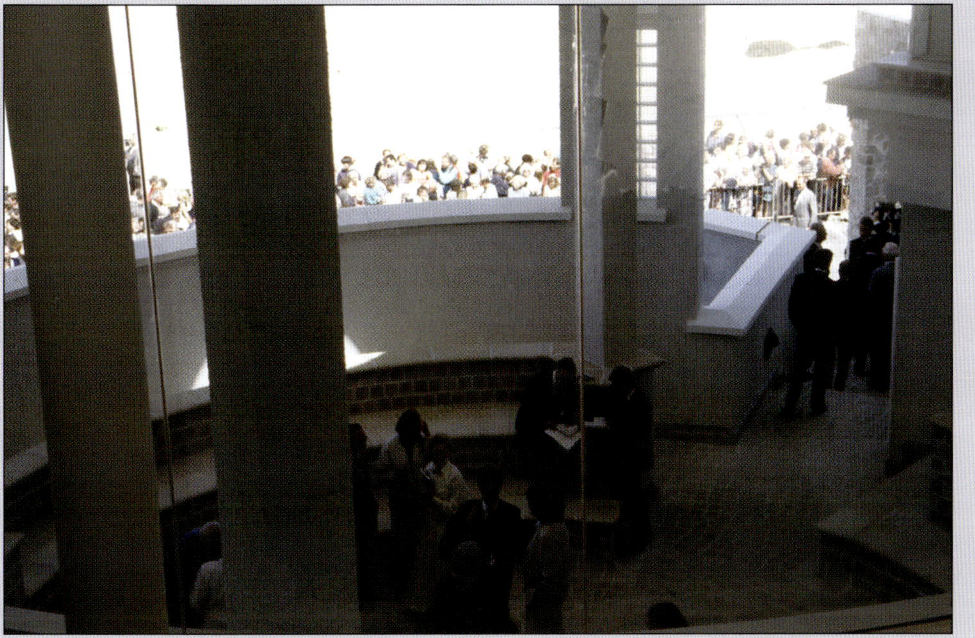

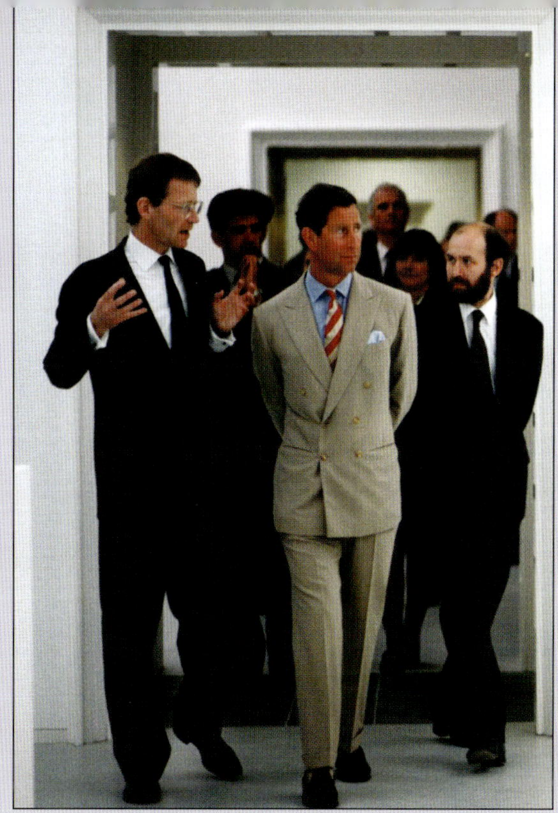

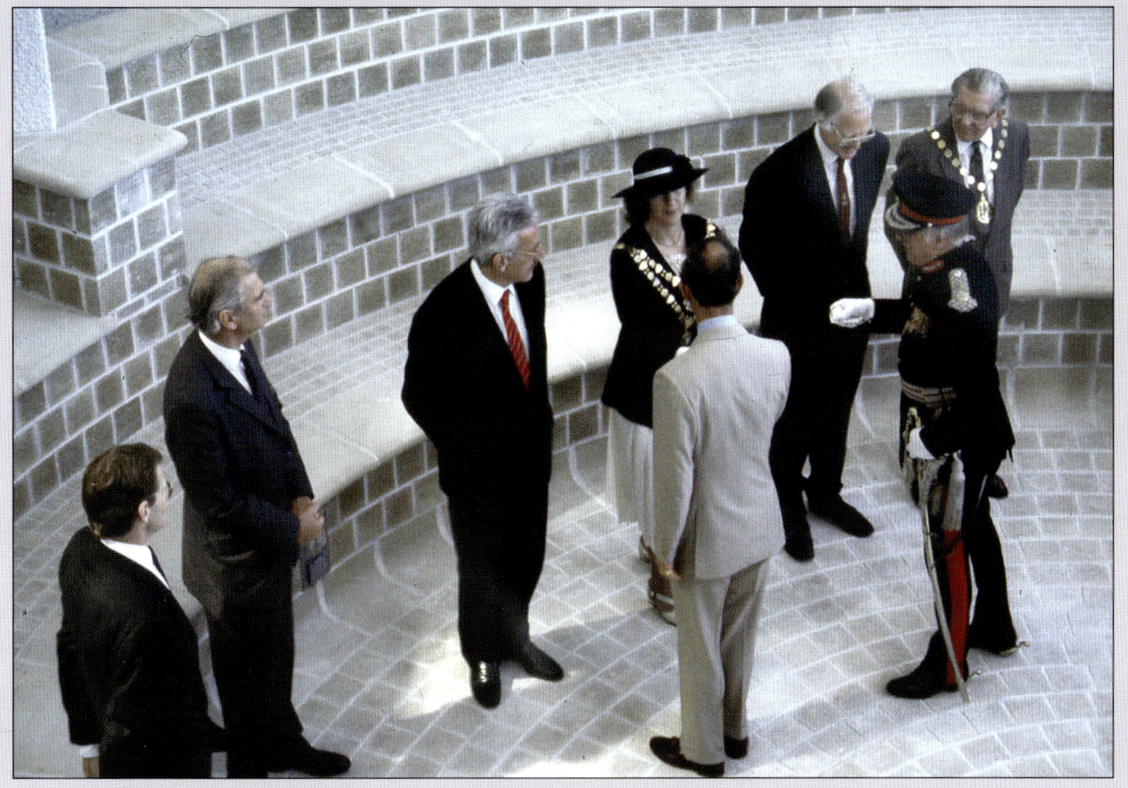

Above left: *Awaiting the arrival of Prince Charles.*

Above right: *Prince Charles with Nicholas Serota, Tate London and St Ives Curator, Michael Tooby.*

Left: *10.30am 23 June 1993. Opening of St Ives Tate Gallery. The Prince of Wales with Lord Falmouth, the Lord Lieutenant of Cornwall. Left Sir Nicholas Serota, Director of Tate Gallery, London; Sir Richard Carew Pole; Malcolm Veal, Town Clerk; Shirley Beck, Mayor of St Ives; Malcolm Furneaux, Director of Central Services; Alan Harvey, Chairman of Penwith District Council.*

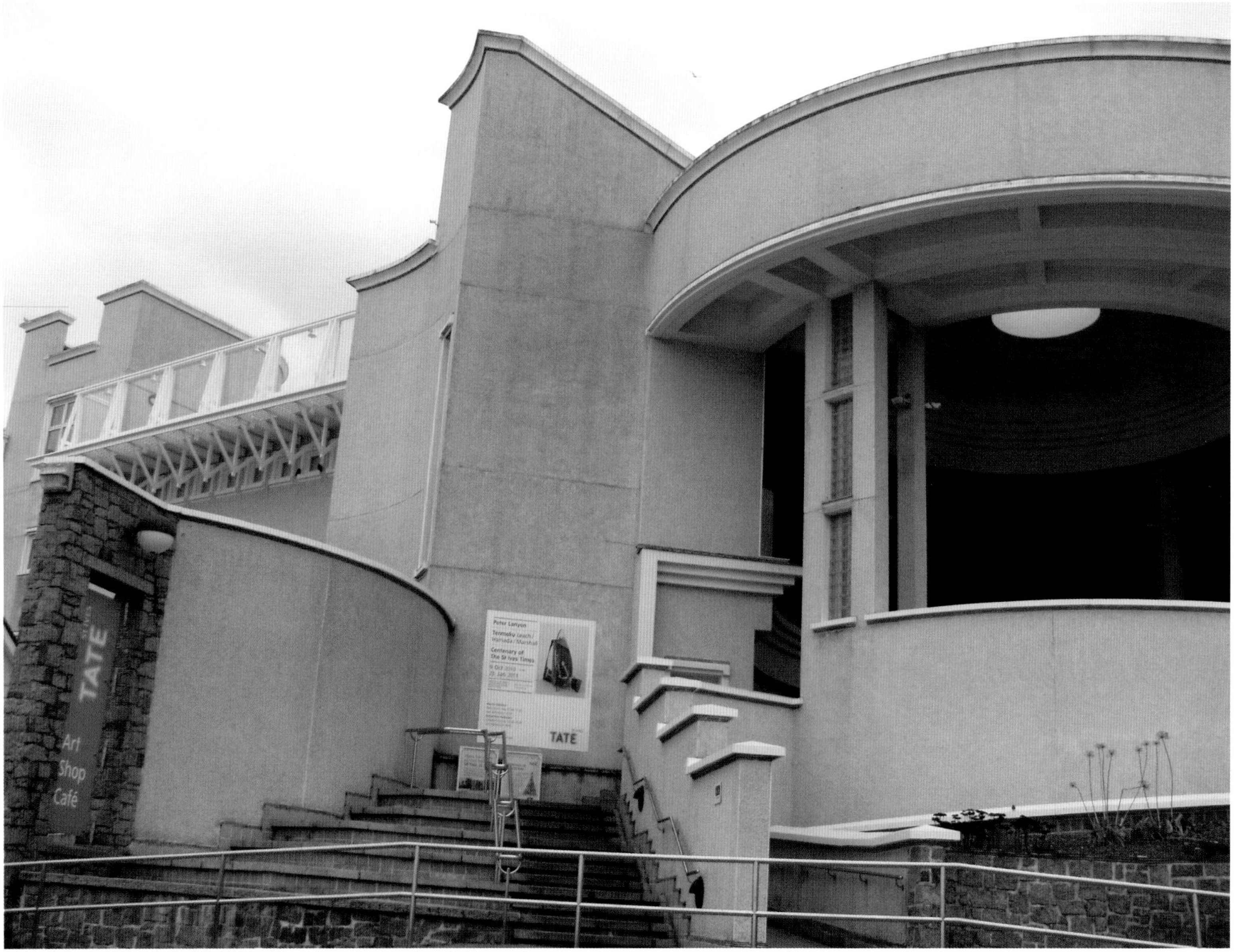

Tate St Ives in 2011.

The building of Tate St Ives in 1993 and the regeneration of the Porthmeor Studios in 2010 confirms Borlase Smart's belief in St Ives as an important art colony and its continuation as a centre of excellence for art, both in its present day painters and its historic heritage. It also fulfilled his desire to create an educational centre; one that would be community minded and would attract the attention of the world of the arts and take its place in history. Smart was truly a man of vision.

It is time for a reinstatement of Robert Borlase Smart's contribution to the many art forms for which he was renowned and which, through time, have been largely forgotten. It is through his devotion to the artists, and the promotion of the societies of artists, that his reputation as a philosopher, idealist and philanthropist remains; and in the memory of the Borlase Smart/John Wells Trust.

Leonard Fuller, wrote of Borlase Smart that he devoted years to the promotion of the art community and believed in its future, *'He had that quality that means so much, both in his artistic endeavours and in his public life, i.e the capacity for taking infinite pains. His characteristic zest is seen in his large and joyous seascapes, his excellent draughtsmanship and his etchings and posters.'* [48]

Ten years after Smart's death, Ben Nicholson declared, *'St Ives is perhaps the most important art centre in Britain after London. This was a fact that was not generally realized in St Ives and it was remarkable that a place as small as St Ives should have attained this distinction.'* [49]

Even with the unshakeable beliefs of Borlase Smart, the love of St Ives by local artist, Peter Lanyon, and the confidence in the modern art movement, which Ben Nicholson and Barbara Hepworth, along with other abstract artists, were instrumental in creating – none of them could have predicted the arrival of the Tate Gallery. It is extraordinary that St Ives, a fishing town on the very toe of Cornwall, could confidently build an art gallery that would not only celebrate the work of the town's modernist art movement but invite international contemporary artists to exhibit. Tate St Ives attracts large numbers of visitors globally to view paintings, sculpture and pottery emanating from artists whose achievements and reputations are recognized world-wide.

Biography

ROBERT BORLASE SMART – RBA ROI RBC RWA SMA

1881	Born Kingsbridge, Devon, 11th February
1896	Studied with F J Snell - Devon
1897	Studied at Plymouth College of Art
Date unknown	Married first wife, who died of illness shortly afterwards
1901	Art Class Teachers' Certificate, Royal Academy
1903-1913	Correspondent and Art Critic for *Western Morning News*
1913	Studied with Julius Olsson at St Ives
1914	Served with Artists Rifles, Machine Gun Corp, London Regiment and The Queen's Regiment
1917	Married Kathleen Irene Godson at Bletchingly Parish Church 31/10/1917
	Met Leonard Fuller
	First one-man exhibition, London: 'From Vimy Ridge to the Somme'
1919	Settled in St Ives
	Elected RBA
1922	Elected ROI
1924	Painted in Venice
1925	Elected a member of the Royal Institute of Cornwall
1926	Lived in Salcombe
	Michael Smart born, Salcombe
1928-47	Member of the St Ives Society of Artists
1929	Member of the Newlyn Society of Artists
	Brian Smart born in St Ives
1933	Secretary of St Ives Society of Artists (also of Newlyn)
1934	*The Technique of Seascape Painting* published
1936	Taught Peter Lanyon
1939-1945	Obtained Mariners' Church for St Ives Society of Artists
1947	Elected President and Secretary St Ives Society of Artists
1947	November 3rd. Died of a heart attack at St Ives

1949	Penwith Society of Arts formed as tribute to Borlase Smart
	Memorial Exhibition at St Ives Society of Artists, Fore Street
1950	Memorial Exhibition at Plymouth
	Borlase Smart Trust founded to purchase Porthmeor Studios
1981	Retrospective Exhibition at Penwith Gallery
2005	Exhibition at The Penzance Art Gallery
2009	Featured in exhibition and memorabilia at Penlee House
2013	War drawings/paintings at Penlee House

Exhibited	London Salon 5 times
	Fine Art Society 38 times
	Royal Academy 16 times
	Royal Cambrian Academy 8 times
	Royal Hibernian Academy 6 times
	Royal Institute of Oil Painters 57 times
	Royal Scottish Academy 18 times
	Royal Society of British Artists 37 times
	Walker Art Gallery 18 times
Others	Imperial War Museum
	Newlyn Society of Artists
	Paris Salon
	Plymouth City Art Gallery
	Royal Institute of Painters in Watercolour
	Royal Institution of Cornwall
	St Ives Society of Artists
Collections	Imperial War Museum
	National Maritime Museum
	Plymouth City Art Gallery
	Royal Institution of Cornwall
	St Ives Library
	St Ives Museum
	The Guildhall St Ives

Notes

1 *Peter Lanyon – The Cuttings.* Andrew Lanyon

2 St Ives Weekly Summary, 1895

3 *The Technique of Seascape Painting*

4 Historical Sketch of St Ives 1896

5 *A Painters Club*, Louis Grier 1895

6 *Architectural Review*, 1920. Frank Emanuel

7 & 8 Visit of Hon. Herbert Asquith. St Ives Times, August 1922

9 Letter from the Palace, 1922. Signed Mary R

10 *The Artist*, September 1933

11 *The Technique of Seascape Painting*, page 11, Borlase Smart

12 & 13 *The Technique of Seascape Painting*, Borlase Smart

14 Letter from Isaac Pitman, Publisher. 17th July 1941

15 *The Western Echo*, 8th September 1934

16 *St Ives Times*, 28th October 1938

17 *St Ives Times*, 30th September 1949

18 *Peter Lanyon – The Cuttings.* Andrew Lanyon

19 *Peter Lanyon, Martin Clark and Mark Osterfield,* Tate Publications 2010

20 *St Ives Times*, 1938

21 & 22 *Ben Nicholson* by Norbert Lynton

23 Letter to *St Ives Times*, Borlase Smart

24 Letter to *St Ives Times*, Charles H Bray

25 Advert in *St Ives Times*, 1946

26 Interview with Katherine Bowtell. *St Ives 1883-1993 Portrait of an Art Colony*

27 *St Ives Times*, 1st December 1944

28 *The Western Echo*, 8th September 1934

29 & 30 Denis Mitchell 80th Birthday Exhibition Catalogue, Penwith Gallery 1992

31 *The Coat of Many Colours*, Sven Berlin. Redcliffe Press 1994

32 *Britain's Art Colony by the Sea*. Denys Val Baker 1959

33 *St Ives Times*, 13th December, 1946

34 & 35 Letters to *St Ives Times* from Borlase Smart, 18th September 1946

36 *St Ives 1883-1993 Portrait of an Art Colony.* Conversation with Hyman Segal

37 *St Ives Times* 19th April 1946. Letter to Winston Churchill

38 *St Ives Times*, 7th November 1947. Leonard Fuller

39 *St Ives 1883-1993 Portrait of an Art Colony*, Marion Whybrow

40 *St Ives Times*, 7th July 1950

41 *Western Echo*, 16th April 1949. Mrs Borlase Smart

42 & 43 *St Ives Times & Echo*, January 1961

44 *St Ives Times & Echo*, March 1959

45 Retrospective Exhibition. Penwith Gallery 1981. Martha Smart

46 *St Ives Times & Echo*, 1961

47 *St Ives Times & Echo*, 9th June 2006

48 *St Ives Times & Echo*

49 *St Ives Times & Echo*, 1957

Acknowledgements

Always, my husband Terry, for script reading, advice and support
Daughters Kim and Tracey.
Special thanks to Brian and Genie Smart for their co-operation.
David Lay FRICS for writing the Foreword
Brian Smart (d.31/12/2010) for writing the introduction.
Janet Axten for her careful reading of the text.
Simon Butler, The Publisher, Halsgrove.
Grateful thanks for support and friendship of Dr Elizabeth Shore
Grateful thanks also to Genie Smart, Michael and Patricia Smart, Diana Smart
Writer friends Ann Kelley and Helen Dunmore for their loyal support
Special thanks to Genie Smart for her unfailing co-operation to provide photos, memorabilia and access to material to ensure the success of the book

Alison Bevan and Katy Herbert of Penlee House Gallery
Barry Fenton of Tate St Ives Bookshop
Brian and Margaret Stevens, St Ives Museum
Chris Hibbert, Borlase Smart/John Wells Trust
Christina Carson and the St Ives Librarians
Eric and Karen Ward
Hayle Gallery, Cornwall
John Allan, for converting my slides/photos
John Keys, St Ives School of Painting
John and Pep Branfield
Jo Bemis for giving me a copy of Borlase Smart's book, *The Technique of Seascape Painting*
Jonathan Brown
Louise Dowe and the St Ives Town Council
M J Long, architect for Porthmeor Studios
Plymouth City Art Gallery
Roy Ray slide collection. Archive Study Centre
St Ives Arts Club
St Ives Museum Collection – by permission

St Ives Times & Echo
Suzanne Newton
The Archive Study Centre in St Ives
Truro Museum and Art Gallery
Tate Gallery Archive
Vince Bevan for photographs
The Sea Scouts
Cyril Bennets
David Daniel
Eddy Bassett
Harding Laity
Jack Murt's daughter, Sarah
Matthew Care
Willie James

Books, articles, interviews

Andrew Lanyon. *Peter Lanyon – The Cuttings 2006.*
Melissa Hardie (editor) 2009. *Artists in Newlyn and West Cornwall 1880-1940*
Borlase Smart. *The Technique of Seascape Painting*
Borlase Smart (1881-1947) *The Man and his Work* – Martha Smart, 1981
David Tovey 2000. *George Fagin Bradshaw, Submariner and Marine Artist and the St Ives Society of Artists*
David Tovey 2003. *Creating a Splash – The St Ives Society of Artists. The First 25 years (1927-1952)'*
David Tovey 2008. *Pioneers of St Ives Art at Home and Abroad 1889-1914*
David Tovey 2009. *The Artists and the Community. A Social History, St Ives 1860-1930*
Janet Axten, *Gasworks to Gallery – The Story of Tate St Ives*
John Pollard, Archive Study Centre: Interview with Brian Smart. Oral history project
Marion Whybrow. *St Ives 1883-1993 Portrait of an Art Colony*
Martin Clark and Mark Osterfield. *Peter Lanyon*, Tate Publications 2010
Penzance Art Gallery 2005. *Borlase Smart, Father, Painter, Teacher*. Exhibition catalogue
Tate Gallery Publications 1985. *St Ives 1939-1964 – Twenty Five Years of Painting, Sculpture and Pottery*
Ted Lever and Nigel Jeyes, *Memories of Wartime St Ives 2005*
The Artist, September 1933
The South Bank Centre 1992. *Peter Lanyon, Air, Land & Sea.*
The Western Echo
The Western Morning News
The Cornishman
The St Ives Times
The St Ives Times and Echo
Willie James interview 1997. 'Down Memory Lane – Aspects of St Ives'. Archive Study Centre

Index